To Make and Make Again

Winners of the Crossroad Women's Studies Award

1992

To Make and Make Again: Feminist Ritual Thealogy
by Charlotte Caron

and

She Who Is: The Mystery of God in Feminist Theological Discourse
by Elizabeth A. Johnson

1991

The Hour of the Poor, The Hour of Women: Salvadoran Women Speak
by Renny Golden

1990

Fierce Tenderness: A Feminist Theology of Friendship
by Mary E. Hunt

1988

Journeys by Heart: A Christology of Erotic Power
by Rita Nakashima Brock

Charlotte Caron

TO MAKE AND MAKE AGAIN

Feminist Ritual Thealogy

CROSSROAD · NEW YORK

1993

The Crossroad Publishing Company
370 Lexington Avenue, New York, NY 10017

Library of Congress Cataloging-in-Publication Data

Caron, Charlotte.
   To make and make again : feminist ritual thealogy / Charlotte
Caron.
      p. cm.
   Includes bibliographical references and index.
   ISBN 0–8245–1249–9
   1. Feminist theology. 2. Ritual—Political aspects. 3. Women—
—Religious life. 4. Religion and politics. I. Title.
BT83.55.C38 1993
264′.0082—dc20   93–12908
                                                                CIP

Grateful acknowledgment is made to Adrienne Rich and to W. W. Norton & Company
Inc. for permission to quote from Adrienne Rich's poem "Natural Resources," from
The Fact of a Doorframe, Poems Selected and New, 1950–1984, by Adrienne Rich, © 1984
by Adrienne Rich, © 1975 and 1978 by W. W. Norton & Company Inc., © 1981 by
Adrienne Rich; and to Beacon Press for permission to quote from the poem "Iamanja,"
from *Ancient Mirrors of Womanhood*, by Merlin Stone.
   The author is also grateful to the following poets for permission to quote from their
work: Jamie Bushell for "theology for me now" and "what to do with jesus"; Kerry
Craig for "The Laying On of Hands"; Linda Ervin for "Groups of Words and Thoughts";
Lorraine Michael for "Easter"; Judith Schenck for "Sacred Ground"; Loraine Mac-
Kenzie Shepherd for "Empowerment"; and Karen Tjaden for "chaos out of order."

CONTENTS

Part 3. Digging Deeper 127

Part 4. Living Out Feminist Thealogy in Ritual and Justice 173

Introduction

MOTIVES AND METHODS

Yearnings for the Holy

After a class in which I had used the term "kin-dom of God" in describing the vision of a world where justice and peace abound and where all of humanity would live as kin, a student asked me, "What if you arrive at the pearly gates and St. Peter says, 'It really is a KINGdom'?" Some time later, as I was reading Nelle Morton's book *The Journey Is Home*, I noticed that she asks the corollary question, "What if we remove the sexism from God and there is nothing left?"[1]

What if. . . . What if religious experience has to have a male bias to exist? What if women's experience of the holy can never be validated? What if God is an old male tyrant with a beard sitting at the top of a great hierarchy, telling archangels and men how to run heaven and earth? What if there is nothing once the sexism is removed?

For feminists, the questions are necessary. If the holy is to have meaning and be that which gives our lives meaning, then the holy must be more than a sexist God. If the holy is creator of, and existent in, this world and is in intimate relations with humankind, then we must ask this question. We must also seek to know this God whose being is not bound up in sexism. It is a challenging inquiry. Historical records show us a God who is bound up and known within cultures that have patriarchal biases. Historical records show much less of the holy free of sexism. But if we discover that the holy is simply a God of the patriarchs, a God that is reliant on male privilege, a God who wants to rule his kingdom, then we have lost nothing by the quest, for such a God deserves no allegiance from women and will, in the long run, contribute nothing of value toward a just, peaceful, and sustainable creation.

---

1. Nelle Morton, *The Journey Is Home* (Boston: Beacon, 1985), p. 223.

If, however, we remove the sexism from God and there *is* something left, then we have gained greatly.

I write with the hope that we can remove the sexism from God, that the integration of women's experiences of the holy will help us to know something more of God than we currently know, and that knowing more of the holy will lead us to a sustainable world order where justice and peace create a kindom of well-being for all humanity and the world in which we live. The theme of this work is one element of that quest: *How can and do religious rituals challenge and nurture feminists in their work for justice and well-being in the world?* My intent is to explore links between ritual and social action, to see ritual as a motivator for social action and activism as a motivator for and a basis of ritual, and to clarify some connections between spirituality, politics, and feminism. It is a study in what I call feminist ritual thealogy.[2]

People, Groups, and Places

Two primary groups inform this work: the Feminist Spiritual Community in Portland, Maine, and the Saskatchewan Christian Feminist Network. Both of these groups started in 1980. In each, some members have remained constant, but overall there has been a high turnover in participants over the years. Each one has a smaller group of very active women as well as a wider constituency of women who come to events, get the newsletter, or are occasional participants. Both groups have commitments to feminist principles and values. Their structures are different, but both work hard to operate within structures and decision-making processes consistent with the feminist values they express. Both were assisted by churches in their formation. The Feminist Spiritual Community received funding and assistance from the United Church of Christ in its formative years but no longer has those

---

2. The term "thealogy," derived from the Greek "thea," goddess, was coined by Canadian Jewish feminist Naomi Goldenberg. Carol Christ describes what thealogy means for her: "When I do theology, or rather thea-logy, reflection on the meaning of Goddess. . . . Two intuitions nourish my thealogy. The first is that the earth is holy and our true home. The second is that women's experience, like all human experience, is a source for insight about the divine" ("What Are the Sources of My Theology?" *Journal of Feminist Studies in Religion* 1, no. 1 [Spring 1985]: 120). For further reflection on use of the term "thealogy," see Naomi Goldenberg, "The Return of the Goddess—Psychological Reflections on the Shift from Theology to Thealogy," *Sciences Religieuses/Studies in Religion* 16, no. 1 (June 1987); and Carol P. Christ, *Laughter of Aphrodite* (San Francisco: Harper and Row, 1987), especially the introduction and the chapter "Why Women Need the Goddess." I use the term here, along with "theology," in order to represent the variety of understandings of the women interviewed. Used alone, "thealogy" indicates that the concepts and reflections grow out of women's experiences of, and insights about, the divine.

connections. The Saskatchewan Christian Feminist Network continues to receive assistance from the United Church of Canada, primarily though secretarial and limited staff program assistance from the Saskatchewan Conference Office of the United Church of Canada. Leadership in both groups is shared.

The Feminist Spiritual Community is a loosely structured community of women who gather

> to affirm women's heritage and our own experiences; to celebrate our dreams and our rootedness in the empowering sources of creativity and goodness; to support one another and learn to value differences; to explore our visions and give voice to them in art, theology, study and action. . . . On each Monday, we participate in a simple ceremony of naming, healing, and empowering. We meditate, sing, tell stories, explore ideas, and plan activities that reflect our values and beliefs.[3]

Besides the Monday evening rituals, there are meetings at other times for conducting study sessions, retreats, social activities, business meetings, fund-raisers, and outreach activities in southern Maine. The Monday evening rituals are the center of the community. The women who come vary in age, socioeconomic situation, sexual orientation, values and political commitments, worldviews, theologies/thealogies, and religious backgrounds and practices. The term "goddess" is used in the community most frequently of the names for the divine; many terms are used, however, and there are many different understandings of who/what/how the goddess is. Some of the women who are part of the Feminist Spiritual Community are active in other religious or spiritual groups such as Christian and Unitarian churches and in New Age, Native, and other feminist spiritual groups. Many women come to the community in times of transition in their personal lives or in need of healing of some kind. One woman described what the Feminist Spiritual Community means for her:

> It has been a major learning place for me. It is a place with a wealth of information, possibilities, and fun. There are a wonderful variety of people for me to get to know. I am able to pick and choose what I want—to change my name and to be with women. I have learned about responsibility and authority as I have worked on committees and offered to do things that needed to be done. It has been a wonderful vehicle for almost everything I needed to learn.

---

3. Feminist Spiritual Community brochure, available from P.O. Box 3771, Portland, Maine 04104.

It has also been a place for getting to know others, and several of these friendships have gone far beyond community.[4]

Others have said, "I am able to receive a lot of healing. There is no pressure to be anyone or anything"; "It is like my mother. FSC is a gathering of women that is home"; the community is "something I do for myself"; "to nourish myself"; it is where I "can be a strong woman and laugh loudly and sing joyfully and dance wildly occasionally. I can imagine incredible things and weep if I need to."

The Saskatchewan Christian Feminist Network is also loosely structured. It has several arms—weekend events, the November event (an annual five-day educational event), *The Unbeaten Path* (a journal of feminist reading material), action groups, and COG (a small coordinating group). The network is a provincial one, and women are geographically dispersed over a wide area. Location of events (other than the November event) depends on local interest and initiative. In terms of intent:

The Network is a visible feminist presence in Saskatchewan; moving from a Christian base; with some particular purposes, such as:
• to share and explore the implications of Christian feminism:
    – to develop and experience feminist spirituality
    – to study women's heritage and unearth her-story;
    – to critique church structure and our connection with it.
• to be intentional about supporting, energizing, and caring for ourselves and each other. This may sometimes mean fighting and loving in honest confrontation.
• to develop feminist models and methods.
• to reach out to other women in the continuing process of consciousness raising.
• to bring a critical feminist analysis to societal systems:
    – by first identifying our own experiences;
    – by raising and expanding awareness of wider women's issues;
    – by bringing theory to bear;
    – by nurturing solidarity with others against oppression.
This is done through organization of women's gatherings and through circulating information.[5]

---

4. I have used a mix of full names, first names, and generalized descriptors in quotes from women interviewed. Some women were glad to have their full or first names used. The vulnerability of a number of women involved in the project, especially as it concerns spiritual and sexual orientations, led some to request anonymity. It seems ironic to choose to have respondents nameless in a project that stresses the importance of naming. However, the project also emphasizes survival and safety as key resources for women's lives.

5. From Saskatchewan Christian Feminist Network information letter, available from Conference Office, 418-A McDonald St., Regina, Saskatchewan S4N 6E1.

Again, women who are part of the group value it. One says:

> It is important because it is long term. It has remained constant during other change and turmoil in my life. It is key as a place to explore my spirituality when church doesn't seem to be that any more. It is also a place for education and social action, which are important to me. My closest friends are part of the network. I also like the age range in the network.

A second describes her experience:

> The Christian Feminist Network brought me friends who were intensely interested in feminism and in women's spirituality. They made me feel less alone, less deviant. Those early gatherings were a comfort and a real joy. And I was made to feel that I had a contribution to make to the group. My ideas and my outlook were appreciated and welcome.
> The early issues of *The Unbeaten Path* offered articles that changed my thinking. . . .
> Today I'm very nearly forty. My younger child is four, and my pastor (although male) is smart and tolerant, so I still go to church. I have rewarding work and secular feminist friends as well as Christian feminist friends. And *The Unbeaten Path* is still very important to me. It has eliminated my special Christian feminist loneliness by putting me in touch with a wide network of like-minded women, and by keeping me in touch with the thinking of leading feminists and the events that are changing herstory.[6]

As in the Feminist Spiritual Community, there is a range of feminist political and spiritual perspectives. The majority of women in the network have now or have had in the past some connections with Christian churches, but others do not. For example, one participant says:

> The November Event is one of the very few experiences in my life when I do not feel significantly marginalized in any way. This is in spite of the fact that the event is organized through a Christian feminist network, and I am not a Christian. I have, nevertheless, always felt that I had a place at the event, and that my spiritual beliefs were welcomed and valued.[7]

Besides the Saskatchewan Christian Feminist Network and the Feminist Spiritual Community, four church congregations have also

---

6. Meredith Cherland, "Editorial," *The Unbeaten Path* 20 (February 1987).
7. Dorothea Hudec, "Justice and Liberalism in the Midst of Diversity: Reflections on the November 1989 Event, January 1990," *The Unbeaten Path* 29 (February 1990).

been part of this project. All of the congregations have commitments to liberal or radical theological perspectives, to action for social justice in church and world, and to being inclusive and caring places for women and men.[8] Interviews were conducted with thirty-six women.[9] The interviewees represented a variety of ages, physical and mental abilities, sexual orientations and commitments, religious views and practices, and geographic, social, and economic positions.

One Feminist Theological/Thealogical Method

The method used for this study is a feminist theological/thealogical method with five components. Although they are listed here sequentially, they are interwoven and spiraling together, rather than linear. The method begins with story-telling, especially around the question, Why do I care about this matter? Second is a defining of the issues, examining what is going on, describing, viewing with a hermeneutics of suspicion, and naming. The third component is analysis—looking at what makes this issue important and how it reflects and portrays class, economics, geography, gender, race, men's power, and women's power. The fourth aspect involves action, the values to be associated with the action, the alternatives, and the strategies. Finally, theological/thealogical reflection and theory formulation are essential, especially looking at how we might convey the theory and theological/thealogical meaning in new ways.

Feminist theology/thealogy is not done by individuals; it is done collectively. Theory arises in community.

Process is also important in feminist methods. Liz Stanley and Sue Wise note that feminist research is more than simply including women in existing social science methods. It involves exploring women's everyday lives, their experiences as researchers in the research situation, and naming how women found out what they did.[10] Content thus cannot be separated from method. How we do things, who we are, and what we bring to situations are critical.

This feminist theological/thealogical method begins with personal experience, with the fact that the researcher and the participant care about the matter in a personal way. The subject must matter, must be based in the experience of women, and must engage the researcher

---

8. The congregations are First United Church in Ottawa; The Peace Church in Portland, Maine; Bethel United Church in Saskatoon; and the worshiping community of St. Andrew's College, Saskatoon.

9. See the Appendix for a list of the interview questions.

10. Liz Stanley and Sue Wise, " 'Back into the Personal'; or, Our Attempt to Construct 'Feminist Research,' " in *Theories of Women's Studies,* ed. Gloria Bowles and Renate Duelli Klein (London: Routledge and Kegan Paul, 1983), p. 196.

in real-life questions. Data, gathered through a variety of experiences, become the starting points and material basis for the development of concepts and theory.

Since the researcher is involved in the research, participant observation is often used by feminist researchers. In participant observation the researcher participates in the daily, ordinary life of the people being studied to observe what happens, to listen to what is said, and to ask questions of the people.[11] While sociologists value objectivity, feminists insist that the researcher is not objective and that her involvement in the struggles of the group is appropriate. Maria Mies suggests that "the contemplative, uninvolved 'spectator knowledge' must be replaced by *active participation in actions, movements and struggles* for women's emancipation. Research must become an integral part of such struggle."[12] Feminist method stresses the "participant" dimension in participant observation; traditional sociology, in contrast, has emphasized the "observer."

Because society has been patriarchal in its perspective (i.e., has taken male experiences and interests as normative and has built a system of power and privilege to reinforce that perspective), research and academic life have reflected male and elitist biases, despite their frequent claim to neutrality or objectivity. Feminist researchers name their biases and their intentions and make no claims to neutrality or universality. They take the need for improvement of women's lives in this society seriously and consider the needs and interests of women in their research work.

Feminist theological/thealogical method begins with *the telling of women's stories* and with the articulation of why the research matters to them. An ability to see oneself is essential to life—to development of a perspective, to adult interaction, and to incorporation of symbols and culture. In patriarchal culture women have often been defined by men and have been unable to see themselves as actors. Carol Christ says that women have not articulated their experiences and told their stories.

> If women's stories are not told, the depth of women's souls will not
> be known. . . . [S]ince women have not told their own stories, they
> have not actively shaped their experiences of self and world nor
> named the great powers from their own perspectives.[13]

---

11. See Howard Becker and Blanche Geer, "Participant Observation and Interviewing: A Comparison," in *Qualitative Methodology: Firsthand Involvement with the Social World*, ed. William Filstead (Chicago: Markham Publishing, 1970), p. 133.

12. Maria Mies, "Towards a Methodology for Feminist Research," in *Theories of Women's Studies*, p. 124. Italics in the original.

13. Carol P. Christ, "Images of Spiritual Power in Women's Fiction," in *The Politics*

In other words, women have not been creators of the symbols of interaction that allow for adequate self-definition. Women and their perspectives must be heard. The participant observer as part of her research can be engaged in what Nelle Morton calls "hearing one another into speech."[14]

The second dimension of feminist theological/thealogical method is *defining the issues.* The naming of starting points and definitions; the collection of the stories or the data; the bringing of them together; the development of categories, concepts, and generalities; and the use of comparison groups are all part of defining the issue. A hermeneutics of suspicion in category and concept formation and in the process of naming is also significant. All feminist research needs to take into account the historical fact of patriarchal control through naming symbols and claiming neutrality in its biases. Suspicion is needed as one chooses the categories, properties, and names given to any data so that the perspective of women is heard. The way in which we describe and interpret situations forms our perceptions of reality. As we create new descriptions, we begin to create new realities. For example, the expression "wife battering" is a term that keeps the focus on the victimization of women, whereas the phrase "husbands who batter their wives" makes clear that the problem is the man's behavior. The naming of the incident is important in the images it produces in the mind of the listener. Theory that promotes the well-being of women needs new concepts and new names for experiences.

The third dimension of feminist theological/thealogical method is *analysis.* Analysis takes the descriptions one step deeper by looking at the data again and interpreting the data in a broader context. Charlotte Bunch notes that *"analyzing why that reality exists* involves determining its origins and the reasons for its perpetuation. . . . We must look at what groups and institutions benefit from oppression, and why they will, therefore, strive to maintain it."[15]

The social sciences have tended toward description that is ahistorical, apolitical, and astructuralist. Feminism looks at concrete historical and material conditions, analyzes structures and the power relations caused by structures, and has a political agenda of serving the interests of women.

Feminist theological/thealogical method also stresses the importance of understanding as it is received through action and therefore

---

of Women's Spirituality, ed. Charlene Spretnak (Garden City, N.Y.: Anchor Books, 1982), pp. 327–28.

14. Morton, *The Journey Is Home,* p. 55.

15. Charlotte Bunch, "Not by Degrees: Feminist Theory and Education," in *Learning Our Way: Essays in Feminist Education,* ed. Charlotte Bunch and Sandra Pollack (Trumansburg, N.Y.: Crossing Press, 1983), pp. 251–52. Italics in the original.

suggests that no research is valid unless it incorporates *action*. Analysis and the theory are influenced and changed by action.

The final dimension of feminist theological/thealogical method is *theoretical and theological/thealogical formulation*. Usually the action component will make clear the areas of substantive theory that can be developed. Because the data is grounded, the theory will emerge. However, the theory may look different from traditional theory based in androcentric paradigms. New theological/thealogical concepts will emerge from the articulation of women's experience, and new dimensions will emerge in the process of revisioning theory through the interactive process of feminist theological/thealogical method. Integration is an important concept at this point. The process must make sense at every level, from data through concepts and theory. The theory must represent a holistic approach to life and to women's life experiences. It must be specific enough to be grounded and general enough to be usable, integrated enough to make sense, and comprehensive enough to add to the scope of understanding of women's struggle for well-being and justice in the world. It must also be clear enough to be understood by laypeople and by those with and for whom the research has been done.

Mary Hunt describes how this method works, using the example of domestic violence:

> They took the problem, domestic violence, and began to solve it directly by providing shelters for women and children. Then they took on the legal aspects, pushing for enforcement of existing laws and the development of new ones. Finally, and only after they had done a great deal of work in direct services, they figured out the theoretical framework in which to make sense of their experiences. Most of all, they involved women themselves, the survivors, at every step along the way.[16]

She notes how different this is from a theoethical method that starts with abstractions and theology and then moves to ethics and, later, pastoral application. Feminist method begins with the experiences and actions of women and only later moves toward theory.

A final note on the process of feminist theological/thealogical method is that it is ongoing. The process is not necessarily logical and sequential. Revision, changes, and redirection may take place at any point in it, as one is challenged and exposed to new ideas. Moreover, once new theory is developed, new layers of patriarchy and of women's

16. Mary Hunt, "Theological Pornography: From Corporate to Communal Ethics" (Lecture at Union Theological Seminary, New York, and Center for Women and Religion, Berkeley, California, Spring 1987), p. 17.

lives that need attention in the ongoing struggle are frequently revealed.

I have outlined the method of this research in some detail because the structure of this book reflects the structure of the method. Each of the sections of the method is the basis for the different parts of the book. Within each of the parts, various chapters elaborate on different elements related to the primary theme of the method. This Introduction presents motives and methods. It contains background explaining why the matter is important and sets the context for the work. Part 1 provides definitions and characteristics of the aspects of the book. Part 2 names thirteen categories of feminist ritual thealogy that emerge from the data. Part 3 moves into deeper analysis of the data, examining what analysis is and why it is important in feminism. Part 3 then takes an analytical look at functions of rituals, at symbols, at feminist spirituality, and at leadership and institutional implications in order to dig deeper into their significance for feminist ritual thealogy. Part 4 explores actions, including criteria for actions and rituals, creation of women's arts and culture, and action strategies. The Conclusion contains theoretical and theological/thealogical formulations in relation to the nature of God/dess, of justice, and of feminist ritual thealogy. The method of the research is also the method of the writing, with the hope that the insights will be grounded in women's life experiences and rituals and that it will be clear that the process of feminist theology/thealogy is as important as the content. This means that the format of the book is unusual. Parts and chapters are of varying length and style to fit the goals of the method.

Context: Why Does This Matter to Me?

The beginning question of the feminist theological/thealogical method is, Why does this work matter to me? Why am I doing this work? I can list several reasons.

First, it is part of my own spiritual interest. I am a person of faith—of Christian tradition, of political theology, and of feminist spiritual consciousness. I live as part of a liberal Christian church, and yet I am on the edges as I struggle with the problems of sexism, homophobia, and liberalism in that church. Nonetheless, it is in that same church that I have come to feminism and to the profound belief that God/dess does not have to be bound up in sexist theology. I want to find a nonsexist spirituality—a god/dess that is life-giving and sustaining, that is amid the concrete conditions and concerns of women's lives, that is in ourselves, our intimate relationships, our longings for sufficiency, peace, and justice for all humanity and the world. I want to know this god/dess in every fiber of my being.

Second, I want a practice that sustains justice and well-being—that challenges and nurtures me and others. I am impatient for justice. To use Adrienne Rich's words:

> *This is what I am*: watching the spider
> rebuild—"patiently", they say,
>
> but I recognize in her
> impatience—my own—
>
> the passion to make and make again
> where such unmaking reigns
> . . . .
>
> this weaving, ragged because incomplete
> we turn our hands to, interrupted
>
> over and over, handed down
> unfinished, found in the drawer
>
> of an old dresser in the barn,
> her vanished pride and care
>
> still urging us, urging on
> our work, to close the gap
>
> in the Great Nebula,
> to help the earth deliver.[17]

I believe our spirituality and our politics must be interwoven so that we can have the impatience and the passion "to help the earth deliver."

Third, being a feminist is the essence of my life. I have a commitment to undermining and overthrowing patriarchy as my lifework. A crucial question for me always is, What does this mean for women's lives and for which women? I have been, and am, an activist for social change in many areas—ecological issues, global issues, reproductive freedom, women's rights, gay and lesbian rights, accessibility for disabled people, and work for peace. I also want ideological change. This project is part of the work of ideological change through revisioning politics, spirituality, and justice and the work of renaming and reshaping patriarchal theology into feminist thealogy.

---

17. Adrienne Rich, "Natural Resources," in *The Fact of a Doorframe, Poems Selected and New, 1950–1984* (New York: W. W. Norton, 1984), pp. 261 and 263.

Part of this desire for ideological change is because I have been a congregational minister in Christian churches and I currently teach liturgy to people preparing for ministry in Christian churches. I have often wondered if worship, and the rituals of the church, really mattered in people's lives—if people were nurtured and challenged in ways that contribute to life and justice and encounter with mystery. Knowing that many women's lives (including my own) have been enriched by the rituals in feminist communities, I wanted to explore the connections. What happens in feminist communities that nurtures and challenges women in their work for justice and well-being, and how can insights from this knowledge be used to strengthen or challenge religious leaders, especially in Christian communities?

Fifth, I love rituals. I love to engage in actions that are evocative and dramatic and life-giving. I also know the power of rituals to reinforce patriarchy and to be destructive or boring. I want to be part of rituals that are playful, profound, and affirming for me as a woman.

I also write as a Canadian prairie woman, and I write with the hope that the Canadian context that envelops me is apparent in this work. I come from a place of wide, horizons that invite looking far into the future and seeing expanding possibilities.

Being from the Canadian prairies means having a hinterland mentality.[18] Saskatchewan has been settled for only a little over a hundred years, which means there is a newness about everything. People have memories of new beginnings and of hope in the face of difficult challenges, of making farms and of living through the Great Depression. People on the Canadian prairies are closely connected with the land. Agriculture, oil, and potash are the primary industries. A resource-based economy means that much of the provincial income is based on sales to other places, primarily eastern Canada and the United States. Prairie people see themselves as part of a hinterland, far from the centers of social, economic, and political influence. They know that the provinces with large populations (Ontario and Quebec) have the most power in Canada and that the federal government is more likely to side with the vested interests of those provinces than with the prairie farmer or resource producer.

These realities have produced a culture of people who are both independent (from the pioneer days of having to be strong and independent) and loyal to community (from the need to survive against powerful outside forces). Saskatchewan is the home of the Social Gos-

---

18. The term "hinterland" is frequently used to describe the experience of being far from the centers of political power and decision-making. For further elaboration on the concept of hinterland theology, see Ben Smillie, *Beyond the Social Gospel: Church Protest on the Prairies* (Toronto: United Church Publishing House; Saskatoon: Fifth House, 1991).

pel, the Cooperative Commonwealth Federation and its successor, the New Democratic Party (a politically left party that operates nationally and provincially), and the first socialized medical plan. Saskatchewan has a long history of political activism in order to provide social benefits for all. Women of the prairies have always been engaged in working for these changes and for the betterment of their communities.[19] Most people on the prairies have done some pioneering, or at least their parents or grandparents were pioneers. So there is nothing strange in prairie women doing the unusual. Everyone who came to Saskatchewan did something unusual. There is a grassroots sense without heros/heras. Ordinary people do what needs to be done, usually in community with a cooperative spirit.

Some of the women interviewed talked about what the prairies mean for them. One said:

> I notice a kind of resilience, a willingness to hang in and a desire to create change against all of the odds. I think it comes out of the desperate times that people have felt on the prairies. There is a connection between the land and spirituality because the seasons are so distinctive.

Another said:

> There is something about the prairie. It is not the center of political and social power. There is a hinterland mentality. There is something positive in that—a humility (though it sounds arrogant to say that), but there is a lack of pretentiousness. There is a simplicity, a lack of sophistication.
>
> We are part of the national church. We often say, as Saskatchewan Conference, "We're here," but they expect us to knock on the door politely. But we are part of the church, so we do not need to knock.

A third said:

> The women I know on the prairie are very resourceful women. They have the strength that comes from so often saying that yes, it can be done. . . .
>
> The geography of the prairies influences us a lot. I think about

---

19. See Rasmussen et al., *A Harvest Yet to Reap* (Toronto: Women's Press, 1976); Georgina Binnie-Clark, *Wheat and Women* (Toronto: University of Toronto Press, 1979); Carol Hancock, *No Small Legacy* (Winfield B.C.: Wood Lake Books, 1986); and *Women of Canada: Their Life and Work*, compiled by the National Council of Women of Canada for the Paris International Exhibition, 1900 (reprinted by National Council of Women of Canada, 1975), for examples of some of the work done by women in prairie history.

how far women drive to be with one another. There is a commitment to dealing with geography and weather, in order to be with one another, and to do the work that it is important to do. We all deal with that all the time.

Canadians value peace, order, social welfare, medicare, education, and negotiation.[20] We tend to believe that there is enough for everyone, so people should not be greedy or grabby.[21] We are morally outraged at injustice in the world but somewhat baffled by stresses in Canada over French-English relations and Native entitlement claims. Canadian women are proud and protective of the inclusion of a clause guaranteeing sexual equality in the Charter of Rights and Freedoms.[22]

This work is grounded, then, in my context as a hinterland woman, a feminist in a country and a part of the country that invites cooperation, that expects pioneering spirits, that assumes pushing against power systems, that calls for creativity and resourcefulness in survival. I come from a place where women have had little to lose by claiming their rights to dignity and justice as women, and as members of society. All of these factors—and the many feminist women who surround me—call me to this task, and call me to keep this work grounded in the politics of Saskatchewan and Canada.[23]

---

20. See Monique Begin, "Debates and Silences," *Daedalus* 117, no. 4 (Fall 1988), esp. pp. 350–54 for fuller discussion of these concepts.

21. See Rodney Booth, *The Winds of God* (Geneva: World Council of Churches, 1982), pp. 53–55.

22. The Canadian Charter of Rights and Freedoms includes the following sections:

Section 15:

(1) Every individual is equal before and under the law and has the right to equal protection and equal benefit of the law without discrimination and in particular without discrimination based on race, national or ethnic origin, color, religion, sex, age or mental or physical disability.

(2) Subsection (1) does not preclude any law, program or activity that has as its object the amelioration of conditions of disadvantaged individuals or groups including those that are disadvantaged because of race, national or ethnic origin, color, religion, sex, age or mental or physical disability.

Section 28:

Notwithstanding anything in this Charter, the rights and freedoms referred to in it are guaranteed equally to male and female persons.

23. Like Saskatchewan, Maine (the second primary research locale) is part of the political and economic hinterland. Both are far removed from centers of political power; both have high unemployment, large Native and rural populations, and resource-based economies; both also have numerous social justice organizations and activists. While they are culturally and nationally different, they share significant similarities.

Limits of the Research

This work is limited. Partly the limitation is by choice, since one project cannot cover every area. It is also limited by my own blindness to areas of life in which I have privilege and by my lack of awareness of lives different from my own.

A primary limitation of the work is in the area of race. I have not interviewed any Native Canadian women, nor have I interviewed any women of color. I have tried to reflect with some sensitivity the problems created by white racism, but the voices of Native women are for the most part not present. At one level, this is appropriate, in that I as a white woman cannot speak for Native women. At another level, since there can be no real justice for anyone until there is real justice for all, the lack of Native voices is a serious limitation in this work.

Francophone and Quebec feminism are not discussed here either. The political and religious issues for Quebec women are influenced by the linguistic and cultural context of being a minority in North America and by the ongoing implications of the Quiet Revolution and the desire for sovereignty. The differences and similarities between French and English Canadian feminists are not addressed here.

Jewish women were not part of the interviews, although there were Jewish women in some of the groups where rituals took place.

Despite these limitations, there was a good cross section of women among those interviewed—Canadian and American, rural and urban, as well as women from various regions of Canada and of various ages, sexual orientations, relationship configurations, and spiritual perspectives. Some of the women were mothers of young children, teens, or grown children; others, by choice or circumstance, had not borne children. There was also a cross section of working-class, middle-class, and welfare-assisted women. Some of the women were physically or mentally disabled; others were able-bodied.[24]

Men were part of some of the rituals involved in the project. However, no men were interviewed. This project primarily addresses women's experience and spirituality; men's experience and spirituality are beyond its scope. The book does not intend to be antimale, although it clearly is antipatriarchal, and it is also prowoman.

Two other dimensions seem important to note in discussing limits. First, a choice was made to work primarily with self-identified feminist women. A few of the women were not strongly committed to feminism, but none were opposed to it. Women with right-wing or

---

24. The demographic data collected regarding age, relationship configurations, citizenship, and group affiliation of the respondents did not prove to be significant variables in relation to the thealogical categories developed.

anti-feminist views were not interviewed. The intent of the work was to look at how feminist women are influenced by religious rituals, and they thus became the target group.

Second, two of the thirty-six women interviewed made it clear that rituals are not important in their lives. Because of the qualitative style of research, it was not possible to see whether, or how, the lives of feminist women who do not value rituals are different from those who do.

Acknowledgments

I would like to thank the Saskatchewan Christian Feminist Network and the Feminist Spiritual Community for their support and cooperation in this project. As well, heartfelt thanks to the women who were interviewed, to the St. Andrews's College community, to First United Church in Ottawa, to the Union Institute in Cincinnati, to those who shared poetry and liturgies, and to many friends who enabled this work.

· PART 1 ·

Describing What Exists: How Does Reality Get Its Name?

Parts 1 and 2 are the portions of the method in feminist theology/thealogy that define the issues involved in the research, describe their characteristics, and name them. Part 1 describes the problems created by living in a patriarchal world and then moves into some definitions and characteristics related to the key subject areas of the book: feminism, justice, and ritual. Part 2 names the categories of feminist ritual thealogy that emerge from the data collected from the interviews and participant observation of the rituals.

Chapter 1

DEFINING THE PROBLEM AS PATRIARCHY

The feminization of poverty is at the front and center of major political issues for women, according to Monique Begin, a former federal health and welfare minister. She notes that women—especially single women, mothers on their own, and the elderly—are poor in Canada. Along with the feminization of poverty, Begin thinks that the work women do in the home, the way public policy and private lives are separated, and child care need to be examined so that new public policy can be formulated. She continues:

> The other issue is violence against women. This is new for me to say this. I used to think this was a very contained problem for a few women—and you know it did not ever get mentioned once in all of the briefs we heard in the Royal Commission only twenty years ago—but I think now that it is a very central issue. Violence is about men's power—it's not in their genes. But how do you address it in a concrete way? Brushing it away like I used to do is not enough. I now think it is a feature of our society; it is an important component of society and it is very dangerous—but I don't know what to do about it—but it would be primary for me if I was in public office now.[1]

Most women's lives are not very glamorous. These realities of poverty, home-work splits, child care concerns, and violence are common. What the feminization of poverty means, in concrete terms, is described by one woman who lives on social assistance. One of her children lives at home with her. Another is going to university and living on his own. Another lives with the father. She cannot invite her children to visit for the weekend because she does not have enough

---

1. Interview with Monique Begin, Ottawa, November 29, 1988.

money to feed them. Last year she filled out the very complex form for the additional assistance available from the government and was given $2 more per month. This year she did not bother to fill out the form. She is quite despondent about the situation and is angry that the government will not provide an appropriate level of help.

Another dimension of the feminization of poverty involves pensions for women. One retired woman said:

> Women's wages are only 60 percent of men's wages. Pensions are a real problem for women. There needs to be some kind of pension for women who stay home. I guess the Saskatchewan government has gotten something going, but you have to have the money to put into it. Husbands should supply their wives who stay home with pensions. There are so many women my age, especially widows, who do not have much of anything. The man was well-to-do when he was alive, but he did nothing to provide for his wife. I was visiting a woman in her eighties who had been married to a teacher, and there was nothing left for her when he died. She has to live on nothing but Old Age Pension.

The problems of ignoring domestic work and child care are especially powerful for farm women, as is pointed out by Nettie Wiebe, president of the Women's Division of the National Farmers' Union. She observes that most farm women keep the farm records, do field work and animal care, care for gardens, manage the household, and look after children. She also notes that 35 percent of Saskatchewan farm women hold off-farm jobs in order to keep the farm afloat. Thus, "On average, farm women put in 100 hours of work per week."[2]

Many women working in the urban paid-labor force also experience limits. One woman interviewed describes her working life:

> When I was working as a landscaper, I worked alone a lot or else with "the boys." It was all I could do to hold my own. There was nothing stimulating about it. Just surviving—all the talk was about the next check, what was on "L.A. Law," or the shit we worked in. When I went to the hospital [as a physiotherapy aide], I wanted to see a place of dignity where patients would be treated as humans. It is not like that—I spend most of my time fixing wheelchairs. But it is sad when a resident has to ask permission of the nurse to go to the bathroom. I can't take the person to the bathroom without checking with the nurse to see if it is OK, and whether the patient needs special assistance, if I have to stay with them in the bathroom or anything else. It feels silly in many ways—they can usually go by

---

2. Nettie Wiebe, "Farm Women: The Triple Day," *NeWest Review* 14, no. 2 (December/January 1989): 29.

themselves. But I would like the hospital to be a place of dignity, where patients could make real choices about their lives and have freedom.

These specifics are typical of the lives of the world's women. According to the United Nations, women compose half of the world's population, work two-thirds of the world's working hours, receive one-tenth of the world's income, and own one-hundredth of the world's property.[3] Two out of three illiterate persons in the world are female. Eight out of ten women in Asia are illiterate; one in five female Canadian adults cannot read and write.[4] Women in Canada earn, on average, 64 percent of what men earn.[5] One out of every ten Canadian families is headed by a sole-support mother, and 50 percent of these families exist on incomes below the poverty line.[6] Women in Canada can expect to live to age seventy-eight; 65 percent of women over age sixty-five live in poverty; widows continue to receive pensions after their husband dies in less than one-quarter of the cases, and those who do usually receive only half of what their husbands have received.[7] The Saskatchewan Federation of Labour indicates that as many as 88 percent of women workers are victims of sexual harassment at some time in their working lives.[8] One in ten Canadian women who are married or in a common-law relationship are battered by the man; one in five Canadian women is sexually assaulted at some point in her life.[9]

What has created a situation where such conditions exist for women? Clearly, there is no single factor; rather, there is a complex interrelationship of ideological, political, economic, psychological, sexual, and religious forces that are combined in the oppression of women. A primary element that surfaces in all of these areas is the ideology and practice of patriarchy. Adrienne Rich defines "patriarchy" as:

> the power of the fathers: a familial-social, ideological, political system in which men—by force, direct pressure, or through ritual, tradition, law and language, customs, etiquette, education and the division of labour, determine what part women shall or shall not

3. United Nations figures as reprinted in *Women's Concerns* (United Church of Canada, Spring 1987).

4. *Canadian Congress for Learning Opportunities for Women Newsletter* (December 1986) and *Women's Concerns Report* no. 72 (Mennonite Central Committee, May-June 1987).

5. *Agnes McPhail Newsletter* (Autumn 1986).

6. *Canadian Congress for Learning Opportunities for Women Newsletter* (December 1986).

7. *Women and Aging* (Canadian Advisory Council on the Status of Women, n.d.).

8. *One Sky Report*, March 1981, p. 15.

9. Linda McLeod, *Battered but Not Beaten* (Canadian Advisory Council on the Status of Women, 1987); and *Sexual Assault* (Canadian Advisory Council on the Status of Women, n.d.).

play, and in which the female is everywhere subsumed under the male.[10]

Rosemary Radford Ruether adds:

> By patriarchy we mean not only the subordination of females to males, but the whole structure of Father-ruled society: aristocracy over serfs, masters over slaves, king over subjects, racial overlords over colonized people. Religions that reinforce hierarchical stratification use the Divine as the apex of their system of privilege and control.[11]

In other words, patriarchy is a system that values male body and mind over female body and mind; benefits males economically, politically, and psychologically; universalizes male experience (especially the experience of white, middle- and upper-class, heterosexual, North American males); encourages competition, hierarchy, violence, and domination; and uses symbols, images, and language that reflect male biases. Patriarchy is a system that oppresses all women and most men, while at the same time benefiting all men and some women through a complex interrelationship of sexism, classism, racism, and heterosexism. Heidi Hartman elaborates by stating that patriarchy is a hierarchical social pattern with a material base (i.e., men control women's labor power). The solidarity of men lets men dominate by excluding women from access to economically productive resources and by restricting women's sexuality. Men receive personal services, sex, housework, child care, and feelings of power from being in heterosexual marriages, especially when the woman is economically dependent on the man. Hartman adds:

> Though patriarchy is hierarchical and men of different classes, races or ethnic groups have different places in the patriarchy, they also are united in the shared relationship of dominance over their women. . . . In the hierarchy of patriarchy, all men, whatever their rank in the patriarchy, are bought off by being able to control at least some women.[12]

Patriarchy, then, is the key ideological framework that underlies the oppression of women in today's world. It is important to note that patriarchy is both the ideology and the practice. It involves attitudes,

---

10. Adrienne Rich, *Of Woman Born* (New York: W. W. Norton, 1976), p. 57.
11. Rosemary Radford Ruether, *Sexism and God-Talk* (Boston: Beacon, 1983), p. 61.
12. Heidi Hartman, "The Unhappy Marriage of Marxism and Feminism: Towards a More Progressive Union," in *Women and Revolution*, ed. Lynda Sargent (London: Pluto Press, 1981), pp. 18–19, 14–15.

values, and the concrete material conditions of women's lives and men's lives.

One of the ways that the ideology of patriarchy is maintained is to give it an ahistorical quality, which is done by using the domination of women as an assumption on which any discussion is based. If patriarchy is assumed to be "reality," then there is no possibility of any other framework. Patriarchy, however, is a historical creation that has changed over time and in different cultural settings. It is neither eternal nor necessary.[13]

In North America, patriarchy adapts to, and is interrelated with, capitalist economic structures. Patriarchy and capitalism (i.e., the economic system of private ownership of resources and means of production) have been linked since the industrial revolution by separating the roles of women and men. Men's roles have been as workers in the public and private sphere. Women's roles are linked to the private sphere of home, nurturing children and husbands, and the role of consumer. However, since World War II, increasing numbers of married women have been part of the paid labor force in order to survive economically. These women question such things as job segregation by gender, sexual harassment, inadequate child care, and the fact that women get paid less than men in similar job categories. Women no longer accept the idea of separate spheres for women and men and thus challenge patriarchal political and economic control. Yet institutionalized sexual, class, and racial biases as well as structures of Canadian society continue to prevent equal opportunity and individual choice. Also, global economic forces are relevant. According to Joe Holland and Peter Henriot, there is currently a shift from national industrial capitalism to control of the economy by transnational corporations and banks. Unemployment and marginalization, class conflict, downward mobility, permanent inflation caused by military spending, high-cost technology and multinational price-fixing, and disintegration of the welfare state will characterize the political economy for the coming years.[14]

Because of the feminization of poverty, women are already feeling the effects of this situation. An article in *Network of Saskatchewan Women* describes some of the problems with the Goods and Services Tax introduced by the federal government January 1, 1991. Primarily, this tax demands a greater proportion of the income of low-income people than of that of wealthy people. Because women have such low

---

13. See Gerda Lerner, *The Creation of Patriarchy* (New York: Oxford University Press, 1986), and Mary Daly, *Gyn/Ecology* (Boston: Beacon Press, 1978), for elaboration on this point.

14. Joe Holland and Peter Henriot, *Social Analysis: Linking Faith and Justice*, rev. ed. (Maryknoll, N.Y.: Orbis, with The Centre for Concern, 1983), pp. 78, 80–81.

incomes (in Saskatchewan, women generally earn 66 percent of what men earn; Native women earn only 26 percent of men's wages), it is women who bear the greatest burden for the Goods and Services Tax. They note:

> Items that will be taxed: children's clothing; children's books; diapers; contraceptives; tampons and pads; baby bottles; soap; heating bills; funeral services. Items that won't be taxed: gold, silver, platinum; international air travel; financial transactions; brokerage fees; dealings with insurance companies and currency brokers.[15]

Capitalist patriarchy affects all Canadian women, with its most drastic toll on those at the bottom of the socioeconomic ladder.

Aside from economics, another means of maintaining patriarchy is to name everything in either-or categories and to create and nurture fear and hostility toward anyone or anything that does not fit on the same side of the either-or equation as oneself. In this way, men and women, workers and managers, nature and culture, sacred and secular, body and spirit, public and private, people of color and whites, gays/lesbians and heterosexuals, and First World and Two-Thirds World are set in antagonistic relationships with each other. This pattern of dualism is also a pattern of hierarchy. One side of the either-or delineation is always more highly valued and has more power than the other side.

Another of the elements of patriarchy is individualism. Although this individualism may come from a number of different philosophical traditions and may be expressed in a variety of ways, individualism is key in North American society, especially in the United States and, to a lesser extent, in Canada.[16] While, on the one hand, feminism is clear that the development of the autonomous person is essential (i.e., women must be free as autonomous persons to make the choices that affect their lives), on the other hand, feminists also assert that context and community are important in decision-making. The goal of human life is not simply unlimited growth and self-fulfillment at the expense of others. Patriarchy's worldview is that individuals who deserve it will rise in the hierarchy and that it is people's own fault if they do not make it in the system of capitalist patriarchy. It is important to patriarchy that this individualistic point of view be upheld be-

---

15. Saskatchewan Action Committee on the Status of Women, "Stopping the GST," *Network of Saskatchewan Women* 5, no. 8 (Winter 1990): 2, 8, 9.

16. See Robert N. Bellah, Richard Madsen, William M. Sullivan, Ann Swidler, and Steven M. Tipton, *Habits of the Heart: Individualism and Commitment in American Life* (New York: Harper and Row, 1984), for a description of sources of this individualism.

cause it keeps people separated from, and competing with, each other, instead of working for collective change in the power structures.

Individualism also affects how men and women respond to the concepts of patriarchy and feminism. Because people are not accustomed to analyzing systems, often individuals become threatened in discussions of patriarchy and feminism because they want to find adequate personal solutions to gender imbalances. Believing oneself to be a person of good intentions and deeds can prevent one from the hard work of looking at the systemic powers and entanglements of patriarchy and can lead to resistance to feminist analysis of the structures and institutions that are seen as normal or real in society. It is important for us to be able to distinguish between individuals and systems—between men and patriarchs and women and feminists—not because we, as individuals, are not bound up in patriarchy, but because the psychology of patriarchy causes us to feel threatened, guilty, and personally responsible or self-righteous about our personal life-styles. When we examine the differences between individuals and systems, we can make clearer choices about how we, as women and men, will live within and resist systems.

Patriarchy is a gender system. In its most overt form, men choose to express their belief in male superiority through violence. A vivid example of the way in which this system works has become a symbol for Canadian women in their struggle to end violence. On December 6, 1989, a man named Marc Lepine walked into classrooms in the engineering school of the University of Montreal and shouted, "I want the women!" After separating the women from the men, he yelled, "You're all a bunch of feminists!" and then shot to death fourteen young women. People across the nation were horrified. Yet, for Canadian women, that day contained no more violence than many other days. One in four Canadian women reports that she has been a victim of male violence at some time during her life.[17] Many other cases go unreported. December 6 has become a day to name violence against women and to rally together for an end to violence against women.

More than simply violence, however, reinforces male gender privilege. Women's sexuality is governed by laws about marriage, prostitution, abortion, birth control, medicare, sexual assault, homosexuality, day care, and welfare. Women's sexuality is governed also by economic factors—most women cannot afford any option but marriage. Family benefits, tax exemptions, child custody, discrimination against lesbians, state regulation of birth control, abortion, and reproductive technologies all benefit married couples and maintain patriarchal control of women's sexuality.

---

17. See Deborah Marshall, "Ministry of Women," *Exchange,* Spring 1990, p. 42.

Even for married women with children who want to live in more egalitarian ways, dilemmas are not easily resolved. One woman interviewed says:

> Raising kids has been one of the greatest challenges of my life. [Husband] and I had talked about shared parenting, but after the birth of our first child I was hit very hard with the reality that I would have to work half-time and that he was not willing to work less than full-time in order to parent. I was very angry, and I raged a lot about that. He was in a job where he was out a lot of evenings, and it was a very demanding job. I raged enough that he changed employment with the goal of having more time at home. But I still spend more time looking after the kids than he does. It is really hard to do shared parenting. . . . The challenges are in the day-to-day working out of our beliefs around parenting and work.

Along with these dimensions comes the reality that patriarchy is also a religious system. Many anthropologists, especially followers of Emile Durkheim, state that religion is for the upholding of the social arrangements of the society and that "God" is created in the image of the powerful in the society.[18] Thus, for example, it has been possible for male rulers, priests, and ministers of Christianity to reinforce the dominant societal perspective that men should have power over women and to use the idea of God's will as the grounds for justification of that assertion. The language of religion has reflected male power (God the Father, salvation through his Son our Lord, the brotherhood of man). It has recorded history through the God of Abraham, the God of Isaac, the God of Jacob. It has diverted attention from the material conditions in this world to hope (especially for the poor) in heaven and has claimed hierarchy as the natural order of reality. Until recently, women have been excluded from leadership roles, as have Native and gay men. The words, actions, and objects of ritual have all worked together to provide the symbolic framework for patriarchal power.

Some feminists note that there is a mix of texts and subtexts in Christian faith. The cultural imperialism and the patriarchy of Christianity can be read either as text or subtext. If one reads the text as the life-giving and liberating stream of Scripture and Christian tradition, and the imperialism and patriarchy as subtexts, then one can continue as a person of faith. If imperialism and patriarchy are the texts, then either maintenance of the status quo and resistance to an

---

18. See Marvin Harris, *Cultural Anthropology*, 2d ed. (San Francisco: Harper and Row, 1987), chap. entitled "Religion"; Edward Norbeck, *Religion in Human Life: Anthropological Views* (Prospect Heights, Ill.: Waveland Press, 1974).

examination of culture or scrapping religion altogether will be the likely options. Rosemary Radford Ruether makes two helpful points:

> I believe that we must recognize two things: (1) Practically all the inherited culture that we have received from a male system of tradition has been biased. It tends either to ignore or directly sanction sexism; (2) All significant works of culture have depth and power to the extent that they have been doing *something else* besides just sanctioning sexism. They have been responding to the fears of death, estrangement and oppression and the hopes for life, reconciliation and liberation of humanity.[19]

Elsewhere, she notes that there have always been two competing views of church. One sees the church as an institution with hierarchies among men and women, clergy and laity, spirituality and politics; the other sees the church as a Spirit-filled community with an emphasis on equality and sharing of gifts and resources.[20] So Christianity can be used as a means of upholding patriarchy or, as will be discussed later, a means of seeking a different vision of power and gender relations.

As already mentioned, patriarchy does not stand on its own. It is important to note some of its allies. *Classism* is the system in which one group of people has economic and social privilege over others. The feminization of poverty, discussed above, shows how this system supports patriarchy by keeping women poor who are not in heterosexual marriages. Classism gives power to those with wealth. *Imperialism* is a system in which one cultural group believes itself to be superior to other groups. The most conspicuous example of this was the imperialism of British colonial power in the settling of Canada, with the denigration of Native peoples and cultures. *Racism* is the system by which one race acts in ways that keep those of other races powerless. White racism—that is, the belief that those with white skins are superior to those with darker-colored skins, and the resultant discrimination—is the most prevalent form of racism in North America. *Militarism* is the system in which the buildup of arms, threats of force, and actual making of war are used to show that one country and its allies are superior to another and its allies. *Ageism* is the practice of privileging one age-group over others—for example, of seeing older middle-aged men as more important than elderly women or children. *Heterosexism* is the result of privileging heterosexual persons over gay/lesbian persons. *Able-bodyism* is discrimination on the basis of whether

---

19. Rosemary Radford Ruether, "A Religion for Women: Sources and Strategies," *Christianity and Crisis* 39, no. 19 (December 10, 1979): 309.

20. Rosemary Radford Ruether, *Women-Church* (San Francisco: Harper and Row, 1985), pp. 22–23.

a person has physical or mental disabilities. A final term that needs to be noted in relationship to patriarchy is *sexism*. Patriarchy is the ideological, socioeconomic, psychological, and religious system of male superiority. Sexism is the effect of patriarchy.

Why is it important to delineate all of these aspects of patriarchy? Without being clear about the extent of problems women face, it is impossible to think about justice for women in the concrete and material conditions of the world, or of a spirituality for justice. To speak of justice without attaching specific meaning to the term will not bring social change. Because oppression is concrete and specific, justice likewise must be concrete and specific. The pervasive ideology, as well as all of the related areas and practices, must be challenged and changed if there is to be justice and well-being for women in the world.

Chapter 2

FEMINISM

Having defined patriarchy and elaborated on its practices, a definition of feminism is needed. To be a feminist is to have a political commitment to the well-being of women in the world and to the creation of just structures. I believe that a just and sustainable society cannot be achieved until women are valued as fully human and are enabled to participate fully and freely in the decisions that affect their lives. Feminism acknowledges that patriarchy is a system of power in which men have more power than women and in which a few men (primarily white, articulate, wealthy, heterosexual men) hold a great deal of power politically, economically, and socially. Feminism says that patriarchy must be eliminated and that the material conditions of women's lives must change in order for women to be able to live fully human lives. Feminism will achieve its goals only when all people have sufficient food, water, shelter, and safety and when they can participate in decisions that affect their lives. Feminists analyze the conditions of women's lives and the interrelationships among sexism, racism, heterosexism, classism, and able-body bias resulting from patriarchy. Feminists then act toward the dismantling of patriarchal powers and the creation of just and sustainable structures and relationships. Feminists envision a world where violence, fear, and poverty are not the lot of most women and children. As feminists, we also laugh and play and create rituals in the belief that we must live into the visions we create in our dreams.

Feminism encompasses four aspects in creating its perspective—women's experiences, modes of analysis, personal well-being, and social change. Feminism begins with women's experience. Women's stories must be told. Women's voices must be heard in all aspects of life, culture, politics, and religion. Women must be able to go deep within and to articulate freely the concerns, experiences, hopes, and fears that are real. Feminism means letting go of patriarchal patterns of thinking and acting. It means a changed consciousness about what formulates reality.

For many women the beginning of this process is some form of consciousness raising, which involves breaking old patterns. It usually begins by recognizing that what women thought were purely personal problems or neuroses in their relationships with mothers, husbands, or bosses were shared by other women, and that in even the most intimate of these relationships women are governed by an unequal distribution of power. Consequently, Gerda Lerner suggests the need for being woman-centered. For her, this attitude means seeing women as always central, assuming that if women appear to be marginal, it is because there has been patriarchal intervention or because there is an illusion.

> The basic assumption should be that it is inconceivable for anything to have ever taken place in the world in which women were not involved, except if they were prevented from participation through coercion and repression.
> When using methods and concepts from traditional systems of thought, it means using them from the vantage point of the centrality of women. Women cannot be put into the empty spaces of patriarchal thought and systems—in moving to the centre, they transform the system.[21]

Eleanor Haney strengthens Lerner's concept of being woman-centered and elaborates on the meaning of women's experience in personal and global terms. For her, being prowoman is loving and celebrating women, grieving women's pain and terror, raging at violence, naming what keeps women separated, seeking connections, and moving toward sufficiency and friendships. She also notes that being feminist means being for ourselves, valuing our resources, and trusting our authority in decision-making, theology, and ethics. Knowing that our own experiences are limited and that our thinking is distorted and biased means that we have to name the ways we gain from the oppression of others, as well as acknowledging the ways in which we internalize our oppression. Being prowoman likewise means challenging the violence of racism, classism, able-bodyism, ageism, heterosexism, naturism, and anti-Semitism.[22]

In thinking about women's experience, it is thus important to "experience our own experience," that is, to be in touch with what is going on in our own lives as women living in a patriarchal culture. It

---

21. Lerner, *Creation of Patriarchy*, p. 228.
22. Eleanor H. Haney, *Vision and Struggle: Meditations on Feminist Spirituality and Politics* (Portland, Maine: Astarte Shell Press, 1989), pp. 1–2.

is also important, as Haney suggests, to recognize that our own experience is not the experience of all women. Women have vastly different experiences in the world, depending on their race, educational opportunities, geographic location, class, age, sexual orientation, bodily capacities, and subjection to violence. Unlike patriarchy, which acts as if the experience of white, male, elite, educationally privileged heterosexuals were universal, feminism acknowledges that women's experiences (and men's experiences) grow out of very different material and ideological places. Feminism takes the issue of accountability seriously. Feminists must determine to whom we will be accountable, in order to choose our actions creatively and responsibly. We need to look at who will bear the costs for our choices, words, and actions, and we must create opportunity together for the participation of those who have had the least opportunity for self-determination previously.

The second aspect in a definition of feminism that seems important is the area of analysis leading to social change. Mary Hunt suggests beginning with the experience of women's oppression in a patriarchal society and considering the racial, class, and ethnic makeup of persons, as well as their sexual preference, social location, and physical capacity, in order to bring about change through equalizing access to resources.[23] Feminist analysis is an approach to life and its politics that focuses on asking questions and seeking answers. The process is as important as the conclusions.

Along with the analysis of women as a gender group, feminism looks to the personal well-being of women in their individual lives. Feminism is the process of seeking healing from personal pain and social injustice, especially as it relates to women; of transforming values toward community, equality, inclusion, and the free and public participation of all in decisions that affect their lives; of discovering and affirming the goodness of creation and ourselves as women; and of finding a new politic and theology of gender relationships. One woman interviewed says:

> Feminism has been so empowering. For example, it helped me to accept my own sexuality and to accept it as part of myself. It allows me to believe I could be a carpenter or mechanic if I want. It gives me the vision to know that I am not alone in my political thinking, that is, that women can do whatever they want. I also know that women in Peru are more caught in survival than in equal pay.

A slogan from the early women's movement—"the personal is political"—remains an important element of feminism. Separations of

---

23. Mary Hunt, "Where Charity and Love Are Not: Contemporary Expressions of Christian Hatred" (Address on International Women's Day, 1990, Regina, Sask.).

personal and political, of public and private, and of domestic and productive are false separations. All of our actions have political consequences, and all of our politics affect individual lives. Individuals damaged by life under patriarchy need healing, just as do the structures and systems distorted by patriarchal practice and abuse. Feminisms based on personal solutions to problems of sexism and capitalist patriarchy are not sufficient, as was noted in the section on individualism above. Donna Hawxhurst and Sue Morrow emphasize this point:

> Feminism is an ideology that insists on social change. We are a feminist community only insofar as we contribute to social change. Women frequently identify themselves as feminists on the basis of their belief in certain values, such as equality for women or loving women. We hope to challenge all who identify themselves as feminists by our insistence that feminism demands action, and that we live in a time when no one can afford the luxury of a raised consciousness without an accompanying commitment.[24]

One interviewee makes the point that "the idea that women can have influence without organizing is ridiculous. Women need organizations to have any influence. We have to keep struggling for women's rights."

Feminism is a movement that seeks social change in all spheres of women's lives—individually, structurally, and globally. There are many different agendas, but they can be broadly termed under the umbrella of "justice and well-being in the world." Feminists hold a materialist perspective, that is, a perspective based in the concrete conditions of women's lives in the world. Economics, politics, family structures, health, education, and many other spheres are the bases for a feminist material agenda for justice. While there are many differences within feminism, all feminists agree that both political structures and personal relationships need to be examined for patriarchal practices. No sphere is exempt from evaluation leading toward change. The Mudflower Collective names an essential criterion for the measuring of justice when it says, "The common good is distorted whenever anyone—women, people of colour, gay and lesbian people, anyone—is not empowered by the community to participate proudly and publicly in the naming and shaping of the common good."[25]

In summary, feminism is a movement that takes women's experiences in patriarchal culture seriously. It places women at the center

---

24. Donna Hawxhurst and Sue Morrow, *Living Our Visions: Building Feminist Community* (Tempe, Ariz.: Fourth World, 1984), p. 123.

25. The Mudflower Collective, *God's Fierce Whimsy* (New York: Pilgrim Press, 1985), p. 31.

as autonomous moral agents, and it considers the variety of women's experiences in the world based on age, class, race, sexual orientation, physical abilities, and geographic location. It analyzes the problems in women's lives, questions the root causes of those problems, and looks for concrete solutions to the oppression of women. Feminism involves personal healing from the damage created to women's lives by living in patriarchal culture, and it involves political action to change the material and ideological conditions of women's lives toward justice, mutuality, and participation in the naming and shaping of the common good.

Streams of Feminism

As already indicated, feminism is not a unilateral movement with only one goal or political agenda. Within feminism there are many different understandings of the nature of women's oppression, the meaning of differences, the appropriate strategies to bring about change, and the effectiveness of different political theories.

While some women in this project identified with a particular stream of feminism such as liberal, radical, or socialist, most did not. Most came closest to what Charlotte Bunch names "non-aligned feminism." Bunch says that feminists need to take stock, and not simply conform to the pressure to be a socialist feminist, a reformer, or a radical. To use the dichotomies of patriarchal thinking—that one must be one thing or another, that one must focus on the material/economic or else the cultural/spiritual—is a distortion and prevents new categories and concepts from emerging. Nonaligned feminism acknowledges the insights of these theories but does not confine one to them. Thus, a commitment to nonaligned feminism means a refusal to polarize and a willingness to examine the subtleties, live with ambiguities, and choose from a wide spectrum of actions available. Nonaligned feminists must examine each situation, taking seriously how each action will affect women's interests and long-term feminist goals, instead of just attaching oneself to a dominant political line. This approach to feminism leaves room for alliances and coalitions around particular issues and for choosing to support or condemn the actions of other groups or governments.[26] It means measuring each action to see whether it will promote justice and well-being for women and identifying which women will be affected. Bunch summarizes the goal of nonaligned feminism: "We need a new social order based on equitable distribution of resources and access to them in the future; upon equal justice

---

26. Charlotte Bunch, "Beyond Either/Or: Feminist Options," in *Building Feminist Theory*, ed. Bunch et al. (New York: Longman, 1981), p. 47.

and rights for all; and upon maximum freedom for each person to determine her own life."[27]

Feminist Spirituality

I would define spirituality as human longing for connection with the universal, with one another, and with the earth—the human longing to be at peace and have integrity within ourselves. At this point in history, feminist spiritualities are emerging from a recognition that women's longings, connections, and integrity have historically not been adequately addressed in religious systems. Feminist spiritualities come in a variety of forms and offer a range of alternatives. Some are connected with various religious traditions; others are new. All are biased toward the inclusion of female experience in any theological/thealogical endeavor, and most support actions toward justice, mutuality, and well-being of women in the world.

Many of the women to whom I spoke felt loss and confusion in their spiritual lives. Some who have identified with the Christian church struggle with what their feminist understandings mean in that context. When asked, "How would you describe your spirituality?" one woman answered:

> Confused! It is like a patchwork quilt. It has lots of little bits and pieces out of different traditions, different parts of life, different experiences. It is not complete; it is being created, it is in the making. I am very cautious about describing it.
>
> Generally I would say it is not Christian. There is no other label that resonates. I am comfortable with goddess language, but it is not really formed at this point. Wicca is interesting, but I am not really there. And I do have a passion for discussion of Christian theology.
>
> I feel like I am always on the edge. I can identify yearnings, and I know what is life giving—but the naming part of that is in evolution. It is one of the most vulnerable parts of my life. I have worked so much in a religious community that is not nourishing of my spiritual life, but I still am part of it. Inside there is knowing but not naming. I have no language to explain why it is so important. I have no concepts to argue from nor identifiable translations.

The need for faith that challenges and nurtures is strong in many women.

The ethical principle of working for justice in the world is also key to feminist spirituality. Feminists want a materially based spirituality

---

27. Bunch, "The Reform Tool Kit," in *Building Feminist Theory*, p. 194.

for justice. We want a spirituality that names the sacred in our bodies, in nature, in relationships, and in transitory moments of life. Chris Smith defines a materially based spirituality as follows:

> For all of us who work for a day when justice will prevail, *intentional transformation* is the cornerstone of our spirituality. Our spiritual lives are in desperate need of rituals that weave the political and the religious together as one fabric. It is important that we give a new name to spiritual praxis. Ecclesiastical structures may never name the spiritual significance of civil disobedience at nuclear missile sites, but many of us must. There are those that know the birth of a child is not a privatized family moment, but a moment of possibility for the world. There are many that understand that the violence that inhabits our homes and our personal relationships can never be separated from the religious and theological expressions of our day. There is no dichotomy between the sacred and political, for the mysterious presence of God moves and acts in the middle of all human life. We are eternally challenged to keep these realities together if our lives are rooted in *transformation*. [28]

Feminists see things organically, sensing the interconnectedness of the whole created universe and people's lives within it. Feminism upholds unity in diversity rather than separation and alienation in difference. Feminists connect personal and political, economic and spiritual, challenge and nurture, into a spiritual politic for justice. For them, differences in beliefs can be enriching rather than detracting from the spiritual quest for justice.[29]

Carter Heyward vividly names the norm for feminist spirituality as justice and justice-making activity. For her, justice means "right-relation between and among people, relation of mutual benefit, created by mutual effort" and "human well-being in a just society." She continues: "Such theology is rooted in faith in a just god/dess. For some feminists, god is the source of justice; for others, the maker of justice; for others, justice itself: god *is* justice."[30]

One concrete example of how this spirituality for justice works is a presentation of the Regina Christian Feminist Action Group to the Federal Government of Canada:

28. Chris Smith, "Feminist Spirituality," *Well Springs: A Journal of United Methodist Clergywomen* 3, no. 1 (Spring 1990): 10.

29. See Mary Jo Weaver, "Who Is the Goddess, and Where Does She Get Us?" *Journal of Feminist Studies in Religion* 5, no. 1 (Spring 1989): 61, for elaboration of the idea that traditional religion offers a perspective based in history, while neopaganism offers a view based in utopianism—but that both are based in the concept of working toward justice and well-being.

30. Carter Heyward, *Our Passion for Justice* (New York: Pilgrim Press, 1984), p. 227.

I represent the Regina Christian Feminist Action Group. As active participants in the women's community in Saskatchewan, we want to join our voices with those of our friends in other groups in protesting against the cuts in the Secretary of State's women's program, in the recent Federal budget. On top of cuts in health care, welfare, Unemployment Insurance; and with more families and individuals facing unemployment and other problems which generate hardship, frustration, and violence, this of all times is not the time to cut projects which are working to fill gaps, and give support and hope to women who so often take the brunt of these upsets.

With the agricultural crisis in Saskatchewan, it is shocking that the Saskatchewan Women's Agricultural Network funding is to be reduced. To give less funds to Saskatchewan Women's Resources, who help organize and facilitate various groups, has a serious effect on the encouragement to groups of women wherever they are in the province, to deal with their own issues. There is crying need for more, not less, funding to the Saskatchewan Battered Women's Advocacy Network, and the Provincial Association of Transition Houses. Above all, the Saskatchewan Action Committee on the Status of Women can be said to be a focal point, a coordinating group for us all in working for the equality of women.

We are talking here of groups committed to justice issues. Included is our Christian Feminist Network. For us, Christianity is very much about justice, ethics, morality in society; feminism is about commitment to women's experience, beliefs, ideas; thus Christian feminists join our voices to calls for justice for women.[31]

A final point about this feminist vision of well-being and justice is that it is global. Women around the world are engaged in work for justice, are involved in spiritualities for transformation. Although this book focuses primarily on North American feminism, it does so with consciousness of the need for solidarity with women of the world whose material and social conditions are often harsh. Pat Krug, an active member of the Saskatchewan Christian Feminist Network, has traveled to several parts of the world as a representative of the United Church of Canada and of farm groups. She also works diligently for human rights in Canada. Pat says:

Having spent time in South Korea where the people have had human rights taken away from them, I think that it's not a good thing for us to ignore when some human rights are being taken away from people in this country. . . .

Women in other countries continually tell us that the way we can

---

31. Florence Bishop, "Opposition to Secstate Women's Program Cuts: News Conference Statement," May 16, 1989.

be in solidarity with them is to go home and look after our own human rights and justice for women.[32]

Global solidarity means we must take action in our immediate locations and contexts.

A Word about Native and New Age Spirituality

Within the feminist movement there is much discussion about Native spirituality and New Age religions. Some feminists believe it is appropriate to use whatever is helpful to their spirituality. Others feel that this is not necessarily so. While New Age and Native spirituality have fundamentally different values and approaches, the issue of the appropriateness of their uses in feminism draws them together here.

There is a current resurgence and development of Native spirituality in North America. For many Native people, learning of their traditions from the elders is giving new life and hope and is allowing for an integrity of personhood and cultural pride that has been severely damaged by life in a racist society. Many white people see aspects of Native spirituality that are appealing and want to be part of them. A conversation between two Feminist Spiritual Community members names the dilemma:

A: The Native people I work with do not want to be anybody's guru and get quite angry when white people come wanting to sit at their feet. Their culture and traditions have been so wiped out for so long in this area that they are only beginning to try to discover what it means to be Native and have a Native spirituality themselves. So when white people want the Native people to lead them to some spiritual truth, it is offensive. I don't know what the answer is.

B: If they have things to share, then I think it is OK to use them. If we listen to them and take them seriously and they offer stuff to us then, why wouldn't we use it, as long as we say this is from the Hopi tradition, this is from the Cree tradition, this is from the Saulteaux.

A: For me it has something to do with the way in which it is approached and also with the context. It has to be used in the political context out of which it comes. So many whites want to take the goodies in a very ahistorical way. They want to use the rituals but not to stand in solidarity with the struggle for justice

---

32. Pat Krug as quoted by Barb Elliott, "Human Rights—in Korea, the Philippines, Saskatchewan," *The Unbeaten Path* 24 (June 1988).

for Native people. If white people are willing to stand in solidarity politically and to take seriously the historic oppression of Native people, then that is different. The same thing is true of people entering Eastern religions. Often they have been very hurt by Christianity and so go to an Eastern religion and claim it to be the way of truth—but they ignore the fact that the culture out of which that religion has come is as sexist, racist, and violent as their own culture.

Canadian Elaine Bishop describes what solidarity with Native people means in her spirituality:

> Being called into right relationships with native people means standing with them on issues like self-determination, self-government, supporting their health care and justice systems, supporting the ways they have of healing themselves which we've helped to suppress, bringing First Nations into the constitution. It also means not requiring that the First Nations educate us, but being prepared to educate ourselves on what the struggles are and then acting on them.[33]

Acting in solidarity with the political struggles of Native people is likely to mean that non-Native people will not use practices from Native spirituality. Because white people have taken land, sovereignty, and economic and political power from Native people, taking aspects of Native spirituality at this point in history seems a further violation.

From a feminist perspective, New Age spirituality contains significant problems. New Age philosophies are broad ranging and differ greatly in detail. However, most are highly individualistic in their worldviews, and thus while claiming to be apolitical, their philosophies and views of social change reinforce right-wing political positions. As Rae Gabriel notes:

> The Catch words or phrases of the New Age movement include: *Create*—as in you create your own reality; *Responsibility*—as in you are 100 percent responsible for everything; *Choose*—as in you choose your parents, your sex, and the life experiences you have had; *There just is*—as in there is no good or evil, there just is; *Negativity*—as in negative emotions, negative energy, negative thoughts.
>
> Therefore, whether it is an abusive relationship, the death of a child, or a life-threatening disease, you created it, you are 100 percent responsible for it because you chose it and it isn't good or bad

---

33. Norah McMurtry, "Solidarity Is Covenant: An Interview with Elaine Bishop," *Women's Concerns,* Winter 1990, p. 7.

anyway. So let's not blame anyone because that's negative and will only create more negativity in your life.[34]

The consequence of this kind of thinking is to blame the victim for his or her situation of abuse, oppression, poverty, or injustice and to reinforce patriarchal patterns of hierarchy and discrimination. The social, political, and economic barriers of capitalist patriarchy are ignored, as are the structures of sexism, racism, heterosexism, and able-bodyism.

Thus there are clear contradictions between (1) the New Age stress on individualism, personal well-being, and creation of one's own choices and realities and (2) the feminist political consciousness, which calls for communal decision-making for global and community well-being and just structures. This analysis shows that much of the New Age religious philosophy and practice does not fit with feminist understandings that require political consciousness and work for justice and well-being in the world.

---

34. Rae Gabriel, "New Age Thinking: A New Weapon of Patriarchy," *Kinesis*, November 1990, p. 9.

Chapter 3

JUSTICE

The various definitions of justice by feminists all embody the same qualities. Pat says, "Justice means that all people in this world have access to a place to live, an ability to grow something, food to eat; they can make choices about their own lives, not to be overrun by some other form of government."

Eleanor Haney describes justice as shared power. This involves enabling self-determination for persons and groups and the creation of structures that value people. It is the power to shape our common future, to have equally shared resources and equal say in decisions about how they will be shared.[35]

Justice, then, is when all people have food and shelter; when each person is treated with dignity and respect and is enabled to contribute to the well-being of society freely and publicly; when health care and medical assistance are accessible to all who need them; when structures are based on human worth rather than color, gender, sexual preference, nationality, age, or physical ability; when violence and fear of violence are eliminated from people's daily living. Justice is known in very concrete and earthy terms and in the present time. Justice for women is particularly important at this point in history because of the structural and material inequalities experienced by women around the world.[36]

Feminist understandings of justice, however, are not the same as all understandings of justice. Mary Daly questions whether the word should even be used while patriarchal society exists:

> Of all the "moral virtues," none is more pompously advocated in platitudes and ponderous tones than "justice." Yet the very idea

---

35. Haney, *Vision and Struggle,* pp. 69–70.
36. See Joni Seager and Ann Olson, *Women of the World* (London: Pan Books, 1986).

that there could be justice within patriarchal society, sustained by phallic myths and ideologies, is a logical absurdity. . . .

The "justice" of the fathers' Foreground is false, elementary, plastic. This is not to say that women should not seek "equal pay" or the "Equal Rights Amendment." It is to say that one should not be misled by such misnomers. To believe that such changes will bring about real "equality," while failing to understand the need for almost ineffable changes at the very heart of consciousness, is to settle for potted "justice."[37]

Three Understandings of Justice

Nonetheless, other feminists choose to use the term "justice," noting that it is helpful to distinguish between procedural justice, distributive justice, and substantive justice. Procedural justice is based on the maintenance of the law. The assumption is that the laws are fair and that the courts are the instrument for the maintenance of justice and for settling disputes in a free society. It is assumed that if the laws are equally applied to everyone, then justice has been done.

Distributive justice goes one step further than procedural justice by suggesting that there would be a fair distribution of goods and services in society if everyone were free to pursue their own self-interests. Robert Bellah and his colleagues question whether distributive justice is sufficient. In distributive justice, different occupations could provide different incomes if everyone could have access to well-paying jobs. However, if not everyone can have well-paying and interesting jobs, especially if lack of access is because one comes from a socially disadvantaged group, then the idea of distributive justice will not work. While resources might be shared so no one falls below a certain level, advantaged groups can rise far above the minimum state of disadvantaged groups in this view of justice.[38]

Substantive justice involves a transformation of every aspect of life. It means the elimination of privilege and achieving the real equality of all people in decision-making that affects their lives. It is more than simple self-interest because it involves the well-being of the community, as well as the consideration of those whose lives are very different from one's own.

Joe Holland and Peter Henriot look at the issue of substantive justice from the point of view of the political economy. They suggest that the changes in capitalism mean that there must be changes in understandings of justice. Under laissez-faire industrial capitalism, the

---

37. Mary Daly, *Pure Lust: Elemental Feminist Philosophy* (Boston: Beacon, 1984), pp. 220–21.

38. Bellah et al., *Habits of the Heart,* p. 26.

focus was on reactionary strategies based in tradition and in the aris-
tocracy. Under the social welfare stage of capitalism, the focus was on
adaptation and freedom, with liberal understandings of justice and
attentiveness to the middle class. Henriot and Holland argue that we
have now moved to a transnational stage of capitalism in which transnational banks and companies govern the political economy. With this
kind of a political economy, they suggest that the kind of justice needed
is a radical transformative view of justice. In this understanding, global
efforts for justice need to focus on the poor, especially the poor of
the Third World. Rather than the self-interest of liberal understanding, there needs to be a utopian cultural vision that is global and is
built on respect for human values.[39]

Two women's visions of justice show what substantive justice would
mean for them. One says:

> In the ideal world there would be more understanding and respect.
> Everybody would be committed to justice. Profit would *not* be so
> important. Multinationals would disappear. There would be no
> people starving. No women and children would be abused. Women
> would be assertive and angry and would have good self-esteem—
> not saying "I'm sorry" all the time. Men would be in touch with
> their feelings—not just anger—and they would be able to cry openly.
> We would rejoice together. All competition would be gone. Coop-
> eration would be a way of life. Any games would be cooperative.
> People would have happy lives lived with meaning and purpose.
> There would be problems, difficulties, and death. But we would be
> able to rejoice in life more than we do now. There would be no
> more bombs or nuclear weapons. When anyone or any government
> took on a project, they would think about the implications of it for
> the rest of the world. Instead of building a satellite, the money would
> go to food for the hungry, for research for AIDS and cancer. We
> would have a real sense of priorities for life. There would be more
> women in power. There would be women leaders throughout the
> world. Women would claim the power that is rightfully ours. But
> we would not operate in men's ways. We would instead ask the
> question, Is this good for our world?

When asked, "What is your vision of a world of justice?" another woman
responded:

> "No crime and lots of fat happy ladies"—I can't remember who said
> that—Flo Kennedy or maybe Gloria Steinem.
>   Justice is shared economic, political, and social power in such a
> way that diversity is accepted and conflict (which I see as stronger

---

39. Holland and Henriot, *Social Analysis*, pp. 84–86.

than diversity) is negotiated and, if necessary, arbitrated, in a way that does not happen now. It means respect for all marginalized people in such a way that we are all valued as much as white middle-class heterosexual men. But it is not a world where everyone would have everything that white men have now. It is not an equal piece of the old pie but an entirely different pie. It would be a world where there is sharing of the work. It would be recognizing that we each have special skills. Doctors would not be valued more than farmers or gardeners. There would be an opportunity in work to use different skills—cognitive, emotional, and physical—if we have the ability to do all of those.

I would like to see social arrangements where sexual monogamy is not seen as the only way that things should be, but that people have real choices around that. There would be complete acceptance of different (but mutual) sexual relationships.

We would not be obsessed by money. We would have more time for leisure. More people would have decision-making power regarding how money is spent.

Personally I would like to live in a community with my own bedroom and meeting space and window box but with a sharing of the household responsibilities. It would have a wide range of ages. It would be a world where the media does not have as much influence in forming one's image of oneself as it presently does. . . . In my household there would have to be lots of toys and kids. "No crime and lots of fat happy ladies."

Biblical Understandings of Justice

The World Council of Churches has named 1988–98 as an Ecumenical Decade of Churches in Solidarity with Women. The aims of the decade are:

1. Empowering women to challenge oppressive structures in the global community, their country and their church.
2. Affirming—through shared leadership and decision-making, theology and spirituality—the decisive contributions of women in churches and communities.
3. Giving visibility to women's perspectives and the actions in the work and struggle for justice, peace and the integrity of creation.
4. Enabling the churches to free themselves from racism, sexism and classism; from teachings and practices that discriminate against women.
5. Encouraging the churches to take actions in solidarity with women.[40]

---

40. Sub-Unit on Women in Church and Society, "Ecumenical Decade of Churches

This kind of commitment grows out of biblical understandings of justice, which is based in concrete human needs and structures.

The Christian call to justice comes from Scriptures such as Isaiah 1:16–17, "Cease to do evil, learn to do good; seek justice, correct oppression; defend the fatherless, plead for the widow"; or Isaiah 65:19–22, 25:

> There will not be weeping there, no calling for help. Babies will no longer die in infancy, and all people will live out their life span. . . . People will build houses and get to live in them—they will not be used by someone else. They will plant vineyards and enjoy the wine—it will not be drunk by others. . . . They will fully enjoy the things they have worked for. . . . Wolves and lambs will eat together; lions will eat straw as cattle do.

It is in this context that Sharon describes her vision of justice:

> It is a very biblical view. Shalom, harmony, right relations with God, earth, one another, and ourselves; a deep peace, connection, valuing, honoring. Not a world where people have power over others but a world where everyone is empowered, where there is a place for everyone's gifts. There would be economic justice and fairness. No one would be exploited. There would not just be one way of looking at things. All would be valued, and we would all learn from each other. There would be no war, but security that comes from means other than the usual military means of war. The earth would be treated as alive, not as possessed. We would know our deep dependence on the earth. And I believe that it is possible.

Clearly, not all Christians hold these views. Many Christians believe that it is God's will for people who believe in Jesus and have a personal relationship with him to have all their prayers answered in a personal way, whether those prayers are for good health, affluence, or the expansion of American political interests in Latin America. Even some Christians who opt for a stance consistent with the scriptural visions of social justice continue to maintain dualistic stances. For example, Mark Searle, a Roman Catholic theologian, has a very low doctrine of human nature and a high doctrine of God. He claims that "human justice, it might be said, is at best a bridle on evil; God's justice is the flowing of the good."[41] Most feminist theologians avoid this dualism, stressing that it is humanity that must embody God's

in Solidarity with Women, 1988–1998" (Geneva: World Council of Churches, n.d.), p. 1.

41. Mark Searle, "Serving the Lord with Justice," in *Liturgy and Social Justice*, ed. Searle (Collegeville, Minn.: Liturgical Press, 1980), p. 16.

justice in this world and that justice created by humans is much more than a bridle on evil; it is good.

Despite the problems with the church and many of the strains of theology in it, Christian feminists continue to claim that the church is a place that allows for this kind of a strong feminist vision of justice to be lived out. As Mary Hunt notes, the Christian community, unlike government, big business, and the university, claims to seek justice, provides an infrastructure for getting the work done, and invites religious people toward a deeper coincidence between word and action.[42] Thus the church is a place where Christian feminists can call people and structures to account, recall the vision of another way, and draw on the historical claim for substantive justice and righteousness. As one Christian woman asserts:

> History is important. That is why I stick with the church. It has been in existence for so long. Jesus had a sense of social justice, and despite what men and women have done since, there has always been a stream of social justice. It is ongoing and continues to lead women and men toward a more just way of living.

Marta Benavides adds a learning from her mother:

> She demanded that our actions be consistent with God's call for justice. It was through these experiences that I started to understand that what we practice must be intentional, directed, planned, and transforming. Justice requires not just action but reflective and responsible action.[43]

---

42. Mary E. Hunt, "Loving Well Means Doing Justice," in *A Faith of One's Own*, ed. B. Zanotti (Trumansburg, N.Y.: Crossing Press, 1986), p. 116.

43. Marta Benavides, "My Mother's Garden Is a New Creation," in *Inheriting Our Mothers' Gardens*, ed. Letty Russell, Kwok Pui-lan, Ada Maria Isasi-Diaz, and Katie Geneva Cannon (Philadelphia: Westminster Press, 1988), p. 132.

Chapter 4

RITUALS

Religious rituals are key in this study. Much of the material was collected through participant observation of rituals. Religious ritual is a way many people create, express, and enact connections with the holy. Christians attend worship services as part of their practice of faith. Witches and goddess groups have circles for rituals. Through the actions of the ritual, people are enabled to get in touch with the divine and see themselves in a new light from those experiences. One woman interviewed in the project says: "[Rituals] deepen daily life. They help me stop in the daily rush. It is like entering through a door and not rushing through that door—pausing to notice. To give meaning to the ordinary. When I have done a ritual, I feel different and see differently." Through rituals, new experiences and ideas are integrated into a person's psyche, patterns of thinking, and theology/thealogy. New attitudes and values can be acquired.

The centrality of rituals in this project means that we need to have some definitions and characteristics of rituals, especially religious rituals.

All rituals involve symbolic actions through their verbal and nonverbal, material and nonmaterial elements. These components are woven into patterns. Richard Schechner claims that "in ritual ordinary behaviour is condensed, exaggerated, repeated, made into rhythms or pulses (often faster or slower than usual) or frozen into poses."[44] The rhythms and poses are set to bear overt and covert ideological messages. Ritual forms, like speech forms, are transmitters of culture that bear inherently political messages—some implicit and some explicit—about power, relationships, and what people can/should do or not do in order to live well. Rituals thus provide frameworks and modes of perceiving. They take people out of the ordinary and frame

---

44. Richard Schechner, "The Future of Ritual," *Journal of Ritual Studies* 1, no. 1 (1987): 5.

the experience in such a way as to limit external influences. Generally, anthropologists and liturgists have concluded that this limiting power in ritual serves as a conservative force emphasizing tradition.[45] In other words, the intent to create a framework for perceiving the culture and its meaning is likely to keep things as much the same as possible.

Nancy Falk, however, adds a different perspective to this idea, suggesting that the values framed in religious rituals are as likely to produce change as to conserve:

> Scholars are now beginning to acknowledge that religion has been equally significant as an agent of social transformation; for that which encodes can recode, framing prophetic new views of human possibility and releasing the enormous bursts of energy that are necessary to move people and policies in altered directions. In fact, as that which alone could alter the root-paradigms which framed the decisions and directions of entire cultures, religion was the most powerful transformative force in society during times prior to the modern era.[46]

Feminists who are seeking change and who are aware that nothing has been left untouched by patriarchal imaginings must critique existing rituals and develop rituals that bring about social transformation.

Another related characteristic is that rituals are concerned with community and with its life and myth. Coming together for ritual is important. Starhawk indicates that when a community gathers for ritual, it can be "a place where they can sing or scream, howl ecstatically or furiously, play or keep solemn silence."[47] Creating a sense of group belonging, a place where people can share their deepest mix of feelings, is important in the life of any group that does rituals. Two women show how the myth and life of their communities are lived out in ritual. The first names the value of worldwide community as a priority:

> One of the rituals of the church that I like is World Wide Communion Sunday. It feels like a ritual of social action because it is a uniting of people all over the world doing the same thing at the same time on the same day. Of course, the problem with it is that it is only Christian, but at least for that one day in October we have a worldwide community.

---

45. For example, see Evelyn Underhill, *Worship* (New York: Harper and Brothers, 1957), p. 35.

46. Nancy Falk, "Introduction," in *Women, Religion, and Social Change*, ed. Y. Y. Haddad and E. B. Findly (Albany: State University of New York Press, 1985), p. xv.

47. Starhawk, *Dreaming the Dark* (Boston: Beacon, 1982), p. 155.

The second woman shows herself as being part of a community that takes people's lives seriously, valuing and caring for them. Her community also believes that new life is possible.

> A woman was sexually assaulted recently. She needed something done ritualistically, some clearing and release so that the event could be turned around and she could know grace in her life again. It was not a broad corporate ritual, but we were able to do that. Or another example would be an incest survivor that I am working with right now. We did a mock funeral as part of the counseling I am doing with her. She needed to bury the horrendous act that had happened to her and to stomp on the grave. I don't know why we stomped, but it seemed right at the time. It just seemed the right way when it came out.
>
> Part of ritual is for healing; that is, it leads to new life.

Cultural anthropologist James McLeod offers several criteria that he believes are essential for something to be classified as a ritual. Rituals must be conventionalized, that is, have certain commonly understood and accepted rules for performance; they must be dramatic, that is, evocative and emotionally engaging; they must be repetitive, that is, involve a series of events in a particular order; they must be communal, or have commonly understood meanings if done alone; they must have higher levels of meaning, that is, go beyond the physical objects used; and there must be an expected outcome of the ritual activity.[48]

Christian liturgies are one form of religious ritual. Christians understand liturgies to be avenues by which one enters the presence of the holy and gives meaning to the circumstances of human life. Marion Hatchett describes liturgies as encapsulating the community's heritage and hopes (i.e., its myth). Liturgy is to remember, to look forward, and to involve the people. Leaders personify the culture that is to be transmitted and are able to lead the long, complicated, but essentially rational rites. Hatchett goes on to claim that "the rites are designed to define, re-define, shape, re-shape, or maintain the communal life. They establish, re-establish, or strengthen communication with the god."[49] Furthermore, Rosemary Radford Ruether notes that "liturgy means lifting up a particular human moment and making it paradigmatic of all moments, focussing in the mimetic reenactment

---

48. James McLeod, "Ritual in Corporate Culture Studies: An Anthropological Approach," *Journal of Ritual Studies* 4, no. 1 (Winter 1990): 92–93.

49. Marion Hatchett, *Sanctifying Life, Time, and Space* (New York: Seabury, 1976), pp. 4–5.

of this moment all our accumulated fears and hopes for this type of event."[50]

Some of the women interviewed did not like the word "ritual," preferring to speak of "liturgy" or "worship."

> I am uncomfortable with the word "ritual." It smacks of paganism and idolatry to me. I am a very traditional Christian in worship. I like the order of service. It has always been important to me. In my early years it was probably related to a sense of belonging and to the kind of community I experienced in my worship family. It was uplifting and empowering and enabling. I still find that in worship I know a sense of the Spirit.

The word "ritual" has been used to designate the broad range of theologies/thealogies and practices the women described. It is used in an anthropological sense of a category in which various forms would be subsumed, including Christian liturgy.

The rituals described in this project fit with some of the categories described by scholars of anthropology, liturgy, and ritual studies. As feminist rituals, however, they sometimes move in other directions and are more likely to involve the unexpected than these definitions would permit.

---

50. Ruether, *Women-Church,* p. 107.

· PART 2 ·

New Names for Theology/Thealogy

Along with definitions, descriptions, and characteristics of patriarchy, feminism, justice, and ritual, the portion of the
feminist thealogical method on defining the issues involves
collecting the data, developing categories and concepts, and naming
them. The chapters in this part describe thirteen categories emerging
from the data that form an understanding of feminist ritual thealogy.
They are beauty, survival and safety, embodiment, naming of self and
experience, community and relationships, diversity, healing, play and
humor, resistance and undermining, vulnerability, loss, vision, and
trusting one's own inner wisdom. The list is not comprehensive—the
ways to know the holy are far more expansive than would emerge
from one small study. Yet these categories for describing women's
experience of the holy resonate with many women. The articulation
of the women in this project brings together ways of talking about
spirituality, of describing what is true and real and meaningful in
women's lives.

This work in no way intends to develop a new systematic theology
that can be universalized. What it does is open the question of the
adequacy of Christian systematic theology, articulating some different
ways of thinking about theology/thealogy. It does this from the point
of view of what would traditionally be called liturgical theology. I have
chosen to call it feminist ritual thealogy because it includes some rituals that would not fit within the framework of Christian thinking
and because it allows for a broadening and a redefinition of the underpinnings of liturgy or ritual. I have chosen to speak of thealogy
instead of theology, since the focus is on rituals growing out of female
experience and feminist understandings of the deity.

Chapter 5

BEAUTY

Why is beauty a thealogical category? What have beauty and spirituality to do with each other? Women name beauty as important in connecting reality and holiness, in seeing injustice, and in being creative and original. The kind of beauty described involves all of the senses, may be transitory, and often involves hospitality.

Beauty is important to women. Beauty as women define it, however, has been distorted or lost in patriarchal culture. In patriarchal culture, beauty is connected with commerce, and thus women's beauty is defined by how many products it can sell. The fair-skinned, blond, thin, young woman of car, beer, and toilet bowl cleaner advertisements, and of pornography, creates the definition of beauty in women. Clear-cut forests, skyscrapers, and cruise missiles define beauty in the environment and in the commercial world. There is no sense of the beauty of natural cycles of aging and of birth-to-death-to-birth cycles in human life or the natural world. As women, we are cut off from recognizing beauty from within, from recognizing the beauty of rage at injustice, from recognizing the holy in the natural world and each other. This is especially true for Christians who have come from a stark Calvinist background where all beauty was seen to distract from true worship and where churches and lives were to be unadorned, lest people focus on the adornment instead of God. Protestant Christians live with the residue of that heritage, and for many, the transformation to an acceptance of beauty and holiness as interrelated is challenging.

In an interview Eleanor Haney describes her experience of moving toward an aesthetic spirituality through rituals with candles, smells, and flowers. She claims that these concrete things "are not just metaphors. They're it."

> I remember one time when we were meeting at State Street Church, we were in the chapel which has dark wood floors. There were fifty

votive candles in their little containers in a huge circle. It was incredibly beautiful. It was one sign post in the transformation of Elly Haney! I guess my spirituality is aesthetic—beauty as a way to holiness. It is in the concrete stuff—not in ideas.

To see the candles, shells, or something to do with the ocean, flowers, plants, all of those [she hesitates] . . . you get embraced by them. You come into the room and it is like being held by all those beautiful objects. It is tangible, textured, sensuous.

For me as a Presbyterian, all of this is so new. Maybe it is not so hard for Catholics, who are used to a more tangible form through icons and incense.

Three other women describe the appeal of beauty as an avenue to holiness. One is part of a small group that does rituals together:

There is a cloth laid out on the floor—a place for us to focus—a kind of altar. It is special because different people bring symbols that are special to them, or on the theme for the evening. Invoking the elements and the four directions is meaningful. It allows a creation spirituality to emerge. The spirit is alive in the elements around us.

Another says: "I like to surround myself with beauty. I write letters to friends, and when I do, I bring out special pictures, stones, shells, and candles. To use a Christian term, I pray for them. Or to put it another way, I become a channel of good energy for them." The experience of the third woman grows out of having recently moved from an urban area to a rural area.

One thing that I have noticed is how much I really appreciate the sunsets. Our house is on the edge of town, so that nothing blocks the view. I often sit on the steps or go for a walk or even watch from inside to see the beauty of the sunset. I hear the birds. I suppose they have always been there, but I just never heard them before. I notice changes in the area that I did not notice in the city.

There is more to beauty than direct connection to the holy through it. Beauty also shows the contrasts present in the world. Again Elly Haney describes what this means:

On Monday nights at Community, when women bring vases of flowers to adorn the center of the circle, the room is transformed. The deep, dazzling, and abiding loveliness of lavender and gold and purple and rose draws one into the very heart of the universe.

Our capacity for beauty and creativity illumines the *unnaturalness* of injustice. When I see and am fed by the flowers at Community,

I also often discover an ache in my soul. Somehow, the monstrousness, the insanity of the possibilities and preparation for nuclear war, for example, are increased in the presence of such innocent beauty.[1]

Many activists recognize the importance of this connection between beauty and justice. The turn-of-the-century women's movement song "Bread and Roses" describes the importance of having both the necessities of life and beauty. Carolyn McDade's recent song "Trouble and Beauty" describes that same sentiment. Alice Walker's essay "In Search of Our Mothers' Gardens" tells of the ways in which black women in American slavery kept beauty alive, in spite of the injustices experienced in their daily lives.[2] The story of the woman who broke the alabaster jar of ointment over Jesus (Mark 14:3–9) shows the valuing of beauty in Christian tradition. Nonetheless, Elly Haney cautions against getting so caught up in beauty that we forget justice:

> For beauty can also be a trap. If creating is not a necessity but a luxury for the privileged, it can be an escape from addressing injustice. Similarly, surrounding oneself with beautiful objects can and often probably does perpetuate injustice; most of the money that buys art, for instance, comes eventually from the labor of other people and the being of the natural world.[3]

An experience in a ritual of the Feminist Spiritual Community adds to the understanding of how ideas involving beauty can further injustice. The ritual was using identification with colors to gain understandings about the internal and external rhythms of our bodies. In the exercise, several people got dark colors—browns, blacks, and grays—and were quite unhappy to have gotten them. One of the members of the community spoke up:

> I am really dismayed as I hear the dislike of browns and blacks. It seems to me that we have been so socialized into seeing these colors as dull and uninteresting. In the Judeo-Christian and other traditions, black is seen as evil. It is amazing how we absorb this so deeply that we even transfer it to people with dark skin colors. We need to be very careful of the way we use browns and blacks in our spirituality, I think.

---

1. Haney, *Vision and Struggle*, pp. 15–16.
2. "Bread and Roses," *SCM Song Book* (Toronto: Student Christian Movement, n.d.); Carolyn McDade, "Trouble and Beauty," in *This Tough Spun Web* (Plainville, Mass. Womancentre at Plainville, n.d.); Alice Walker, "In Search of Our Mothers' Gardens," in *In Search of Our Mothers' Gardens* (San Diego: Harvest Books, 1983).
3. Haney, *Vision and Struggle*, p. 16.

So our definitions of beauty are important, and we can use beauty in ways that draw us into holiness, or we can use beauty in ways that perpetuate classism and racism and the systemic evils that reside in our current world.

Janet Walton helps to expand the definition of what beauty is and how it can be lived out in our spirituality and our world. She indicates that music, architecture, and ceremony are the usual forums for beauty in worship. However, beauty also includes what is truthful and original. Beauty as originality comes through artists and inventors, but also through those who create new patterns, whether in the area of work (e.g., through job sharing), in models of relationship (e.g., single parents adopting unwanted children), or in presentation of ideas (e.g., teachers using new methods). Thus, challenging convention is often one way of exposing a deeper beauty than what is seen on the surface.[4]

In noting that beauty occurs in many different forms, Walton suggests that not all beauty needs to be permanent. Elizabeth Dodson Gray focuses specifically on this idea. In discussing some of the beautiful and artistic endeavors of women, she says:

> Think of the anonymous designs for quilts, the patterns for dresses, the recipes for wonderful food, the table settings, the flower arrangements, the countless insights into better ways of childrearing and keeping house. Think of the knitting knots devised and the patterns of knitting ranging from argyle to cable that women have created. Think of the crochet knots and patterns, think of the needlepoint and embroidery stitches. All of these "women's arts" have been freely donated to the culture, and the originator never recorded. . . . Women's creative impulses are invested in perishable foods, fleeting flower arrangements, sensitive relationships with people who grow old and die, in rearing children who grow up and go away.[5]

Not all beauty is permanent. Another example comes from Carol's life.

> A lot of things I do everyday are part of my ritual. I do not just get up in the morning, shower, and prepare for the day—instead, as I do these things, I am preparing myself for life and for who I am to be that day. I also like having bouquets of flowers around or, when flowers are not in season, to have some other decoration in various

---

4. Janet Walton, *Art and Worship: The Vital Connection* (Wilmington, Del.: Michael Glazier, 1988), p. 62.

5. Elizabeth Dodson Gray, *Sacred Dimensions of Women's Experience* (Wellesley, Mass.: Roundtable Press, 1988), pp. 8, 9.

places in the house. They are focal points or areas of beauty. The wearing of clothing that I like and colors that I like is ritualistic for me. The ordinary stuff of life is part of the ritual for me.

Most of the rituals in feminist communities in which I participated over the course of this project were rituals that were created for a particular setting and a particular context. They were not necessarily recorded for herstory or for reuse. Their importance was in the moment of their use. The space was made beautiful with ordinary things. The words, actions, and feelings were woven into a cloth for that occasion. Rituals, then, call our attention to beauty—the candles, stones, shells, and altar cloths are concrete signs of all that is beautiful in life, and at a deep level they remind us that we too are part of that beauty. Even when we come feeling desolate, the beauty of ritual can touch a chord deep inside. Part of the vision of a just and peaceful world includes chocolate, pretty jewelry, bright clothing, outrageous humor, and sensual pleasures of sight, sound, touch, smell, and taste in feminist spirituality.

Another example of beauty comes from a woman who says:

> I try to create a home for myself, my family, and to offer hospital-
> ity. I always have many people in my home. I always have plenty of
> food and drink and a well-ordered and pleasant living room. I grow
> flowers to bring into the living room. I have often had the beauty
> of hearing, "I have never been in a white person's house before." I
> often wonder how that can be in this day and age. I want to keep
> up with the practice of hospitality.

Many women go to great lengths to create hospitable environments. Food is often a large part of gatherings and sometimes is included in rituals. Eating together creates community, and the foods are often festive or symbolic to express shared commitments or values. Opening their homes to people needing a place to stay is also a form of hospitality common to many women.

Elizabeth Dodson Gray points out what she perceives to be a difference between women's perspective on caring and hospitality and men's perspective on it:

> Male religion has always stated *from a child's point of view* its central
> image of God-the-Father as caregiver. Care giving has always been
> reflected upon from the position of the one *receiving* the care. Once
> again male theology discloses how it is permeated through and
> through by the limitations of male life-experience.
>   The truth is that since males do not usually give care, they are
> severely limited in their capacity to reflect upon how care giving

may be sacred. They can only and have only reflected upon the sacred nature of *receiving* care. There has not yet been a theology imaged and written by those who *give* care.[6]

Women thus connect the care giving done in their experience with the care giving of the divine. This care giving, this creation of hospitality, is part of the sacred experience of women. It is part of the creation of beauty, part of the challenge to create an environment that is hospitable even with very few resources, part of the way of bringing hope for justice when so much injustice exists.

Beauty, then, is a thealogical category—a way of experiencing the holy, a way of seeing what justice and injustice means, a way of offering sustenance and hope in a broken world.

---

6. Ibid., pp. 68–69.

Chapter 6

SURVIVAL AND SAFETY

Closely connected to the idea of beauty are the concepts of survival and safety. The Mudflower Collective chose their name because, in their challenging quest for justice, it became quickly apparent that "flowers do not grow easily in mud."[7] Oftentimes, more mud than beauty seems present. Yet women are survivors, and this is one of their spiritual strengths.

Although survival has been key in women's lives and culture, it has not always been considered as a category of theology. Eleanor Haney suggests that within Christian tradition, survival has been viewed as selfish or cowardly. She claims that in the lives of women and other oppressed groups, survival is often a positive principle of moral action, a creative response to the historical moment in which we find ourselves. Often, survival means "that we do what we need to in order to live with some measure of dignity, security, and integrity" by such strategies as "deceiving and outwitting the oppressor—'closeting' ourselves, for instance . . . [by hiding our] anger and frustration, play[ing] some of the games and accommodat[ing] on certain issues in order to survive." She concludes, "Surviving is a necessary and important principle. We should live."[8]

Vicki puts this into a Canadian context:

> There is a strong history of prairie women facing the elements. They had to be tough to survive, and so that survival meant that the spiritual and the political, the personal and the global, had to come together. The history of the C.C.F. [Cooperative Commonwealth Federation] and those roots formed Saskatchewan. The strong independent spirit of those pioneer women lives on. There is a real

---

7. The Mudflower Collective, *God's Fierce Whimsy* (New York: Pilgrim Press, United Church Press, 1985), p. xi.
8. Haney, *Vision and Struggle*, pp. 70–71.

strength of surviving here that has affected the politics and the women's movement here.

Unfortunately, survival continues to be the most important and time-consuming activity for many women. In fact, for most people on the planet, poverty and the lack of clean water, food, shelter, and medical assistance absorb life. Oppressive governments, trade policies, and international relations force the poor world to be at the mercy of the rich world, preventing any semblance of well-being or justice and demanding that all energy focus on economic and family survival.

Caroline La Chapelle shows that survival for Native Canadian women stems from their socioeconomic status. Often, Native women are not involved in the women's movements because all of their energy is directed toward meeting basic needs. Using the example of demands for equal pay, La Chapelle notes that "while white women are striving towards ensuring their work is valued as the equivalent of a man's, Native women are trying to seek employment in order to feed their families."[9] Survival means different things for people of different races and classes and even of different geographic locations.

White Canadian prairie women talked about the influence of rural living, past and current. The following comment is typical:

> Many women have had to endure hard times on the farms. A lot of women grew up in the depression and were miles from any other women and had no transportation to be able to get to other women. They had to be either strong or dead.
>
> Sometimes it is really lonely for prairie women because of the isolation. There are things I would like to go to, but they are too far away. The farms are closer together than they used to be, but women can still feel isolated.

In the current farm crisis, the loneliness and isolation are not always based on geography. They are sometimes based on fear or discomfort. Farm people who are in danger of losing their farms or who have lost them because of banks' foreclosing often find it very hard to share the fact that they are in financial trouble. There is embarrassment, anger, shame, and concern at having no way to repay deeds of kindness when the crisis is on. Sometimes neighbors do not respond, even when they know that a farm family is in financial trouble, because they do not want to interfere or do not know what to do or say or are afraid because they know they may be next to lose their

---

9. Caroline La Chapelle, "Beyond Barriers," in *Still Ain't Satisfied,* ed. Maureen Fitzgerald, Connie Guberman, and Margie Wolfe (Toronto: Women's Press, 1982), p. 261.

farm.[10] This isolation makes survival for farm women and their families very difficult.

Often, however, it is for the sake of their families that women become involved in political actions. Farm women will do many things for the sake of their families that they would not do for themselves. In many spheres, women will assume great power when they see their children or grandchildren being threatened. Women have strong urges to survive and to help their children survive.

Clearly, survival is also a key resource for victims of patriarchal violence. Being survivors of incest, childhood molestation, or rape or having struggled through adult sexual assault or battering by a partner means that the resources and will for life are strong. Women who come face to face with such violence find strength in the reality of having survived and are often encouraged by the survival of other women who have known similar violations. In the face of violation it is easier to turn inward and to live as a victim than it is to see survival as a spiritual resource. Reliance on those who have caused the violation, although it is a pattern maintained by many women, does not provide the spiritual nurturance needed for healing and for becoming a healthy person who has survived an unhealthy situation. Turning to other survivors is often a new way of coming to terms with survival. Women can look to other women as sources of hope—to find inner strength, to find companions in their rage and grief, to find those with whom to weep bitter tears, and to find silent strength emerging from sorrow and brokenness.

Alyson Huntly adds hope as a need for survival against incredible odds. She wrote on the day the Gulf War began:

> It is January 15th [1991] as I write this. Not a time to write . . . a time to march, pray, stand in silent vigil . . . but surely not a time to write. Whatever I say may be meaningless before it reaches you. I turn the radio on, hoping for news. Hoping not for news. Hoping that peace may somehow have won out over violence. I find only hockey games!
>
> And then I write on. Every woman who writes is a survivor! All of us who write, who challenge injustice, speak out for change, new vision, hope, survive. We create. Out of the charred ashes of our lives, individual and collective, so scarred by violence, we create fertile ground. We continue to name the violence, in all its forms. . . . We hold fast to hope. We dig out spaces where we and others can build homes and live in them, plant trees and live to see them bear

---

10. See Nancy Painter, "The Emotional Side of Farm Foreclosure," in *Fighting the Farm Crisis*, ed. Terry Pugh (Saskatoon: Fifth House, 1987), for more details on this phenomenon.

sweet fruit. Spaces where justice can flow like water and peace like an everflowing stream. [11]

It is important not to romanticize survival. It is a spiritual resource only out of necessity, not out of choice. In a just world, where everyone had the resources needed for sufficient daily living and had freedom from violence, survival might be accepted as a given. But in the patriarchal culture of domination, degradation, and violence, it is amazing that survival has happened, especially for those who have lived with double and triple oppression. Audre Lorde, a black American feminist, graphically names this reality.

> But most of all, I think, we fear the very visibility without which we also cannot truly live. Within this country where racial difference creates a constant, if unspoken, distortion of vision, black women have on the one hand always been highly visible, and so, on the other hand, have been rendered invisible through the depersonalization of racism. Even within the women's movement, we have had to fight and still do, for the very visibility which also renders us most vulnerable, our blackness. For to survive in the mouth of this dragon we call america, we have had to learn this first and most vital lesson—that we were never meant to survive. [12]

Several of the women talked about the need for communities where survival is valued and about how rituals help them to survive in their daily living. One woman, who often feels as if she speaks a different language from the people she works with day-to-day because of her different values, says:

> [Rituals] are empowering. They help me to realize that I am not alone. God is with me in the midst of this. Other people, especially women, are with me in the midst of this. They understand. They will weep with me, laugh with me—and I don't have to spend two hours explaining to them what I want to say. Rituals sustain me. They hold me for a long time—I can go back to them in my mind when I feel there is not a lot of support for me where I am.

Another connects her rituals with her work:

> I worked with women who had become pregnant but wanted to finish high school. Some of them were like thirty—and had three kids but were totally illiterate. They had terrible stories to tell of

11. Alyson Huntly, "From the Editor," *Consensus*, January 1991, p. 1.
12. Audre Lorde, *The Cancer Journals* (San Francisco: Spinsters, 1980), p. 21.

rape and sexual abuse and devastation. I really needed meditation when I worked with them, just to keep myself centered.

Many women value safe ritual space in their struggle for survival.

It is frightening to rename the spiritual resources in ways that are at variance with the ways of the dominant culture. Several of the women that I spoke to described what Merlin Stone calls "the bolt of lightning phenomenon." Stone describes sitting in a small room in Oxford typing the text for *When God Was a Woman*. She had done extensive research over a number of years studying the excavation sites and museums of the Near East. As she typed, Stone suddenly felt sure that a bolt of lightning was about to strike her. She says:

> I mention this bolt of lightning syndrome because so many other women, those who now have an interest in the Goddess, have told me that they've had that same fear, that fear of questioning and challenging early religious training, that fear that a bolt of lightning would descend from above and strike them dead, just as they uttered the word "Goddess." [13]

Some described incidents such as Stone's naming the goddess; others, the fear of being struck down for entering the pulpit as a woman; others, the sudden flash of consciousness that life might not be as they had perceived it to this point. One simple example of the latter would be the sudden consciousness that it was possible for this particular woman to exert some control over her environment.

> One of the things that has helped me be more responsible is when I hear others saying no. I remember the first time that I was in a situation with gossip going on and one of the women simply said, "I do not want to do this." It had never struck me that I could say that. So I have learned to be more responsible.

While some of the experiences of the bolt of lightning were drastic fear that the person might be struck dead, the sudden flash is also important in situations of new insight.

But the drastic state is real. Many feminists, especially those who remain in the church while struggling with new forms of spirituality, live with real fears that someone will find out what they really believe. This tension led Ann Naylor to coin the phrase "closet spirituality." Ann was in a church-staff position that related to women in ministry. Often on late Saturday nights she would receive phone calls from women who were dreading having to preach or teach Sunday School

---

13. Merlin Stone, *Return of the Goddess* (Montreal: C.B.C. Transcripts, 1986), p. 1.

on Sunday morning, not knowing how to say what they really believed. Along with the anguish over their integrity as Christian ministers, the women would be asking what goddess books they should be reading as they sought nurture for their own spirits. Ann continues:

> I was in the process of coming out as a lesbian. The processes parallel each other. There was naming going on. The fear of being discovered was so real. Sharing about our spirituality is like sharing about our sexuality. You begin to share a little, then a little more and more. There is naming. There is a struggle with what will be the consequences of telling the truth, with what will happen if I say what I believe. It is very hard to share.

Women who live with closeted spirituality need safe spaces where they can be real if their spirits are to be nurtured.

Creation of emotionally and physically safe space is essential for women's ritual needs to be met, especially because so many women are survivors of incest, rape, and abuse, or they are in alcohol and drug abuse treatment or have physical disabilities. Women with mobility difficulties need easy physical access in buildings and smooth paths outdoors. Women who struggle with drugs and alcohol need to be safe from compromising situations. Survivors of violence, who feel threatened by physical contact, need to know that group hugs or other forms of contact are not going to be forced onto them.

It is the goal of the Feminist Spiritual Community and the Saskatchewan Christian Feminist Network to provide safe spaces for women. Often, the ritual leader at FSC will start a guided meditation with something similar to this one, which was used one January evening:

> When we are doing the meditation, if you end up not feeling good about where we are going, or if something bad happens, stop. You do not have to go anywhere you do not want to go. Just go somewhere else, or have a nap, or whatever you want, and come back when we are finished with the meditation. Now let's take a few minutes to relax . . . concentrate on your breathing . . . breathe slowly in through your nose and out through your mouth . . . in through the nose and out through the mouth . . . in through the nose and out through the mouth. Now go to a safe spot, somewhere that is very beautiful and feels like a safe and magical spot to you. Enjoy it.

A member of the Saskatchewan Christian Feminist Network says:

Rituals can bring me back to my rootedness, my center. When I am there, I am better. Sometimes I am really really well. Sometimes there is so much pain, ambiguity, uncertainty, insecurity. Rituals provide safe space. They help me come back to my center. If I feel like I belong and am free, there's not much that can get me down. Rituals help me keep my energy and move with it.

One of the terms Pat McCallum has used to describe FSC is "domestic sanctuary movement" for women. The sanctuary movement helps refugees from Central America who are entering the United States, afraid for their lives, and in need of some means of survival. To think of FSC as a domestic sanctuary movement is to think of it as something that provides a safe, renewing, and sane space for women confronted by chaos and alien values in other dimensions of our lives. In a number of the interviews and conversations I had, when I asked, "What role does FSC play for you?" the immediate response was, "It saved my life!" and the women went on to say how FSC has been a safe space to be oneself, to sort out values, in which to be nurtured while going through very difficult life transitions. One woman said, "It was a place I could go where I did not have to put up a front—a place where I could most be myself"; another says, "It is safe to be there—safe to grow there—safer than most homes!"

At this point in history, survival and safety are critical elements in feminist spirituality. Survival involves living in an unjust world and recognizing the power of having survived injustice. Survival of injustice of economic disparity, racism, geographic isolation, farm foreclosures, violence, and abuse is amazing. And yet, women together are survivors, have hope even against the odds, and create communities and rituals of sustenance. Women choose strategies that will allow for survival, such as closeting and creating accessible and safe space. Survival and safety are where many women can look to see the divine in themselves and to love her with tenacious tenderness.

Chapter 7

EMBODIMENT

Our bodies are ourselves. We know nothing of this world and of human life other than what we know through the experiences we have in our bodies. The dualism of Western culture has encouraged people to believe that body and soul are separate, that the body is associated with nature, and therefore that it is of lower value than the spirit, which is connected with the divine. Women have often been associated with body, men with spirit. Women, body, and nature have all been devalued. Feminist spirituality suggests that if the world is to survive, women, body, and nature must all be highly valued and that the dualistic mode of thinking and separating must end. Women and men must come to know their body-selves, recognizing that it is through these embodied selves that humanity participates in the divine. It is through our embodied selves that we live and know about life.

Jeanne Brooks Carritt speaks of what this means as she gets older:

> Nevertheless, overall I am rather enjoying the aging process. This body is still me, the one I entered the world with, and the one I will take with me when I leave. In the deep lines on my face, I can now see my brother, my father, and my maternal grandmother, none of them now living. Yes, my body is myself, and related to the universe. It is indeed sacred.[15]

Our bodies are where we live. It is through our body-selves that we have consciousness of ourselves, of our surroundings, and of our relationships.

This is not to imply that society does not also influence the way our bodies are and our perceptions of them. Cultural expectations re-

---

15. Jeanne Brooks Carritt, "Our Bodies Are Still Ourselves As We Age," *Woman of Power* 12 (Winter 1989): 75.

garding dress, grooming, movement, weight, aging, feeding, sleep, and exercise all influence how we adapt bodily to our environment. Although women's bodies vary in size, shape, color, and range of potential activities, our culture determines how we are supposed to look and move. Thus, creating body image can be a revolutionary strategy for feminists. Choosing to affirm our bodies in whatever form they exist, dressing comfortably, expressing ourselves through our clothing and jewelry, walking as freely as we are able, moving in the ways that give self-assurance rather than the ways of the ideal give women a sense of power and well-being.

Feminist spirituality also suggests that we need affirmation for our bodies. One woman described her day:

> I had to go downtown this afternoon, so I stopped in at the Bay to buy a new bathing suit. I said to the woman, "I need a bathing suit that has some support because I have low-slung breasts." She said to me, "Well at least you're honest." I said back to her without even thinking, "I like my body just fine!" I refused to be put down. Then I went to buy some face cream, and the clerk there said, "You'll want the anti-aging stuff." It was about the tenth comment I have had this week to remind me that I am no longer in my twenties. I am offended by the ageism of it. But I am not stewing about my age.
>
> I guess that is part of what ritual in feminist community has done for me over the past fifteen years. It has affirmed me as a woman, and as a woman in the image of God or of many different goddesses.
>
> I know I come away from rituals affirmed as a woman, and I feel affirmed in my female body. That is different than years ago. I am appreciative of women's rituals and women's bodies.

Two of the women interviewed talked about bathing as a ritual. One says, "The most important [personal ritual] for me is having a bath. When I bathe—at least 90 percent of the times I bathe—it is not just to get clean. It is a ritual of my womanhood—touching my body, cleansing myself; it is a very spiritual experience." Another woman echoes her: "Bathing is also a spiritual experience. I light candles, burn incense, and put oil in my bath; I celebrate my physical being in the bath."

Women from the Feminist Spiritual Community also acknowledge the importance of women's body-selves. Enfolding happens each week, so that everyone who comes is welcomed with a hug. Singing time involves joining hands with the alternate person in the circle so that joined hands rest on the belly of each woman. Hands are held in energy circles, and bodies are touched during healing rituals. At FSC retreats, the first evening involves a ritual of footwashing. People get into pairs, soak their feet in warm, epsom-salt water, then in turn dry, oil, and massage their partner's feet. An additional element is the painting of toenails with brightly colored nail polishes and sparklers as a sign of commitment to outrageous actions.

Susan Sorensen describes an activity at an event of the Christian Feminist Network that indicates a different kind of bodily awareness. She says:

> Even the way we did "analysis" was different. For example, as we explored different understandings and perspectives on family (conservative, liberal, radical, feminist) we first described each perspective in words and then with our bodies. We built a tableau with each one in turn—Mr. and Mrs. Conservative and the various people and relationships in their life were modelled using ourselves as the material for the still life. The ways we chose to represent the relationships and place ourselves in the scene opened for us a whole new way of understanding of family. It helped us see and *feel* the oppressive structures that keep it in place and it helped us recognize and identify our feelings and reactions to it.[16]

Through using our bodies, we can come to new understandings of feelings and of our options. Women's bodies are very diverse. All are different, and none conforms to the perfect standard set by patriarchy. As we learn to love our bodies, we can do things with them and learn from them information that will help us be whole. As we listen to our bodies and trust their messages to us, we will know far more about what is safe and healthy and positive for us than if we are simply heads, totally out of touch with our bodies. We can get in touch with a deepened spirituality through our connectedness as a whole person.

Our sexuality—that is, our erotic arousal and our way of being women or men in the world—is also a dimension of our body-selves. Our feelings about ourselves and the roles we appropriate in society are deeply connected to our sexuality. Our modes of expressing affection and our patterns of making love are part of our body-selves.

One woman connected her sexuality and spirituality:

> In personal relationships I have a strong sense of spirituality. I am a lesbian, and I find in loving and in relationship I have a strong sense of God's love. I have learned a lot about God's love through

---

16. Susan Sorensen, "Beyond Survival—November 6–11 at PCTC," *The Unbeaten Path* 11 (February 1984).

this relationship—about steadfastness and faithfulness. I experience those attributes of God through being loved.

Two of the women interviewed talked about the importance of women's bodily cycles. One says:

> I did not know the moon and its connection to the menstrual cycle until I was involved in wicca. I think that when women are involved in doing rituals there is a connectedness to others and a sense of being connected to our bodies. So, for me as a woman, I am more conscious of the moon, of the seasons of the year, of "my moons" waxing and waning in my body. As a woman, I am more in touch with my self and my body, mind and spirit.

Another put it this way:

> Women are more in touch with the changing of life cycles or of seasons because of our monthly cycles. Just the changes in women's bodies means that we go through different stages in our lives. For example, in a group I am part of, we plan rituals around birth-giving and menopause, around puberty. (I wish we would do more on this one.) I think the neatest thing is the croning. Those events are really significant in women's lives. When bodies change, capabilities are different. It is amazing to think that there is a time when you cannot be pregnant, a time when you can be pregnant, and then another time when you cannot be again. Our bodies determine what we are capable of and what we are free from. I think as women, because we experience these changes in our bodies, we are aware of the changing seasons, night to day, day to night, phases of the moon.

Rituals connected to these cycles are important to women. One describes a ritual:

> A ritual involving a birth canal held great meaning. It was important because it was like a new ritual of belonging to this new community, this new spirituality. It was like an initiation into and honoring and valuing of an ancient tradition that had been lost or never found. It was like birthing to me.

Reproduction is part of women's lives and concerns, ranging from all of the concerns with a normal healthy pregnancy and birth of a baby to the medical system's treatment of pregnancy as an illness and to birth control, unwanted pregnancies, miscarriages and stillbirths, abortions, and reproductive technologies. All of these affect women's sense of health and well-being. All are political issues related to justice for women in the world. All are, or can be, interrelated with women's embodied spirituality.

Another area that affects women's body-selves is the reality of violence. At some point in their lives, most women experience male violence—if not in fact, at least through fear of male violence. Far too many women know it as a reality. The injustice of violence against women must not be underestimated, nor should its effect on women's self-image and perception of themselves in the world be minimized. Sexual harassment is designed to keep women in low-paid, ghettoized jobs. Violence on the streets is designed to keep women fearful and in need of male protection. Violence against adult females and children in the home is an expression of male power. Violence in pornography and the media is designed to perpetuate the illusion that violence against women is appropriate and expected behavior. Violence in war is an expression of the national ideology of power, dehumanization, and domination as a way of life.

A key demand of the feminist movement is that male violence in every sphere must end. Women's lives cannot be fully and freely lived while violence continues, neither can they be as long as women are excluded from political processes and decision-making in the naming and shaping of the common good. Thus, there is a strong need for healing spaces for women who have been violated, for women who are in recovery of some kind, and for women who need the courage and affirmation that will allow them to live as fully self-accepting body-selves, in spite of all the messages and pressures to the contrary. Beverly Harrison and Carter Heyward suggest that women (especially Christian women) are trained to live for others. This means that many women cannot even imagine that they deserve to be well treated in relationships, or that they should have physical or emotional pleasure in their lives. Because of the ethos of sacrifice, women live lives alienated from their body-selves, out of touch with their sensual desires, afraid of violence, and ambivalent about their own feelings about their bodies.[17]

For many women, one of the ways to move out of patriarchal views of women's bodies is to move from allegiance to a male God to understandings of God in feminine form—a female God or goddess. One of the rituals of the FSC involved each women present looking into a mirror and saying aloud, "Behold the Goddess!" Such a radical act of seeing oneself as goddess is an experience readily available to men each time they hear that they are made in the image of God.

---

17. Beverly Harrison and Carter Heyward, "Pain and Pleasure: Avoiding the Confusions of Christian Tradition in Feminist Theory," in *Christianity, Patriarchy, and Abuse*, ed. Joanne Carlson Brown and Carole Bohn (New York: Pilgrim Press, 1989), p. 157.

But for women, to look at themselves and see the goddess is to re-image what it means to be a woman. It invites women to see the sacred at every level of their being and to see the holy as embodied in themselves in concrete and specific ways. It calls equally for a reimaging of what the divine is like and for a reimaging of ourselves and the meaning of our bodily existence.

We are our bodies; our bodies are ourselves. We as body-selves are affected by society, consumerism, ageism, movements, touch, sexuality, menstrual cycles, reproduction, and violence. We are also affected by being in touch with ourselves; by making choices about how commercialism will affect us; by participating in rituals that let us see our body-selves as holy, our minds, bodies, emotions as connected, and our sexuality and its potential as good. Knowing our body-selves is thus a thealogical resource for women.

Chapter 8

NAMING OF SELF AND EXPERIENCE

Some of the rituals I do are really important—washing my face is the first thing I do every morning, and I have to do it before I go to bed. I don't ever miss a day of doing that. It is important for me to look at my face in the mirror and see who I am today.

Looking in the mirror to see who one is, is important to many women. Women's search for identity, and their affirmation of that identity, is an ongoing process.

The religious and psychological questions of women often revolve around the questions Who am I? Who are we? Such questions are phrased in a number of different ways and focus on identity, finding one's voice, self-respect, naming of one's experience, or autonomy.

Patriarchal society has encouraged women to be other-identified—to base their identities on men and male approval (especially of fathers, husbands, lovers, and bosses) and on their relationships with their children. Patriarchal society has not encouraged women to name themselves or their experiences. Yet women need to be the subjects of their own lives.

Carol Gilligan, who writes about the moral development of women, suggests that women move from an early stage of self-centeredness (which she also calls survival) toward responsibility and social participation. Rules, seen as sanctions, set aside in the first stage, are seen, in the second stage, as a way to live by society's values and get society's approval. The primary ethic of this second stage is the ethic of care for others. Gilligan suggests that North American society, based in male patterns of moral development, has encouraged women to remain at this stage of moral development all their lives. One woman describes her mother's choice to stay at this stage: "My mom had thoughts and desires, but she never acted on them. Everything she did was for the good of her family or for the good of her husband, not for the good of herself." Gilligan, in contrast, sees women moving toward a third stage of moral development that has not been valued in male moral development theories—that is, a stage in which there is a new mix of what others think along with one's own inner judgment. One woman describes her transition:

> For a long time I believed that in order to be in a relationship with anyone, I had to give myself up, or give up something of myself. I did not know that anyone would want to be in a relationship with me unless I gave up something of myself to them. Until I was able to see this as a value that I held, I could not get into relationships easily or be free to be myself. But once I was able to see that it was a value that I held, I could change it. I could decide whether to throw it out or keep it.

In the third stage of Gilligan's model of women's moral development, self-sacrifice and care are held up along with, and in contrast to, the power of women to choose, value themselves, and accept responsibility for themselves along with others.[18] This stage of moral development in which women claim their own autonomy along with their responsibilities to care for others is what is meant by being subjects of our own lives.

The researchers who wrote the book *Women's Ways of Knowing* also look at the different ways that women come to "know" and to make moral decisions. They describe the importance of women's being able to name their experiences, or use their own voices, as part of identity formation. They discovered that "voice" was a strong metaphor in women's development. Such expressions as speaking up, being silenced, not being heard, really talking, feeling deaf and dumb—"all having to do with sense of mind, self-worth, and feelings of isolation from or connection to others"—were repeated over and over again as women spoke of their intellectual and moral development. "The development of a sense of voice, mind, and self were intricately intertwined."[19]

Thus, it is not surprising that several of the women interviewed talked about the importance of speaking and of being heard. A woman who is part of a small group that gathers for feminist ritual says:

> It is a place where I can trust that my spirituality and searching and questioning and celebrating will all be valued by everyone else in the community. No one will think that I am stupid. I am valued. It

---

18. See Carol Gilligan, *In a Different Voice* (Cambridge: Harvard University Press, 1982).

19. Mary Field Belenky, Blythe McVicker Clinchy, Nancy Rule Goldberger, and Jill Mattuck Tarule, *Women's Ways of Knowing: The Development of Self, Voice, and Mind* (New York: Basic Books, 1986), p. 18.

is important to me because it is not everywhere that I can talk about this.

Another woman talks of not yet having found her full public voice:

> I think I probably could be more effective if I really believed in myself. I get really scared when I think about that. What if I really believed in myself? I know deep down inside that I am capable of being a leader. Some days I wish I would let myself out of the cage and let myself do it. But I won't let myself do it. I am afraid— maybe because I am a woman—although some women do it.

One of the ways that ritual allows women to find their voices is through naming circles and through check-in. For example, in FSC each week the ritual starts with a naming circle. The naming involves going around the circle. Each woman states the name by which she wants to be known as the sacred space of the circle is created. This is powerful for many women who rarely hear their own names but are known only as "Mom" or "Mrs. John Doe" or by a label ("girl," "employee," "lesbian," "wife"). Also, choosing names is important especially for women who have always been pleasers or who have been violated by those who gave them their birth name or married name.

Equally important as the use of women's own names is the naming of experiences. A woman talks about the Regina Book Club, which is composed of SCFN members: "We do have the ritual of checking in. We may have all read something and come prepared to discuss it— but often one woman has an unbearably urgent need, and so much of our time will be spent with her. So check-in is an important ritual."

Women need to say what life is really like—to tell the truth about their lives. In rituals, women talk about traumas, pain, suffering, and joys, and they celebrate the milestones in relationships, work situations, the creation of home environments, and spiritual discoveries. For example, at one ritual three women spoke about work—one was quitting an unfulfilling job to start a business of her own; the second was exhausted from a hard day at work; another, with no resources to live on, was desperately looking for a job. Another night, four women talked about what it is like to be getting older in an ageist society. Others told of experiences of violation, sexual abuse, and incest as they sought healing. Another woman spoke of how being part of feminist rituals had allowed her to shift her priorities from money to enjoyable work and had given her class awareness and global awareness that she had not previously had.

Talking freely about these aspects of women's lives and naming them as resources for spiritual strength and survival in community have not been part of patriarchal religion. Feminist communities encourage truth-telling—naming of the experiences that are real in women's lives. In these settings there are no correct doctrines into which women have to try to fit their experiences, and so, as the truth-telling goes on, new ways of describing women's spirituality emerge, and new sources for survival and strength are named and incorporated into women's spiritualities.

One example of using a ritual for the naming of experience was a sermon preached in a Christian congregation by Sally Boyle, a member of SCFN, in which she names publicly that she is a lesbian woman. Using the scriptural image of sowing seeds (John 12:24), she spoke of the seeds in our lives that need nourishing to be brought to blossom. She says:

> God instilled in me a seed of difference, a seed of opportunity to view the world from a different perspective, a seed of difference in sexual orientation and once upon a time I thought that I could let that seed lie dormant until I died and only God and I would know. But God is like my Dad and my grandfather before him. If the seed didn't grow you went and coaxed it a little, you poured on a little fertilizer, you added a little water and if all else failed you turned the soil again. God was just that persistent. While I denied and refused to grow, believing that if I did I would grow to something ugly, and shameful and too awful to look upon, while I refused to grow God devised more ways to encourage growth. And after many years of feeling like my heart was being shredded and my innards cut up (on some occasions quite literally since I had numerous surgeries for imagined diseases) I finally took the risk one day in the midst of an alcoholic stupor. I gave up. It was just that simple. I gave up—I chose to let the seed be nourished and produce life and in so doing I opened myself to the experience of death.[20]

She then went on in the sermon to speak of what it means to be a lesbian and a Christian, and to know oneself loved by God.

Speaking and silencing are political acts. The late Audre Lorde made this clear in *The Cancer Journals*. Lorde had cancer and thus had become aware of her own mortality. Reflecting on her life, she found what she regrets are her silences.

> Of what had I *ever* been afraid? To question or to speak as I believed could have meant pain, or death. But we have all hurt in so many different ways, all the time, and pain will either change, or end. Death, on the other hand, is the final silence. . . .

---

20. Sally Boyle, "Does a Lesbian Belong in the Pulpit?" *The Unbeaten Path* 28 (October 1989).

I was going to die, if not sooner, then later, whether or not I had ever spoken myself. My silences had not protected me. . . .

We can sit in our corners mute forever while our sisters and our selves are wasted, while our children are distorted and destroyed, while our earth is poisoned, we can sit in our safe corners mute as bottles, and we still will be no less afraid. . . . [Or] we can learn to work and speak when we are afraid in the same way we have learned to work and speak when we are tired. For we have been socialized to respect fear more than our own needs for language and definition, and while we wait in silence for that final luxury of fearlessness, the weight of silence will choke us.[21]

We have the choice to be silent or to speak.

Lorde believed that we must speak the truths we have discovered in our lives, as part of the process of naming. When we speak of what is real in our lives, we know our own truth. We also discover that truth is a social construct rather than an objective quality or state somehow disembodied from experience, or rather than being a description of "reality." The political consequences, rather than the disembodied ideal, are what make something true. For justice to take place, the multilevels of truth must be discovered.

Truth-telling, as it is being described here, also carries with it a level of discretion and choice. One feminist activist mentioned that she had learned, in preparation for civil disobedience, that "we have the right not to tell what we do not want to tell." This was a new learning. She had always assumed that she must tell everything for it to be the truth. It was hard for her not to tell people why she was going to Honduras, when she went knowing that she would be committing acts of civil disobedience while there. It was especially hard to decide how much to tell her children, yet it was essential that this intent to act in ways against the law be kept only among the participants in the delegation if it was going to have the desired political effect. Truth-telling and truth-knowing-without-telling are political actions of great consequence in the task of seeking justice.

The political choice to speak out, the political action of naming ourselves and our realities and truths, is an essential element in feminist thealogy. But it is a long hard journey for many. The Mudflower Collective says that it is particularly hard for "white women of the upper social strata, whose experiences have been dulled by the false lessons that race, gender, and class are irrelevant to our lives and our relationships,"[22] because we have been taught in patriarchal culture

---

21. Lorde, *Cancer Journals*, pp. 20, 22, 23.
22. Mudflower Collective, *God's Fierce Whimsy*, p. 69.

to forget ourselves. This insight connects with what Pat McCallum says in describing FSC:

> This community may be viewed as part of a *domestic sanctuary movement*. While women who seek out the Feminist Spiritual Community are or may be seen as members of a culture of privilege, they are also those within that culture who have been taught, as Nelle Morton phrased it, "not to experience their own experience." While the larger liberation struggle calls for the decision to stand in solidarity with those who are different, many women have not experienced truly standing in their own shoes. Thus, as delicate as the balance may seem between "self-absorption" and becoming a self, I am using the goals, structure and process of this community as a particular manifestation of indigenous liberation community which offers potential to enable some women to develop a *voice* to raise with others, and a *self* to dedicate to the wider struggle.[23]

Becoming a self, and knowing who one is, gives power to speak the truth, to challenge assumptions, and to be persistent in naming the political implications of what is going on.

For most women, being self-reflective and self-affirming are key in this process. Women need to know and believe that they are valuable. A woman talks about learning to value her work in the process of self-affirmation. As a potter and liturgist, she occasionally does a service that involves making a clay man and a clay woman facing each other dancing at creation.

> Now I like to do the same theme two or three times to deepen it. If I am doing two or three retreats, as I did last Lent, then the handouts and the ideas are the same, but it is different each time because of the context and the people involved. It has been hard for me to learn to value our own work, but I have decided that it is worth keeping and worth reusing. I used to just do it and throw it away. But I am slowly learning that it is good and worth a lot.

Learning to name one's own value is challenging for women in patriarchal society.

Naming of self and experience in terms of women's spirituality is also important. Florence says:

> I think spirituality is being me, my whole being, who I am. It is an unfinished definition—but I can get into it from that perspective— by thinking of it as the essence of who I am—someone with dignity,

---

23. Pat McCallum, American Academy of Religion Liberation Ecclesiology Panel, December 6, 1987, printed in Liberation Theology Group Working Papers.

purpose, a belongingness and humor, with intellectual capacity (that is a big part of me!).

Another woman, who is part of a small group, says:

> Part of it is women *friends* gathering to do rituals. It has been important to me over the last few years. It has allowed for a broadening for me (which I did not know how to have) take place. I like the small group and the spontaneity. I like how we can name what is going on for us, how we are feeling personally, and about what is going on globally—how we can name the hurts, joys, vision, dreams. It is important to say out loud what is really important to me and to all of us. We have common bonds in that sharing.

Naming oneself, naming one's experience, speaking out, and affirming oneself and one's identity and autonomy as a political, spiritual, and moral agent are indeed significant parts of feminist ritual thealogy.

Chapter 9

COMMUNITY AND RELATIONSHIPS

Relationships and being in community were pointed out by almost all of the interviewees in this project as being very important elements in feminist spirituality. One woman says:

> Relationships are like water. You can't live without them. I need to be in relationship—in a variety of relationships. A spiraling circle of relationships. Sometimes they are closer, sometimes further away. But I need a community to belong to so that I can be with others in order to find myself. When I do find myself and others in dynamic relationship, I get a profoundly sacred sense of life.

This comment is typical of the value women attribute to the relationships in their lives. The women spoke of many different kinds of relationships, but friendship was certainly a common thread. Mary Hunt defines friendship as "those voluntary human relationships that are entered into by people who intend one another's well-being and who intend that their love relationship is part of a justice-seeking community."[24] Unlike heterosexual marriage, Hunt reminds us that friendships are available to everyone. She suggests a norm of replacing quantity with quality—groups rather than couples, communal ethics in various circles. Friendship, to her, is the interrelationship of love (intending that one and self are more in unity than not), embodiment (all friendships are mediated by being in the concrete world), spirituality (full attention), and power (sharing of resources).[25]

All of these qualities of friendship are important, but it is especially significant for friendship to be available to everyone, as people with difference seek relationships. For example, age need not be the de-

---

24. Mary Hunt, *Fierce Tenderness: A Feminist Theology of Friendship* (New York: Crossroad, 1991), p. 29.
25. Mary Hunt, "Being Church Means Loving Well" (Event at Prairie Christian Training Centre, March 9–11, 1990).

termining factor in friendships. One woman talked about her son a great deal and about the importance of passing on to him something of value. There is a sense of the friendship of this mother and son as she talks about the rituals they do together: "I like to do them because they give me a sense of peace and pleasure. I feel connected to my son when we sing and pray and connected to something greater—the Creator or whatever. It brings reverence into my life—and gratitude."

A middle-class woman tells of her friendship with a woman who lives out of the local laundromat and on the street. It took a year of gentle approaches before the homeless woman would talk to her. One hot summer day the middle-class woman saw the other woman and asked her if she could buy her some ice cream. The woman busily scrubbed off a place in the laundromat and invited the middle-class woman to sit down beside her. It was a turning point in the relationship, and the middle-class woman knew that it was because she had given the other the choice of whether or not to accept the ice cream, rather than assuming she would want it. From then on, they were friends.

Memories could be added to the concept of friendship—we have friends among the heros/heras of the past and present. Traditional Christianity has named this quality "the community of saints" and elaborates as follows:

> We cannot serve God in isolation. We need the inspiration, strength and joy that come from fellowship with those who love and serve Christ. We have fellowship not only with believers here on earth, but we join with the apostles and saints and martyrs, the brave and the good and the wise of all ages, and our loved ones who have gone before us, in offering our adoration and praise to God.[26]

One of the women interviewed, named Linda, described what this concept means to her in day-to-day life:

> There is lots of pressure as a political activist. I have had to be an extremely strong person. Often when I was going to speak, I would play a song before I went out about the women who have gone before and the ones who have spoken and taken brave and courageous steps. For example, I image Rose, a prostitute that I worked with in the prostitutes' organization, who was brutally murdered in 1987. I would then go to the rally with these pictures in my mind of Rose and other women so that I would remember that I was not just doing it for me or to satisfy my own ego or power-desires. I

---

26. United Church of Canada, *Companion to the Catechism* (Toronto: Board of Evangelism and Social Service, 1944) (pages unnumbered).

would think about Nellie McClung's call for justice and equality for all, about the discrimination Rose faced as a Metis woman and of my nieces because it is not yet a world where there is equality in the home and in the work place. It is a kind of remembering.

The Amanecida Collective adds a global aspect to our understanding of friendship—when we begin to "see, think about, and act in solidarity with a world in which most people are not white, educationally privileged, or economically secure."[27] Making decisions in our lives, with the lives of others in mind and with accountability, is important in feminist community. The practice of lighting a candle each week at FSC for the women of El Salvador is an important reminder of the solidarity with the women there, and a reminder of the personal and political connections between members of FSC and the village women of Guarjila. A woman also talks about an insight from a friend's global connections: "I have a friend who is going to South Africa with her partner. She is wanting support. The thought came to me, 'What better way to go into the face of evil than in the arms of the beloved.' It is a wonderful force to take into the powers of death."

But as women talked about community, it was not just the "joy of being together"—it also included pain. One woman relates an experience:

> At my stepfather's funeral, the religious ritual was a terrible experience. So after it was over, my family did the rituals that we needed—not in an organized way. But our being together was the ritual—telling and retelling the stories, naming of our experiences and feelings and our pain; doing the things we had always done together was our ritual. The religious ritual was so devoid of acknowledging our reality, and so we needed our own rituals. Healing happens when we name brokenness and name the vision.

Janice Raymond adds another dimension to pain in friendships—the pain of feeling betrayed by other women. Often, women are very deeply hurt and disillusioned when a woman who they expected would support them does not. Raymond says that we need, as feminists in a woman-hating world, to know that sometimes women will hurt us and that horizontal violence comes more easily than support from other women schooled in victimization. We need to reinforce all the acts of gyn/affection that we can.[28]

27. Amanecida Collective, *Revolutionary Forgiveness* (Maryknoll, N.Y.: Orbis, 1985), p. xxiv.
28. Janice Raymond, *A Passion for Friends* (Boston: Beacon, 1986), p. 198.

Mary Daly identifies fear of separation as another issue that often is problematic in women's lives:

> Terrified of the dreadful thing which in fact has already happened (although this event is unacknowledged), that is, of separation from their Selves, women in the Possessed State dread separation from their separators/fracturers/batterers/flatterers. Therefore they are horrified at such words as the label "separatist."
>
> Women confined in the phallic State of Separation, then, are characterized/crippled by inability to identify the agents of Self-blocking separation. They are victimized by the strategy of reversal. Just as the label "man-hater" in Woman-Hating Society functions to stop thought, so also the negatively charged use of the label "separatist" within the State of Separation hinders women from Be-Friending. [29]

Although women are encouraged to identify themselves with particular males in order to gain identity and are taught to fear aloneness or seeing themselves as separate autonomous persons, women themselves name relationships as central to their lives. For feminists, then, community is an essential element. The feminist movement calls us to a shared commitment to transform the situation of women in the world. We recognize that as long as women do not share their experiences of violation, exploitation, joy, and longing together, and as long as women accept theology and theory based on male experience as if it were universal, we cannot act together for justice in the world. We need community.

A SCFN woman also emphasizes the importance of a caring and active community in what she calls ritual:

> There can be no ritual without community. Ritual can take place only in community, although the numbers don't matter.
>
> Going to an abortion demonstration is an example. To get fired up for it, we have to be together. The serious purpose of what you are doing is fed by the joy of being together. I'd hate to be the lonely picketer. In fact, the demonstration exists so that people can be seen together.

In patriarchal society, women's community has not been encouraged (except for service to others). Thus, the creation of women's community that is self-defining, that seeks for truth in women's lives, and that encourages friendships that are fun, outrageous, and deep is a revolutionary act. "To act together provides sustenance. To al-

---

29. Daly, *Pure Lust*, p. 363.

ways fight alone is to risk our sanity and our ability to remain true to our identity and central commitments."[30] Building community, of course, takes hard work. Feminist groups that choose participation, consensual decision-making, and shared leadership often have real struggles to work effectively. Keeping accountability clear in nonhierarchical groups demands direct dealing with one another, which is scary for many women who have been taught to submerge their own feelings for the well-being of others. Recognizing that there will not be a savior to deliver the group from its problems and conflicts means self-conscious choosing, by the group, of how it will deal with responsibility, personal issues, and group maintenance.

Carter Heyward suggests that God is powerful in the world only if we make God alive in human history. She notes that it is only as we effect love in relationships and justice in society—by providing food for the hungry, liberating the oppressed, living out our commitments in our families, spending our money thoughtfully, and making our decisions ethically—that we know God's power. In other words, God's power is known only in and through humans, in interaction with one another.[31] Susan describes what this means to her: "In my teens and twenties, I had a real sense of God in relationships and in conversations. That would be the one constant between my life now and then— that sense of the holy in the midst of intense conversation and relationship. I remember the physical response as a child."

Jan talks about the importance of ritual in community for her:

> Good ritual puts me in touch with the holy—with the sacred dimensions of life. I become aware that those sacred dimensions are not out there, but they are in me. I become aware of the sacredness, the holiness, of life—and I think that is what we acknowledge in rituals. Sometimes the holiness is created by the people gathering. It is just in the essence of being together. Something happens between people when you gather to share symbols of what is most important to you. This is especially so when the ritual is planned so that each person has a rightful and respected place, through the acknowledging of the sacredness of each life.

Another woman talks about family rituals, saying:

> I have all kinds of rituals with people in my family. For example, I always rub the kids' backs the night before they have an exam. I

---

30. Lois Grace Stovel, "A Woman's Path to Power as a Sacred Process," in *Sacred Dimensions of Women's Experience*, ed. Elizabeth Dodson Gray (Wellesley, Mass.: Roundtable Press, 1988), p. 29.

31. Heyward, *Our Passion for Justice*, p. 117.

feel terrible if I don't do it. It is the strength I am offering to them.
Connections with my immediate family and with other people are
very important to me.

Many of the women I interviewed spoke of solidarity with the natural world as well as with humanity—friendship and solidarity with
the animals, birds, sea creatures, flowers, trees, and rocks. The interdependence of creation is important; justice must be for the whole
universe. Priscilla names her experience this way:

> Connecting with nature is important to me. I have a wood stove,
> and gathering twigs to keep the fire going is important. I have two
> large trees in the back yard, and I call them Grandmother Tree
> and Grandfather Tree—and there are the little trees around them.
> When I moved in, I cleaned up all the trash around them. I love
> the trees and feel strengthened by them.

Others spoke of the importance of stones. Several mentioned the sense
of personal power gained from carrying stones in their pocket and of
being able to reach in and hold them whenever a reminder of strength
or courage is needed.

Only one or two of the rituals attended in the project were outdoors. One was a very beautiful summer solstice ritual by a lake:

> It was dark by the time the ritual started. A candle for each woman,
> a small cauldron, and a piece of wood (a gift from the earth) were
> placed on a flowered cloth (to represent the fullness of the summer
> season) on the water's edge. We sat facing the altar and the last rays
> of the sunset over the water. During the ritual the waxing moon
> came up over the water to the south of us.
>
> The goddesses of the four directions were invoked, noting the
> abundance of each, in the invocation. We took time, silently, to
> ground and center. Each woman stood on one of the rocks in the
> water and spoke about the cares she wanted to be free from. Then
> she floated her "boat" made of large leaves, branches with many
> leaves, or cow pies away. Some were floated gently, while others
> were hurled into the water, depending on the feelings of the woman
> speaking. The cares ranged from problems in work environments
> to concerns about unknown futures.
>
> After a time of silence, each woman had opportunity to use wild-
> flowers as a symbol of her wishes. Each flower was placed into a
> bowl of water with our wishes about keeping in touch with each
> other, about the new adventures for some in the coming year, about
> personal relationships, about decisions soon to be made about issues
> we care about, about the need for all of us to know and follow our
> woman-wisdom. When all of the wish "boats" were in the bowl, one

woman read the poem "Iamanja" from Merlin Stone's *Ancient Mirrors of Womanhood.*

> . . . Your holy spirit floats
> along the cresting waves of the water,
> as we walk out upon the sands,
> night time closing on the longest day of the year,
> and join together in small circles
> around the sacred boats
> that we shall send you,
> each whispering our prayers to a flower
> that we lay upon the boat,
> for Iamanja, Holy Queen Sea. . . .[32]

After the poem was read, another woman poured the wish "boats" from the bowl of water into the lake with a prayer for fulfillment of those wishes of our flowers and our hearts.

Along with outdoor elements of nature, many of the women in this project have animal friends that are extremely important in their lives, especially cats and some dogs. Justice for nature, and ecological concerns, were also strong among most of the women.

Community, then, is a very complex but essential part of women's lives, of what they describe as important in their thealogy and spirituality.

---

32. Merlin Stone, *Ancient Mirrors of Womanhood* (Boston: Beacon, 1979), pp. 96–97.

Chapter 10

DIVERSITY

Along with the concept of community goes that of diversity. Community does not mean everyone is alike. In fact, communities are richer when there is difference in them. Often, Christianity has insisted on assent to correct beliefs as the only appropriate spiritual expression. Sameness, rather than difference, has been valued in Christian doctrines. But feminist spirituality allows for differences in worldviews, beliefs, spiritual practices, and life-styles. It suggests that all people affected by decisions should be able to participate in those decisions, that no one person or group has the right to determine what others should believe or do. As long as the ethical practice of looking to women's well-being personally and globally is central to the participants' lives, then the actual differences of women and their experiences can enhance life and spirituality.

Diversity is an element of both the Feminist Spiritual Community and the Saskatchewan Christian Feminist Network. The media image of the young, sleek, able-bodied heterosexual girl is challenged as we gather—young and old, with many body shapes and sizes, with our varying disabilities and strengths, our spectrum of sexual orientations, differing economic means, and our many strong opinions about the life-denying policies of our governments. The ritual of croning celebrates the wisdom and life experience of older women.

Thealogy needs this kind of diversity and must not be simply inward-looking at our own experience. Within the diversity, there must be respect for, challenge of, engagement with, and conflict with others. Assent to correct doctrines is not as important as the ethical practice of seeking justice. One woman says:

> I want to have much more of a world in which we are learning to live together—to be together in the world and in community. Whatever religion promotes life-giving, caring justice has to be OK. We

do not have to agree with the specific components if this is what it does. If it is destructive, it is useless. Every major religion has been both.

The doctrines differ, but the point is the same. Actions of justice are the norm.

Uma Narayan expands the idea of diversity. She says that in groups with a variety of races, classes, sexual preferences, or other differences, there needs to be a recognition of the differing experiences of oppression present. It is easy for those who face less oppression (e.g., white women in comparison with black women) to violate unintentionally the members of the more-oppressed group. She suggests that the burden is thus on the one who has more privilege and power to acquire knowledge of the situation of the more oppressed and to assume that as an outsider "what appears to her to be a 'mistake' on the part of the insider may make more sense if she had a fuller understanding of the context."[33] The more privileged thus need to exercise caution not to offend, even though that takes some effort on the part of women who are accustomed to speaking to other women like themselves with ease. Discovering the intelligence and integrity of those whose lives and voices differ from the dominant voice is hard for most women of privilege.

Some women in the interviews talked about the difference that class makes in their lives and in their working relationships in feminist communities. In SCFN, there is less consciousness of class than of urban-rural distinctions. Women in urban areas can go out to supper together, give each other a call, or travel occasionally to other cities where we see other groups of feminists. For rural sisters, in contrast, access to materials and people is more difficult, and feminist energy is used up in trying to help others catch a new vision of the roles and realities of a changing consciousness of women and to survive as the only feminist for miles around.

Age also makes a difference in the way groups operate and in the values and priorities they choose to live out. One woman describes what the transition to a different age has meant to her:

> I have changed so much. It was fourteen years since those sociology classes [where I first learned about feminism]. I wonder what the next ten years will be like. I always thought that one of these years I would get it all figured out—but when I do, the questions change. I thought that if I could just get my head around this, if I could just get this done, if I just did this better, if I just had the money—

---

33. Uma Narayan, "Working Together across Difference: Some Considerations on Emotional and Political Practice," *Hypatia* 3, no. 2 (Summer 1988): 38.

then I would have happiness and satisfaction. I thought we would change the world in my generation. Now I am moving into middle age, and I find myself going for the journey as well as for the ends—and that is where the chocolate fits in. I like a life that is scheduled—and I know it isn't going to be that way. Life is good, and there is nothing I can do about a lot of the things that I worry about. I have moved toward an attitude of come what may.

Another of the differences mentioned by women was around different faith perspectives. In both SCFN and FSC there is diversity among the participants' religious orientations. SCFN women often spoke in reference to Christianity—either from engagement in the Christian community or from the difference in their religious views from that presented within Christianity. FSC women tended to speak more often of different worldviews, within the context of what the goddess means to them. The women interviewed make different choices of how to live with diversity. For some it means honest dialogue about meaning, which may lead to confirmation of one's own position or to changed perspectives. One Christian woman talked about a dilemma for her, related to being Christian:

As a woman in a pluralistic society, being a Christian seems very imperialistic. Native people have been denied in their spirituality and in their right to survive. Christians went to Asia and did the same thing. What Christianity did in denying people's spirituality was to cause them to lose their identity. Maybe it is too much of a generalization to blame it all on Christianity, but we are so indoctrinated in it across Canada, and it has so often been used as a weapon. So it bothers me to identify myself as a Christian because of all of this.

Because of this kind of consciousness, some women choose to suspend discussions of beliefs so that concrete actions can be shared. Others synthesize a range of beliefs into their ritual practice, such as one woman describes:

I found a little clearing in the woods and made a circle there. My spiritual director came with me that last day [of a retreat] and shared with me as I went through my rituals which incorporate the Buddhist, Native American medicine wheel, and feminist spiritual practices. I took him through the medicine wheel, and we peeled and shared an orange at the end of it.

Each of the traditions is important—has so much to offer—and I want to bring them together. I pray to the Christian God (You Who Are Here—I call those my "youwho" prayers), the Buddhist prayers of abandonment, the four directions of the medicine wheel, and I have the feminist sense of connectedness and community and commitment to others.

Differences do exist, and it is important to acknowledge the differences and to find ways of living with diversity. Clearly, not all women's lives are the same, and yet, in spite of the challenge of working with different races, classes, sexual orientations, rural-urban views, ages, and faith perspectives, women can and do work together on common causes. Women have the power to bring about change in the world. But it is hard work and requires a strong commitment to acknowledge and value differences. Encountering differences often means that one must change. One must confront one's own limits. Along with the internal changes in one's own personality are the political changes growing from new consciousness of class, race, imperialism, age differences, awareness of differing physical and mental capacities, and thealogies. In light of these realities, the wisdom Starhawk brings is helpful:

> Diversity is highly valued—as it is in nature—in a polytheistic worldview which allows for many powers, many images of divinity. In ecological systems, the greater the diversity of a community, the greater is its power of resilience, of adaptation in the face of change, and the greater the chances for survival of its elements.[34]

Finally, it is important to note that valuing difference does not mean relativism or having no substance. It simply means difference. Moral judgment and testing all beliefs and action against the criterion of whether they contribute to material, ideological, and spiritual well-being of women and to justice in systems is essential in all communities, heterogeneous or homogeneous. Feminism is not value-neutral, but its central values do not include uniformity. Diversity in community is one of the central values in feminist spirituality and ritual thealogy.

---

34. Starhawk, "Ethics and Justice in Goddess Religion," in *The Politics of Women's Spirituality*, ed. Charlene Spretnak (Garden City, N.Y.: Anchor, 1982), p. 417.

Chapter 11

HEALING

Women are healers. Women have always been connected with giving birth, nurturing, feeding, and caring for the sick and dying. These acts of caring are the basis for healing. Diane Mariechild claims that healing goes even deeper: "Healing is a journey deep within oneself—a search for soul, the essence of the self. It seeks to balance the inner and outer worlds, to connect and to integrate. Healing is the reuniting of the body, mind and spirit."[35] Healing is circular; it involves both the healing that women are able to give and the healing that women need. Both of these interrelated dimensions are part of women's spirituality.

The need for healing, as Diane Mariechild describes it, is obvious. The reuniting of body, mind, and soul; the balance of the inner and outer world; and connecting and integrating are all important for women's health and well-being in the world. Women have been fragmented and distorted by the powers of patriarchy. Violence through incest, childhood molestation, adult sexual assault, and battering of wives by husbands destroys women's health in every way—our connectedness with our bodies as good, our self-esteem, our belief in ourselves as capable persons able to function freely and publicly in society. Poverty means insufficient food, anxiety about how to survive, and no energy for creative endeavors. Pollution and environmental destruction mean unhealth. Work environments create high levels of stress in women's lives, especially where women have no control over their lives and are always subject to the demands of others; where we are expected to compete through productivity, dress codes, and constant threat of layoff; where we are subject to sexual harassment. Feeling misunderstood or being trivialized, discredited, and devalued simply because of being female lead to dis-ease. The excessive use of

---

35. Diane Mariechild, *Mother Wit* (Trumansburg, N.Y.: Crossing Press, 1981), pp. 58–59.

alcohol, the high rate of addiction to prescription drugs, and the commonness of eating disorders are all symptoms of the lack of unity in body, mind, and spirit and frequently are signs of the destructiveness of the society turned inward. Healing in such a world is desperately needed.

The resources for healing women's lives are limited. Although not all healing needs to be done with the aid of the medical profession, access to adequate medical services is essential. Yet access is uneven. Ginette Busque describes the situation in Saskatchewan, where farm people make up 19 percent of the total population and 44 percent of the rural population. Yet, in all of rural Saskatchewan, with a population of 405,145, there is only one psychiatrist, one pediatrician, and four gynecological obstetricians. Lack of services for children with disabilities and for the elderly, lack of information about family planning, and lack of abortion-related services are worrying to women. Busque goes on: "In addition to congenital malformation, other kinds of reproductive-related problems—such as spontaneous abortion, stillbirths, and premature births—can be attributed to exposure to certain products used in agriculture. As well, women may develop irregular menstrual cycles."[36]

Women thus need access to medical services, as well as healthy environments, in which to live their lives. But some women have very negative experiences of medical procedures and hospitalization, feeling that much of what now needs healing in their lives was caused by medical procedures and professionals. This was especially so for the women interviewed who had been diagnosed as mentally ill and had at some point been under psychiatric care. One woman, who has been hospitalized in a psychiatric ward several times, describes what a world of justice and well-being would be like from her perspective.

> It means peace and autonomy for all members of the family of nations. It means life-supporting actions and speech by all individuals and nations. It means health and rejuvenation little short of immortality for everyone. It means respect for the environment—social, physical, emotional, spiritual. It means bliss for everyone and harmony everywhere. It means naturally virtuous people and naturally peaceful nations. It means no more poverty, disease, ignorance, prejudice, war. It means no more need to escape from reality for anyone through drugs, alcohol, etc. It means mutual supportive interaction in families, friendships, and other relationships. It means that none of our friends is on a psychiatric ward *ever*. In the past

---

36. Ginette Busque, "The Needs and Resources of Farm Women," in *Growing Strong: Women in Agriculture* (Ottawa: Canadian Advisory Council on the Status of Women, 1987), pp. 24–25.

92 New Names for Theology/Thealogy

year we've had five friends (one twice, and another ending in death) on a psychiatric ward or in [hospital]. It means honesty, sincerity, courage, and patience among individuals and society. It means smooth (not necessarily easy) resolution of all problems known to the human family.

This longing for a world that has bliss for everyone is common to women. The healing of the world, as well as of personal problems, is frequently mentioned by women, but often healing—especially through psychiatric services—has not recognized the need for healing of more than the individual. Helen Levine insists that feminist counseling must link the personal and the political. She suggests that depression may be a response to killing roles and expectations; drug addiction may be a response to narrow and suffocating lives; poor women's apathy and anger may be connected to their powerlessness and to lives controlled by the state. Unlike many "male-stream" counselors, who focus only on the individual, Levine looks at social causes as part of her feminist counseling practice. As women come to political consciousness, they can work for both personal and social change. [37]

But therapy, even good feminist therapy, is not adequate alone as a healing resource. Rosemary Radford Ruether suggests that:

> While professionals are important at these moments, they are often beyond the financial means of violated people, and they also fail to address the deeper dimensions of such crises—the sense of being alienated from human communities of meaning and of being rejected by God. Thus healing from violence demands a deeper liturgical dimension that enfolds violated people in a supportive community of meaning and assures them of divine love. [38]

Rituals that address the spiritual needs, bringing balance and healing to body, mind, and spirit, thus are important.

The Feminist Spiritual Community recognizes this need in women's lives and offers healing circles on a semiregular basis. When a woman asks for a healing circle, she and anyone else feeling in need of some extra healing energy or emotional strength lie in the center of a circle of those present. Those acting as healers surround the woman (or women) and gently lay their hands on her. After a time of silence to gather energy and focus, the healers begin to chant or sing as they are moved to do so. The healing continues until a stopping point is

37. Helen Levine, "The Personal Is Political: Feminism and the Helping Professions," in *Feminism in Canada: From Pressure to Politics*, ed. Angela Miles and Geraldine Finn (Montreal: Black Rose Books, 1982), p. 200.
38. Ruether, *Women-Church*, p. 109.

spontaneously felt. Hands very gently and gradually are withdrawn, excess energies discarded by shaking the hands away from the healed one's body, and the healing is quietly ended.

After one healing circle I attended, there was time for conversation about the experience. Some of the comments reflect the mood: "It was wonderful"; "It made me realize how rarely I am touched. It feels so powerful, and to be touched by strangers at such a deep level is amazing, a real experience of grace"; "I was floating in the universe among the stars and galaxies"; "It was really nice for me. I only got scared a little bit and had to open my eyes two or three times for reassurance, but it was good." Someone asked a pregnant woman if there was anything special that the community could do for her. She said, "No, just being here is enough. I think I'll try to deliver on a Monday night so that all your energy will be with me."

Another woman describes healing rituals that are important for her:

> I like looking back at the wiccan year and going through the sabbats and the holy times. I feel steeped in the old religion when we do that. There is something about being in touch with the old religion that is holy and ancient and healing. When I leave, I feel different than when I came. The rituals are a way to participate in an event that seems very timeless and healing. I let go of the stuff that is weighing me down. There is healing that happens through the process of ritual.

In group healing rituals it is important that some criteria be named for the practice of healing so that it in fact leads toward healing and not to deeper unhealth. Some healing rituals have tended to blame the victim for her or his own problems; others have been irrelevant to people or have harmed the person instead of assisting in their well-being. Jane Doull and Mary Jane Hudgins have drawn up a helpful list of criteria:

Rituals need to acknowledge the deep pain, suffering, silence and death involved in people's lives and in healing.

The ritual is just one aspect of the healing. God is in the whole healing process, in the journey, in the ongoing support and informal care after the ritual.

Healing takes place best in community, in relationship, in groups with shared meanings and symbols.

Healing needs to be requested/desired (as opposed to "done to") and needs openness to life energies and to results.

It is important to have a vision of healing/wholeness and hope on which to focus. Creation of healing images for oneself can help the healing process.

Healing is not necessarily dependent on what theology we hold—
but hopefully rituals for healing will be life giving for the person and not blame the victim.[39]

While all of the criteria raised are important, it seems helpful to
elaborate on a few of them. First, Doull and Hudgins point out the
need for acknowledgment of the deep pain involved in people's lives
and in healing. One of the women interviewed speaks of this quality
in rituals along with the importance of community:

> Healing happens when we name the brokenness and name the vi-
> sion. Ritual allows that to happen and allows us to do that in rela-
> tionship. It is a shared tangible experience of doing that with other
> women—although sometimes the other women are only there in
> spirit—but it still acknowledges relationship.
>   For me it is also important to acknowledge others who have been
> there, who have also experienced the pain, violation, despair, and
> hope—to acknowledge their presence and gain their spirits—to keep
> their spirits alive.

Ritual is not a solution to all problems. Barbara Walker notes that
rituals did not cure the plague, smallpox, diphtheria, and the many
diseases that have been controlled by modern medicine. She suggests
that healing rituals are to listen, to allow the person's emotional state
to be strengthened, and to offer care. She summarizes, "Rituals should
give the patient room to express her pain or her need, to acknowledge and respect it, and then distract her attention from it in an exercise of kindness."[40] Elaine Ramshaw adds that healing rituals can
be helpful in times of ambivalence. She says that the church has tended
to deal with ambiguity by holding up one side as the positive option
and downplaying the other side of the dilemma or conflicting emotion. A more helpful route, from Ramshaw's perspective, is to provide
a safe space for expression of conflicting emotions.[41] This seems especially important for women who are often caught in situations of
conflicting emotion, such as how to deal with one's own needs in relation to the demands of family, anger at injustice while feeling powerless to change the situation, or loving someone while experiencing
them as hurtful.

A second aspect of the criteria above is the importance of commu-

---

39. Jane Doull and Mary Jane Hudgins, "Religious Rituals in Human Life" (Class
presentation at St. Andrew's College, Winter 1991).
40. Barbara Walker, *Women's Rituals* (San Francisco: Harper and Row, 1990), p. 169.
41. Elaine Ramshaw, *Ritual and Pastoral Care* (Philadelphia: Fortress Press, 1987), pp.
30–32.

nity. Mary Pellauer notes the importance of this factor in recovery from rape. Pellauer found that healing happens most readily for women who have a supportive network of people around them. Having a group of listeners seems to be the key factor in the length of time needed for recovery; "women without social support had still not come to terms with the crisis *four to six years* after the assault." Pellauer adds, "In the face of a world which allows and encourages the victimization of women, rape victims also need action that can heal the wounds in the social order which perpetuate such crimes as surely as they need a sustaining personal presence to heal their own wounds."[42]

A third point of elaboration is very simple. Doull and Hudgins mention the need for openness in order for healing to take place. Taught to be givers and caretakers of others, women have learned only to give and not to receive. Many women find it difficult to admit publicly that all is not well in their lives and then to be the center of attention while other women offer healing love to them in concrete ways. This openness to receiving the healing gifts that others offer is needed if deep healing is to take place, if the flow of healing energy is to be maximized. But it is hard work for many women to be able to come to a place where such openness can happen, and it needs to be in a space perceived as being safe. One woman talked about how healing had come to her through new understandings of community. She had been a devout Christian, living a very controlled life with no trust at all in her own emotions. Joining the charismatic movement opened a powerful release for her blocked emotions. But when her theology shifted and when she began to get in touch with her lesbian sexuality, she lost the powerful spiritual experiences and highs she had known. She tried many forms of meditation and spiritual activities, but none filled the vacuum. She began to get involved with different community groups and entered a healing and healthy relationship with a woman.

> Last summer I realized that the vacuum that I was trying to fill with all this meditative high was happening in a different way. These needs were being met in community and in my partner. I have strength, solidity, and centeredness that are deeper than I have ever had before. I realized the vacuum had been filled.

So healing does not always bring us the expected or desired results—but healing for women is often at a very deep level.

It has already been mentioned that healing rituals are not a pana-

---

42. Mary Pellauer, "A Theological Perspective on Sexual Assault," *Christianity and Crisis* 44, no. 11 (June 25, 1984): 254–55.

cea and that they can sometimes cause harm. It is important that healing rituals be grounded and be in community. Much of the New Age ideology (which stresses that people are responsible for their own illnesses and disabilities because they have things to work out in this incarnation) has little grounding in the concrete and material conditions of human life, nor does it take seriously the social context of patriarchy, oppression, and violation that are uninvited by the person in need of healing. New Age believers do not, for example, admit that the primary problem for persons with disabilities is bad social planning and lack of communally based resources for assisted living. Thus, the individual with the disability is seen as responsible for her situation, rather than recognizing that the problem is a productivity-oriented capitalist society that is not interested in anyone who cannot produce in the mainstream patterns. From a feminist perspective, a healing circle with a person with disabilities is more likely to invite expression of the rage at an unjust society and at the lack of resources and understanding available than to seek to "cure" the disability. Then the energies of the circle will be mustered to seek "cures" in the society with its distorted values.

Healing, then, as a spiritual resource for women needs to be seen in a broad context. It is not simply a medical term. It is a term that involves personal and global well-being. It involves envisioning wholeness in community. It involves holding people in love and respect so that their integrity as a person can be nurtured and so their body, mind, and spirit can be united in an ongoing process of healing.

Chapter 12

PLAY AND HUMOR

Play and laughter are qualities of feminist thealogy that are closely connected with healing. In a world where there is so much injustice and so much evil, it is a resource for spiritual strengthening and a gift to join with others in play. For many feminists, rituals are one way of playing. They are an opportunity to mix seriousness and delight in ways that hold up the rich moments of women's lives. It does not matter if everything turns out as planned in feminist rituals. What matters is that women are together and engaged in what they are doing. Barbara Walker notes that when the feminine was suppressed by patriarchy, the sense of play, the feelings of fun and the laughter that create interpersonal bonds and make up the quality of love, were lost. Laughter is not shallow or frivolous but provides a release from the excessive physical and mental control of patriarchy. [43]

According to Sapphire, rituals are important because "they are a way of paying attention or of making note of things. They are a way of doing serious play." Ruth simply says, "Rituals are pleasurable. I like the fun and beauty."

Lanie Melamed has done a recent study on play. She says that play has been defined in male terms since the time of Plato and Aristotle. Play, for men, involves games, competitions, joke-telling, sports, and activities. She suggests that for women, play "seems to involve small, often inconsequential happenings," brief stories "describing a special moment and good feelings," balancing sadness and pain with playfulness and laughter.

> Our humor tends to be in the shape of informal story-telling that describes the foibles of our personal lives and which generally takes place in groups where we feel trusted and at ease. . . . To be play-

---

43. Walker, *Women's Rituals*, p. 6.

ful is to approach life with a sense of wholeness, spontaneity, and
connectedness. Playfulness is an affirmation of life itself since we
choose to invest ourselves fully, willing to face the risks and the
challenges of the unknown.[44]

Feminists enjoy laughter that grows out of the situation—that lifts
up and affirms and that brings healing. Feminists become sad or angry when people are hurtful to each other or when people use humor
as a means of oppressing others by keeping them "in their place"
through racist, sexist, or heterosexist jokes. Well-being and affirmation are high values, and therefore laughter can never be at the expense of another person or group.

Humor plays many roles in our lives. Sometimes it is to lift up a
moment in its pain, absurdity, or joy and to laugh at it. Sometimes it
simply bubbles out of us in spontaneity, without particular purpose.
Bob Parrott also suggests that "laughter destroys the power of non-
being. Humor exposes the powerlessness of meaninglessness. Thus
humor remains a meaningful act of courage."[45] Lanie Melamed also
claims that "when playfulness leads to thinking for ourselves or acting
defiantly in the face of oppression it becomes a radical act. Joyful,
creative and spontaneous behavior can be threatening to those who
value order, conformity and control."[46]

A number of women spoke of humor, some giving examples of
incidents that were humorous in their context and showed that quality of ordinariness. In many of the rituals there was much laughter,
either because something went in a different way from how it was
planned, or because the atmosphere invited laughter. Eleanor Haney
describes this aspect of the Feminist Spiritual Community:

> We laugh a lot at Community. We may be struggling with a very
> serious issue, and suddenly laughter will erupt. We play and dance
> and laugh with the sheer joy of being spontaneous.
>   Our laughter often highlights the absurd side of patriarchy.
> Sometimes a joke enables us to get distance and freedom from con-
> trol by others.
>   Laughter also cleanses, releasing tension, frustration, resentment
> and fear. Such laughter helps to heal us and empower us for the
> next day's challenges.[47]

Another FSC member says, "Many women say that they come back
because of the singing. It is not just the leaders or the good singers

---

44. Lanie Melamed, "Living and Learning: The Choice to Be Playful," *Women's Education des Femmes* 8, no. 3/4 (Winter 1991): 27, 28, 30–31.
45. Bob Parrott, *Ontology of Humor* (New York: Philosophical Library, 1982), p. 43.
46. Melamed, "Living and Learning," p. 32.
47. Haney, *Vision and Struggle*, p. 27.

but doing it together. You can feel included, even if you do not know the words. And it can be playful."

A SCFN woman says:

> There is lots of laughter in church—and there would be in a just world. [My partner] or I often make a mistake, and it almost always allows for laughter, for a moment of grace. It is wonderful that God does not expect us to be perfect. Ritual helps me realize that it is OK to make mistakes.

Laughter and play allow for creativity. They allow for new ways of seeing things and for release of emotion. They let people be themselves and become community. They give courage and inspire people toward action. They create disorder that allows for options that never would have come through rational thought.

Sandra Brown makes a final point in relation to ritual and play: "When creating ritual it is well to remember that play and ritual are really the same thing. . . . The genuinely sacred stays lighthearted, flexible, and sincere as a child, so that ritual form never overpowers the spiritual content."[48]

Play and laughter are thus another dimension of feminist spirituality; in play and laughter there is another way of knowing the holy.

---

48. Sandra M. Brown, "Creating Ritual," *Sage Woman* 3, no. 10 (Summer 1989): 5.

Chapter 13

RESISTANCE AND UNDERMINING

Resistance and undermining have some of the same qualities as play—they can produce the unexpected, and they rely partly on bringing chaos where order existed. Their intent is to put a stop to something. Feminists have a clear political agenda to resist and to undermine patriarchy.

It is also true that patriarchy has an agenda to resist and undermine feminism. Patriarchal backlash against feminism is seen in the media mockery of feminism, in the 1989 violent murder of fourteen Montreal female engineering students, in the unrealized hope of the present Canadian government to recriminalize abortion, and in the refusal of the (male) prime minister of Canada and the ten (male) premiers of the provinces to consider seriously the demands that the Meech Lake Accord and subsequent constitutional proposals be amended so that women's rights could not be overridden by the "not-withstanding" clause guaranteeing French Canadian rights. The political agenda to undermine and destroy feminism is real. But feminists also are involved in activities with the intent to resist and to undermine patriarchy. Much of this resistance is at an ideological level. One is the naming of patriarchy as a historical creation. If patriarchy is not a historical necessity, then there can be change. There can be a world where women are valued and structures are just to all people.

Besides recognizing patriarchy as changing and unnecessary, another element in ideological resistance is the claiming of a history of resistance. Adrienne Rich decries the lack of historical consciousness and also the lack of resources to help women know that they are not the first to resist patriarchy. She says that even though women have been writing history for centuries, their history has been ignored, buried, and erased. This means that women have no knowledge of what other women have done in the past—the ordinary acts of survival and the communal acts of resistance. She says that women suffer from "historical amnesia."[49]

Lois Wilson describes learning one form of historical resistance common to women:

> We are in a very real sense subversion specialists. I certainly was, before we came into this era where we are working towards building the community of women and men. Certainly I learned it at my mother's knee through osmosis, how to get around men, over men, under men—how to get men to do things, manipulate—that was subversion. There is a sense that this also can be turned to good use. I think Puah was the first subversion specialist—read Exodus again—she was one of the midwives and Ramses had instructed the Hebrew midwives to get to the Hebrew women who were bearing children and make sure they don't get delivered. And Puah came back to Ramses and said, "Oh Ramses, I'm sorry. I didn't get there on time!" So we know how to do these things and I think that is alright. Because the gospels radically question and threaten the way things are.[50]

As Wilson notes, women's theological resistance is a reality coming out of Scripture. Catherine Madsen gives another example of theological resistance:

> Is it so strengthening to have an image of God who nurtures us? How much more strengthening to have an image of God we can stand up to: whom we can argue with, whom we can exhort, to whose face we can insist upon justice and nurturance and wisdom and every great thing we want to be capable of. How much more strengthening to strive with God. The story of Jacob and the angel may look to women's eyes like just another masculine tussle in the dust, but it contains this truth: that it will not destroy us to strive with God, that we can wrestle and prevail, that even against God's will we can exact a blessing.[51]

Starhawk describes political and systemic resistance as refusal to be negated by systems of control. As we refuse to leave or disappear, we can create alternatives. By giving feedback to systems, the systems change—first by trying to regain stability, and then, through transformation. War and domination require obedience, construction of an

---

49. Adrienne Rich, "Resisting Amnesia," *Woman of Power* 16 (Spring 1990): 18–19.
50. Lois Wilson, "Building a New Society" (Talk at the Well, World Council of Churches, Vancouver 1983).
51. Catherine Madsen, "If God Is God, She Is Not Nice," *Journal of Feminist Studies in Religion* 5, no. 1 (Spring 1989): 105.

enemy, and enormous resources—and they also require undermining for change. "When our vision of what we want is clear, each act we take *against* an aspect of domination can become a positive force *for* the alternative we create."[52]

A group of Maine women are involved in political resistance and change. The Legislative Committee of the Women's Lobby meets for breakfast every other week to talk about what bills are coming up in the legislature and about the strategies they will use to keep women's agendas on the floor.

Eleanor Haney suggests some other political and economic actions for the undermining of patriarchy. Boycotting and "buycotting" (supporting businesses that are seriously trying to change); seeking legal ways to constrain and restrain organizations that pollute, exploit, harass, and exclude; and engaging in civil disobedience, such as massive tax resistance, are all strategies for undermining patriarchy.[53]

Another form of undermining is through creativity. Mary Douglas notes that disorder both spoils and provides the potential for patterns. Order means restrictions have been made and limits set. Disorder means no limits, patternlessness, and chaos. It destroys existing patterns, but it also shows potential. In other words, it "symbolizes both danger and power."[54] Karen Tjaden wrote a poem that names the problem:

chaos out of order

they said ORDER ORDEr ORDer ORder ORder Order order
til it echoed
through the centuries
and moments
we might o.d. on order
choke on it
be burned by it
why doesn't it feel right
to think right?

we are frightened
are we free?

---

52. Starhawk, *Truth or Dare: Encounters with Power, Authority, and Mystery* (San Francisco: Harper and Row, 1990), pp. 86, 314.
53. Haney, *Vision and Struggle*, p. 113.
54. Mary Douglas, *Purity and Danger* (London: Routledge and Kegan Paul, 1966), p. 94.

in the midst of order
crushing, stifling
holding us in hierarchy
she has called
through the centuries
and moments
she calls us
into chaos
meets us
in chaos

are you frightened?
are you free?

Being called into chaos allows for potentials to be opened and explored, for the absurdities of patriarchy to be exposed, and for freedom from the usual constraints and expectations in thought, action, and systemic patterning.

A concrete example of this kind of resistance through chaos comes from Iceland, which is noted for its feminist activities. October 24, 1975, was a particularly significant day, for that was when Icelandic women across the nation took a day off. Fully 90 percent of the women in the country joined in the symbolic action, leaving men to look after children, not going to their paid jobs, and not doing the home works that they usually performed. Instead they held meetings and celebrations all day!

Symbolic actions that disrupt the usual state of affairs, in both public and private spheres, are disconcerting at the very least. They show the potential for undermining patriarchy in a visible way.

A final means for undermining patriarchy is through ritual. While the symbolic actions of ritual alone are unlikely to be sufficient to overthrow patriarchy, rituals allow transformed perspectives on reality and potential. They expose the ill-formed ideologies of patriarchy and also envision concrete changes that would embody values and principles consistent with feminist visions of justice and well-being. Several examples elucidate this point.

In 1989 the Women's Alliance for Theology, Ethics and Ritual (WATER) held a series of Easter rituals. On Maundy Thursday evening it is traditional in the Roman Catholic church to have a service involving footwashing. The bishops in Washington, D.C., had built a new "palace" during the year. They had also declared that, since Jesus had washed only male feet (of the disciples) on the night before his death, only men's feet should be washed at the Maundy Thursday services in the diocese. WATER women went to the steps of the bishop's palace and washed the feet of passersby in basins of water with bubble bath, plushy pink towels, and laughter. On Good Friday, they spent the morning with the Co-Madres protesting U.S. intervention in El Salvador, and in the afternoon they celebrated the "stations of the cross" by going to the different embassies and marking the horrors and atrocities perpetuated by the different countries. On Easter Eve, there was silent fasting and then the lighting of the paschal fire. On Easter Sunday, they went to an art exhibit of black women's photographs and then to see a performance of the Dance Theater of Harlem. The next morning they were back at the I.N.S. because one of the Argentinean women from the Co-Madres march had been taken to be deported.

Bubble bath footwashing, solidarity with the Co-Madres (who march daily against the laws of their countries), naming the atrocities of the countries of the world, valuing the culture of black Americans, and protesting deportations are rituals whose intent is to undermine patriarchy—to show its absurdities, weaknesses, and injustices to all who have eyes to see.

A second example comes from the Fellowship of the Least Coin, an international organization formed by women early in this century, with the inspiration of Shanti Solomon from India. Members of the fellowship donate the least coin in their currency once each month to the fund, which is then distributed to projects that assist women who have the least in society. The richest of First World women cannot give more than twelve cents per year, and the poorest of women can give, with sacrifice, twelve of their precious small coins. All are invited to the ritual of giving and of prayer.

Women all over the world—giving to help other women, giving in equal amounts, giving with the ritual of prayer—undermine a system that allows the rich to dominate the poor, pits country against country, demands the biggest possible projects, and gives aid to those projects that will benefit the donors.

Another example comes from a recent winter solstice ritual. At the ritual, the women discussed a theme that is usually a focus of Christmas church services—Christ as the light of the world. Over the past few years the group had become conscious of how the imagery used in Christian tradition that equates light/white with goodness and dark/black with evil perpetuates racism by insinuating that people with black/dark skin are evil, and people of white/light skin are good. The solstice ritual therefore focused on the goodness of the dark, on going into the dark, on taking things into the darkness to be transformed there, and on receiving gifts from the darkness.

It is hard to measure results that happen from a small group of women who befriend the dark. Yet each step to eliminate racism is a step toward undermining a patriarchal pattern based in domination and submission, such as structured racism.

A final example of feminist rituals' undermining of patriarchy comes from using "goddess" imagery. As an iconoclastic way of asserting that God is not male and as a way to be free of patriarchal influences and images in understanding the holy, use of the term "goddess" can be freeing and health-producing for women. Using "goddess" can help women catch glimpses and visions of a world not yet in existence— one that is consistent with feminist values.

Use of "goddess" is an act of ideological resistance, an act of affirmation for and of women, an act that increases the capacity of women to be self-determining in the world. Such acts undermine patriarchy.

We do not know how long we feminists will have to keep up the work of resistance and undermining, or how many rituals we will have to make, before patriarchy collapses. As Esther Broner says in the National Film Board film *Half the Kingdom*, "These ceremonies we make for the first time. There's no cartography." But these rituals give us power and courage. They invite our creativity. They enable us to be who and what we want to be. They help us keep hope as we continue the creation of chaos out of order, through resistance and undermining.

Chapter 14

VULNERABILITY

In Saskatchewan, vulnerability is made real by the geography. The prairie land is flat. There is no hiding—only open land and sky. The farmers are vulnerable to the whims of the weather. The amount of snow in winter affects moisture level in the spring. There is the vulnerability to winter too—it gets very cold. In Saskatchewan, the wind is bitter. And on the prairie there is nowhere to hide. This geographic reality of openness in a northern climate influences the way Saskatchewan women think about life and thus about spirituality. We recognize vulnerability easily.

This was evident at an event of the Saskatchewan Christian Feminist Network called "Making the Connections: Feminist Spirituality, Theology and our Global Community." The vulnerability expressed at the event occurred at four levels.

First, there was personal vulnerability. Because each Christian Feminist Network event is a new group (even though some participants have attended other events in other years, with other groups of participants), everyone needs to know where they will fit. At a structural level, Sister Groups, composed of four women each, were formed at this event to give everyone a place of belonging to return to each day. At a personal level, however, women still felt vulnerable about where they would fit—perhaps because as feminists in ordinary life, within patriarchal structures, we never quite feel as though we do belong, and so when we come together, we want to be accepted and valued.

A second area of vulnerability was in the area of spirituality. In the network, experiences of spirituality and faith expressions vary considerably. For those who are part of the church, being a Christian feminist in daily life means constantly raising issues of sexism, pushing for change, and frequently sensing displeasure from other Christians who hold a more traditional interpretation of Christianity. These women want to come to a safe space "where we can tell our stories, ask our questions, and be cradled and comforted by other Christian feminists." For those who have other spiritual expressions, there is the hope that a gathering of feminists will include others who understand their spiritual longings and practices. Women want to come to a place "where our spirits can be nurtured and where it is safe to name our spiritual experiences"—even those that are not within the scope of traditional patriarchal Christianity. Time is needed for personal story-telling. We need to talk about what is real for us with others who will listen deeply. Questions of institutional commitment or loyalty are part of the group's life and vulnerability. As women, and in groups such as those at this event, we live out our feelings of vulnerability in a variety of ways. Some women who clearly name themselves as Christian felt silenced at this event. Some women talked about spiritual practices (goddess or wiccan) in the group that they do not want talked about in other circles of their lives. Some women moved into patterns of nurturing those who were hurting. Some women chose to have private conversations, instead of speaking in the larger groups. Some women spoke openly about their spirituality in the total group. Our spiritual diversity and vulnerability, seen in a variety of responses, is thus part of the Christian Feminist Network's life together.

A third level of vulnerability at the event was sexual. A conversation about confidentiality raised a number of issues. A primary concern was that there needs to be extreme care around the vulnerability of lesbian women. Some women are more open at the event than in other spheres of life, and so people need to be very careful in their comments both at, and following, the event—about who went where, with whom, and when, and about innocent-seeming remarks that can cost someone her job, home, or children. One lesbian participant said:

> You probably get mixed messages from us. We say "trust us," at the same time as we sound like we are saying we do not trust you. But the experiences of our lives make us aware of the costs we pay each time someone accidentally brings us out of the closet or we deal with a homophobic society. We know that you may not mean to do something that causes harm and that you feel hurt when we do not want you to know who is and is not lesbian among sisters, but it is we who pay the cost, and so we need to have the choice for anonymity even here.

Not only lesbian women feel vulnerable at the event. Some heterosexual women are struggling with what feminism means to their relationships with male partners. For example, one woman talks of the dilemma of liking Mary Daly's philosophy but living with a male partner:

> I especially like Mary Daly because she comes through with a vision. So many writers give a really great critique—and you end up devastated and overwhelmed, with nowhere to go. But Daly is concrete. She gives constructive ideas of how to go. I find her hard to take, and I am never quite sure what to do with my choices about my life after I read her. I have chosen to live with a man, which is such a contradiction from Daly's point of view.

Some women are also sorting out how to survive in creative ways as single women, especially in rural areas, or in ordered ministry. Some women are sorting out identity, changes in circumstances, and relationships with families of origin, extended families, children, and new forms of kin structures. We also try to live embodied lives as part of the event. In a world that does not value women, to enjoy women's bodies—through hugs, touch, dressing up for a party, having a clothing exchange, or wearing expressive jewelry—rates highly as part of the time together.

A final focus of vulnerability expressed at this event was in relation to conflict. We find it hard to fight—to address differences directly— and so we often choose to continue the process, the agenda, the tasks, working together in whatever ways are possible. We did not take time to have a total group session to address differences and conflicts and to determine appropriate strategies for personal and community well-being. In a list entitled "Things that were not good for you," one participant noted "how anger/angry issues were handled—not talked through." She suggested that "a chance for personal stories around this could have been more meaningful." We had conversations about diversity but did not quite know where to go with the differences that irk us. The ways in which we deal with conflict make us feel vulnerable also.

Women feel very fragile when coming together. In patriarchal society women's community has not been encouraged, except when devoted to service to others. We have not learned to be clear, to name our circumstances and needs, and so we feel vulnerable as we try— and many of us fear conflict because we have been taught to be reconcilers and to submerge our own truth, needs, and ideas in order to save relationships. So when we try to tell the truth in community, we feel vulnerable about whether we will be "politically, spiritually, or sexually correct," about our inarticulateness, about whether the risk will lead to love, healing, or rejection.

Nancy Van Scoyoc's study *Women, Change and the Church* showed that church women often feel vulnerable. Women want the comfort, safety, authority, and values of the church, but they also feel that it represents unattainable standards and a potential for rejection. Thus, many women reveal only the parts of themselves that they feel are acceptable to the church.[55] But women in ministry are trying to shift this perception. Mary Thomas, a United Church minister in Alberta, writes:

> Authentic liturgy takes seriously and reflects our understanding of God as Living Creator, as Depth within our history, as Spontaneous Freedom. Authentic liturgy therefore moves, leaps, lifts, surprises and frees people—as well as enlightening them. . . . Authentic liturgy gives us a sense of wrestling with God, shakes us to the core, surprises us, expresses our feelings, brings together loose ends, awakens us to a concern and propels us toward decisions. Authentic liturgy is a foretaste of the new community of God in which all barriers will have disappeared.[56]

Sharon Moon of First United Church in Ottawa says:

> Once we are comfortable with our own brokenness, then we are comfortable with the brokenness in other people's lives. So much healing happens just through listening and valuing. I really do value people for what they are. I see the richness in people's lives—often before they do—I don't know if that is Christian or feminist—but it involves turning things around—an "upside-downing of the structures" so that the ones not viewed as important see the gifts they have, and that they have as much as the tight-asses who think they have everything together as they climb up the economic ladder.

Sharon preached a sermon focusing on suffering that gives a theology of vulnerability. She began the sermon by speaking of a number of different images of God from the Scripture and hymns—God as rock, as comforter, as eternal source of strength, as wind, as rain on a desert bringing forth blossoms, as a parent, as one giving birth, as the creator of life—but said that the image of God as one who suffers is not one that is often upheld. Theologically, we have moved away from the idea of a terrible God of vengeance, a Father God who demands the death of his own Son to appease him for the sins of the world, and yet we have not made the move to see a suffering God—even though Scripture and human experience point to the God who suffers with us.

This different image of God points to a God of vulnerability, quite unlike the omnipotent, almighty, victorious God that has often been

---

55. Nancy Van Scoyoc, *Women, Change, and the Church* (Nashville: Abingdon, 1980), p. 64.

56. Mary Thomas, "Authentic Liturgy," *Practice of Ministry in Canada* 4, no. 5 (January 1988): 6.

upheld in much of Christian faith. But it is important to note that a
God who suffers is not an invitation into suffering, nor is it a theological justification for suffering. *Christianity, Patriarchy, and Abuse,* a
book edited by Joanne Carlson Brown and Carole Bohn, delineates
the extreme distortion caused in women's lives by viewing Jesus' suffering as model for their lives and for the appropriateness of abuse
inflicted on them. Marie Fortune points out that there is never justification for involuntary suffering, for it never serves a greater good.
Instead, it is inflicted upon one person by another and creates only
destruction. She notes that victims of sexual and domestic violence
frequently want to find some reason, cause, or explanation for their
suffering in order to regain some control over their situation and
to find meaning in their lives. But seeking meaning or causes in oneself will not necessarily help the victim of abuse come to terms with
the real problem, which is the abuser's behavior toward a vulnerable
person.[57]

Thus, the image of God as one who is vulnerable and one who
suffers needs to be used with great care so that it is clear that God's
suffering is known as "suffering with," in the midst of evil and sorrow, not an invitation into suffering, a requirement for salvation, a
justification for suffering, or a judgment from a God who sits in the
sky meting out punishments of suffering onto innocent people.

Because of the history of abuse of women in the name of the Christian God, it perhaps would be better to refer to divine vulnerability
in images of the goddess only—the power within, the knowledge of
the grace that can come in vulnerability, the life-giving and sustaining
force. In vulnerability, there can be growth in individual lives and in
community. There can be new discoveries about life, meaning, and
power. But vulnerability is a spiritual resource because it is present in
women's lives. Unlimited vulnerability is no better than unlimited suffering. Women feel, and are, vulnerable in patriarchal society. When
women talk about their spirituality and the things that are real in
their lives, they talk about vulnerability. They talk, too, about protection needed in settings where vulnerability is present but unlikely to
lead to positive results. This comment is typical of several women's
voices regarding the need for rituals of protection:

> My rituals that I do alone too are important—like surrounding my-
> self with mirrors or prisms if I am going into a heavy meeting,
> especially if it is with men that I don't like. I use it with women too.
> I have had to sort out a lot of ethical stuff around it. I tend to be

---

57. Marie Fortune, "The Transformation of Suffering: A Biblical and Theological
Perspective," in *Christianity, Patriarchy, and Abuse,* ed. Joanne Carlson Brown and Carole
Bohn (New York: Pilgrim Press, 1989), pp. 142–43.

suspicious of all men, and too vulnerable, especially with feminist women. I have found myself needing to keep centered. I want to honor and support these feminist women, even when they have different ways of doing things than I do. Or I want to be able to keep in touch with women who have been good friends in the past and by whom I have been deeply hurt. So in order not to feel suppressed, oppressed, or repressed, I often do protective things before going into those situations.

Vulnerability is risky. Vulnerability can allow closeness and challenge. It demands accountability and the willingness to lay oneself open to the challenges of others, about one's own racism, sexism, and patterns of oppression. It means listening to others and being heard. Eleanor Haney elaborates:

> Being vulnerable means being open to others' voices, perspectives, pain and joy. It is being open to lupine, dolphins and rocks and to one's enemies as well as friends. It is being willing to seek out the voices and perspectives of others struggling for justice, whose programs are different from and may be in conflict with one's own. . . .
> To be vulnerable, finally, is to be willing not always to be "politically correct," but rather to question accepted ideologies, including feminist ones, and of course to run the risk of rejection once again.[58]

Women are vulnerable in many ways in patriarchal society. We are vulnerable in our personal lives, our spirituality, our sexuality, our ways of being in conflict, our experiences of suffering, our longings for authentic rituals and liturgies that will touch and move us deeply, and our willingness to challenge and to be challenged. In vulnerability we search for meaning and ask profound theological/thealogical questions. Thus vulnerability is a category of women's thinking, feeling, and knowing faith.

---

58. Haney, *Vision and Struggle*, p. 75.

Chapter 15

LOSS

As was noted in chapter 14, "Vulnerability," the categories of feminist ritual thealogy are not all entirely positive. Vulnerability is often a dangerous state for women. As a spiritual resource or thealogical category, loss lies in this ambiguous field as well. Loss always involves some pain, some giving up. In a society that suggests that the acquisition of goods is the most important value and that staying young and vigorous is a high priority, there is little room for seeing loss in positive ways.

Goddess spirituality differs from capitalist patriarchy in that it sees life in cycles—birth to death and death to birth. It uses the image of the crone as an image of the cycles of loss. The crone is the hag, the old woman, the bringer of death, and, when necessary, the destroyer. The crone recognizes that loss is natural, inevitable, and a part of the life cycle in an ongoing universe. The crone is free to rage and grieve. She is not constrained by the pressures of the mother—the nurturing and caring for others that is needed and appropriate—nor does she live with the freshness, freedom, and idealism of the maiden. The crone has seen life, its injustices, and hurts. She has nothing to lose by seeking change.

The image of the crone is one that can be very helpful to women in their spiritual journeys. The crone image need not be confined to old age—one does not have to be old to experience loss. But as an image, the crone can give assurance that loss is natural, that women survive through losses, that uncertainty is part of human existence, that grief and rage are appropriate responses, and that living into the losses is part of women's wisdom. As with suffering and vulnerability, loss is not necessarily to be sought after, and it is not noble.

Many women talked of deep losses, especially losses in relation to their faith, losses not filled by some new faith or any kind of hope. They are simply losses. They are often confusing and leave one feeling very vulnerable. A poem by Jamie Bushell sets the context for hearing from several women about loss in their lives.

theology for me now

it is like
going on a journey
to a place
using a map—
(someone else's map)
and discovering that
the map is wrong
and you didn't even start out
where you thought you were
and you can't get to where
you thought you wanted to be
from here.

and not knowing
since it's not the same place
you thought you were going
whether
you want to get there, now
anyway.

Jamie describes the period of her life in which that poem was written as a time of "spiritual jet lag." Intellectually she had moved to new theological alternatives through her discovery of Christian feminism, but her emotions could not move so fast, leaving her spirit bewildered and with an acute awareness that she had lost the strong faith of the past, without clarity in her future direction. [59]

Judith Schenck describes her experience in beginning to study theology in similar terms:

And then at seminary, happily charging full steam ahead, I crashed head first into the wall of male exclusive language. I splashed and splattered and bled all over the place, and it has been the most excruciatingly painful experience in my life. And the pain is not over. There is an immense grief in this pain, a loss of a place to pray, a loss of the ability to hear scripture in the same way, a loss of the ability to sing the old songs, a loss of that which once was near and dear and sustaining. Consciousness has a great price and

---

59. Jamie Bushell, "Christology" (Paper for Christology class, St. Andrew's College, Winter 1986), p. 1.

we can not go home again once our eyes have been opened. We can only go on and trust that the Spirit has led us to this new place for a reason.[60]

This movement from what is known to what is unknown involves deep senses of loss, even when one knows that the new direction is right and certain. We rely on the familiar, especially when the familiar has been the framework that has given our life meaning. Many of us also struggle with keeping some elements of the old, while letting go of other elements. A woman who has been part of the church for many years states:

I am in a different space now. Being through the family crisis with Mum and my brother becoming seriously ill, in two weeks of each other, and then when Mum died, I have had to think about a lot of things. I have nothing to put in the place of what does not fit any more. There is a loneliness and a scariness about that. It probably has been that way for a long time, but I had not identified that so much of it was not meaningful. But to totally disconnect feels like ripping out a part of my roots—yet a lot of what is going on is destructive. A lot of women's predicament is perpetuated by Christian tradition. But where did I get the ideas of love and justice, if not through Christian tradition? Goddess worship just doesn't do it for me. I can't create a religion on my own.

For some, the loss is deep and permeates every aspect of life. Another woman describes her experience:

I never thought that I could feel nothingness. But in the past few months I felt nothingness. I was terrified. I didn't know what to do. I prayed. Not for release but for endurance and understanding. I wanted to live. I prayed to God, to the Goddess (they sometimes go together for me), to get me through this. I prayed to have insight, wisdom, peace, and harmony to get me back on track so that I could believe in myself again. In church, there is time to offer myself and to pray for others. I had prayed for years, but I did not know what it really meant until I found myself in this situation.

A woman who has shifted from involvement in the Christian church to a goddess-centered spirituality says that without the old patterns and routines, ritual is not present in her life in the same way. Although she is active in a small ritual group, the new kinds of rituals are not in her bones in the same way as the traditional church rituals

---

60. Judith Schenck, "Shekinah" (Paper for "Religious Ritual in Human Life" course, St. Andrew's College, Winter 1990).

were. She especially misses the singing and has moved away from playing piano and guitar because she does not have a group of like-minded people with whom to create music. There is a real feeling of loss as she says, "Talking about music touches something very deep."

Another woman who has no institutional religious connections and has no community for spiritual nurture expressed real grief, wondering what she can pass on to her son and unsure how to keep centered and peaceful in her own life. She was disillusioned by her lack of influence for change in the 1960s.

> I could not change the world—and so I decided to focus on my own life. I have been married to a black man and am married to a German man now—I think that grew out of my '60s upbringing and desire for difference—but both of them have had very different backgrounds from me. It is hard work to keep a marriage going when the backgrounds are different. So that is where I put my energy.
>
> I despair for a community. It feels alone. It feels like a band-aid—it is not a viable way for real change. I have such a deep yearning for community and for knowing the way to go. I do despair about where I am going and for community.

Some women turn to Scripture to find resources in loss. Renita Weems sees the biblical story of the daughter of Jephthah as a story like many women's stories and claims that women need to be together in the face of such loss. In the story, Jephthah makes a pledge to sacrifice the first living thing that comes to greet him after his war victory. When his daughter greets him and he tells her of his pledge, she asks for two months to lament in the hills with her female friends. The women's sorrow at such betrayal and violation is bottomless.

> But more than a young woman's virginity was lamented out there on those mountains. The daughter of Jephthah and her girlfriends huddled in a circle and wept over much more than children unborn and ecstasy unexperienced. Each of her girlfriends knew that what was about to happen to Jephthah's daughter could happen—without warning—to any one of them.
>
> For every woman who lives in a society which values notions more than it does women lives with the risk of annihilation.
>
> So the women cried inconsolable tears that day. They wept for Jephthah's daughter. They wept for themselves. And they wept for their daughters' daughters.[61]

---

61. Renita Weems, *Just a Sister Away: A Womanist Vision of Women's Relationships in the Bible* (San Diego: LuraMedia, 1988), pp. 58, 60–61.

A contemporary situation, reminiscent of the story Weems describes, was told:

> Some women did a ritual about divorce in which they wrote all of their losses on pieces of paper, and then we burned them. A lot of them were hanging onto stuff and needed to let go of it in order to go on. It wasn't that they just lost the dork they had been married to—they lost their dreams. We need to mourn our losses and the loss of our dreams. If we can do our grieving through rituals, we can be freed from the pain and be transformed into the life-giving. People who are depressed can mourn through rituals and then often be transformed and work with others who are depressed. Sometimes the ritual helps us to realize the possible before it happens by visualizing the strength in our unconscious. It is a birthing. It happens in the prayer group where the latent qualities in people are brought out through their meditations. That is justice making—when the fragile, weak, and seemingly useless are able to own our own holiness.

Grief needs to be lived with. The loss of faith, loss of hope, and loss of dreams need to be mourned. It helps if they can be mourned in community. Rosemary Radford Ruether suggests that we need rituals that help us toward decrease of our capacities, cessation of fertility, cessation of paid employment, sickness, despair, dying, and death. We need to let go of the dream of ever-upward-and-ever-onward self-actualization that is perpetuated by patriarchy, living openly with our insufficiencies, decline, incurable realities, and eventual death.[62]

In a poem entitled "The Laying On of Hands," Kerry Craig names sadness and memories as two of the resources present in this thealogical search amid loss.

The Laying On of Hands

We lay our hands on the
ashes of a woman who has
known birth, who has known life.
We cradle fondly the memories
of love and togetherness—holding
them for one last time in our arms
and let them go—let her go—ashes to ashes
earth to earth and dust to dust.

---

62. Ruether, *Women-Church,* p. 112.

How sad it is—the time when
loving arms must cradle
memories instead of the warmth
of lived life.
How tenderly do fingers
touch one last time and
gently pull away.
Ashes to ashes and dust to dust.

Loss comes to women in many ways. The poignant and deep feelings expressed by the women here show loss as a place of women's searching, women's living, and women's despairing. Loss of faith, loss of what was once meaningful, loss through death of loved ones, loss of the familiar, loss of community, loss through annihilation, loss of the telling of women's stories, and loss of dreams are all part of women's realities.

We need images, maps, and resources that will allow us to enter fully the cycles of life, including loss. Some of the images and resources emerging here are seeing cycles of birth to death and death to birth, connecting with natural cycles of life, drawing on the image of the crone, prayers for wisdom and endurance, Scripture and stories about women coming together in loss, rituals for cessation and decline, weeping together, sadness, and memories.

Loss, as a thealogical category, invites entering into pain in a search for resources that will bring wholeness and meaning to all the cycles of life.

Chapter 16

VISION

Another quality of women's spiritual experience is visioning. Vision is the capacity to see beyond the current situation as it is. For feminists, visioning often involves seeing beyond patriarchal practices and structures. It means imagining other ways that life might be. It allows new options to emerge and new values to be explored. It involves all the senses—sight, sound, taste, smell, touch—and intuition and imagination to work together in an integrative way.

Mary Ann Beall remarks that visioning is not an abstract intellectual exercise. If one envisions an orange, one senses the roundness, smells the oils, feels the dimpled skin, hears the sound of separating segments, feels the cool sticky juice, and tastes the clean sharp flavor. She suggests that "visioning gives us a tool to begin to recover experiential reality untainted, simply as it is, and to use imagination and imagery as a way to establish our vision of a truly woman-centered future," and to fulfill the dreams in reality.[63] Visioning is a way to create possibilities and to break out of our old molds and patterns of thinking and perceiving. Visioning allows us to change our lives and our attitudes and allows for radically innovative possibilities.

Feminist spiritual communities are visionary communities that act as if women's full participation and well-being were part of everyday life in society. Time is spent envisioning the new society of peace and wholeness where social and economic security exist; where everyone has food, shelter, and freedom from violence or fear of violence; where everyone experiences mutuality in relationships and participates in decisions that affect her own life. There is time to laugh and cry, to know moments of tenderness and moments of rage, to try to treat

---

63. Mary Ann Beall, "Dangerous Vision" (pre-reading for "Dangerous Visions: Leaping Past the Edge," an event of the Saskatchewan Christian Feminist Network, 1986), pp. 4–5. A slightly different version of this article appears in *Woman of Power* 2 (Summer 1985).

each other with respect, and to hear the realities of each other's lives and the ways we seek to find meaning. We struggle with finding our way when there are no paths. We do not know what the just and peaceful society would look like—there are no models other than the ones we create. We create these models in the belief that they open rich possibilities for a transformed world.

The visions of a just world, for most of the women interviewed in this project, had some similarities, but each adds her own unique elements to the vision. Several examples will give an idea of what the visions might mean for a transformed society.

According to one woman's vision of a just world:

> Everybody would have enough food and clothing, and there would be no one who was extremely rich or in dire poverty. There would be peace and cooperation. Countries would be assisting each other for health, peace, and living conditions that are conducive to developing intellectual and artistic and spiritual life. There would be a development of human potential. Now in so many countries there is little hope that a child will even live to maturity, let alone develop his or her potential.

Another says:

> We would have to do a better job of living with difference. That would be part of the equitable sharing, since poverty and deprivation of various kinds breed hostility when they are imposed by others. Gender would not be an issue. Women would be valued for the stereotypically noted qualities but would have a freedom to be fully who we are. Our whole range of strengths, contributions, and abilities would be recognized.

A third uses Christian terms:

> I often preach: "Let justice flow like a mighty river." In the Philippines, women could not wash their clothes in the river any more. Life was torn apart, and the village was decimated. But even then the people had a dream of peace. I dream of peace, respect, and honor for each person.
>
> The just society—Trudeau's phrase—would mean that people would live in safety, harmony, and peace, in a world where people can go to bed at night without fear of break-in, where they are safe, with a home, food, and clothes to meet their needs. It would mean that there would not be some who have much and who make slaves of others. It would be a world where men are taught not to beat women. Women would be able to work at whatever job they choose

to. There would be farm land, and agricultural production would come ahead of military weapons.

All people would be able to be who they are. Gays and lesbians would be respected. It would not mean that you would have to love everyone, but it would mean having to honor everyone and thereby ultimately honoring the whole society. This would bring a transformation to peace.

I do not want simple change. I want substantive change. The economic system needs to be turned upside down. It needs to be changed totally. The just society will be a long time in coming. It is like the kingdom—partly here and partly not yet. We have to keep working and encourage young people to think in new concepts and to honor one another.

Doris Anderson, in addressing a conference of the Canadian Advisory Council on the Status of Women, adds some concrete political implications to these visions. She dreams that child care, homemakers' pension plans, and adequate housing would come ahead of domed stadiums and nuclear submarines. She says she would not worry about an affirmative action plan for men until women had at least 95 percent of the seats in provincial legislatures, 90 percent of seats in the federal government, and 98 percent of the judgeships. "I wouldn't worry about affirmative action too much at all, because men have had affirmative action—a very good affirmative action plan—that's been in place for 2,000 years."[64]

Visioning gives opportunity to imagine the world as we want it. It allows for creation of a new order where women's lives are taken with seriousness and where peace, justice, and personal well-being are priorities. It allows testing of how to live into the visions and spurs action toward a just and creative future.

---

64. Doris Anderson, "The Power of Women," in *Fine Balances* (Canadian Advisory Council on the Status of Women, 1988), p. 8.

Chapter 17

TRUSTING OUR OWN
INNER WISDOM

A final and central aspect of feminist spirituality that I want to engage is the capacity to trust ourselves. Hallie Iglehart Austen sums up what this means:

> Women's spirituality is a process of demystifying spirituality. It is about making spiritual practice accessible to each one of us in our everyday lives. We can write our own scriptures, create our own rituals, since each of us has access to the inner wisdom from which all the great practices come. . . . We always need to come back to our own inner selves where the heart of wisdom resides. [65]

It is possible for women to believe that they have within themselves the resources to make the appropriate decisions for themselves and that they do not need to be told what to do by external authorities. Women are wise, and in community the inner wisdom they have can be brought to life and nourished. It is essential for us to listen to our inner wisdom and to trust ourselves to know and do what is right and just and good for ourselves and in relation to the world in which we live.

This being in touch with the inner core of one's being, with one's inner wisdom—or, as some would say, with the goddess within—is essential in feminist consciousness. It is what gives courage for analysis and for action. If women know, in their being, what is true and can name it, they can keep on track, in terms of commitments to justice for women. One woman, when asked about her spirituality, said:

---

65. Hallie Iglehart, "Women's Spirituality from the Roots to the Heart," in *The Womanspirit Sourcebook* (San Francisco: Harper and Row, 1988), p. 107.

I guess it is those things that give me life—literally to be in touch with the ground, to have time alone. I need time mostly to integrate, to think through experiences and get ready for more. It is for reflecting and connecting. I read our scriptures a lot and try to connect them with my experiences, to put the experiences in some perspective. I like to examine how I could be acting more "faithfully" toward a life that is more inclusive and has some movement toward justice—or at least seeing that it is not at odds with that goal.

Women experience their need for time alone, time to integrate, time to reflect in a variety of ways—some through active thinking, some through certain activities, some through various forms of meditation done alone, some through guided meditation done in groups, some through prayer, and some through other techniques of relaxation or devotional activity. One woman describes her meditative experiences as follows:

Swimming is more than just a physical thing. It is a time to meditate. The water is cleansing, healing, and comforting. When I don't do it, I miss it. I also use driving as a personal ritual time. I drive a lot, and I use my driving time on the open prairie to look at the horizon and meditate. Sometimes I listen to meditative chanting-type music. I have found ways to make driving time useful. I do, in the car, what some people do at home.

The ways that women talked about their meditation time reflected the importance of these activities in their lives, even though they took many forms.

Some of the Protestant Christian women talked about prayer as a form of reflection and about how it has helped them. In Protestant theology, it is understood that all individuals have direct access to God. No mediator, priest, or minister is needed to gain access to God, so many Protestant women have had strong prayer lives. They count on the interior strength and inner wisdom that they have gained through prayer, devotional acts, and personal experience. One woman talked about prayer in her life:

I do lots of rituals in my ordinary life. I think that things become sacred as we are mindful of them—for example, when I am standing at the sink peeling carrots at my cabin. It is a moment in which I am very present, unlike in the busy days, when carrot peeling is just another task to do.

Each morning I give thanks for personal, emotional, and physical health, for my friends and family, and for my community, my nation, and the planet. Then I offer prayers for all of the people of the world. I do this by going through the map of the world and seeing all of the people of the different countries of the world.

Another woman, however, does not find that prayer reveals inner wisdom to her:

> As a teen I prayed religiously. I did devotions every evening. Now I don't pray at all. Even when I was doing it all the time, it didn't feel real. It felt like I was talking to myself. It made more sense to me to talk to a real person.
>
> Prayer was always a funny thing to me. I often felt like I was having to give up something of myself to do it. In prayer groups I would fight with myself. Whenever I would close my eyes, I would be in tears. I didn't feel like it was a valid way of dealing with stuff or of having one's needs met. You weren't going to be heard. The prayers were going into the air and then being lost to the wind.

Many of the women interviewed would not describe their reflection time as prayer. More would call it meditation and would see it as a going inward, focusing of the self and connecting with the divine within, instead of gaining inner strength through praying to an external deity.

Many of the women like to use guided meditations or creative visualization. Diane Stein describes how, in guided meditation based in visualization, women can let go of ordinary concerns. As they are guided toward their inner self, women can create, through the powers of will and mind, a transformed universe, a place of beauty and safety, a space where they can meet the Goddess, a spirit guide, or their inner self, where they can receive a message, an image, a solution to a problem, or a gift.[66]

The Feminist Spiritual Community uses guided meditation most weeks as a way of entering into a state of openness and receiving new insights. There are a variety of purposes for the meditation. Sometimes it is primarily for centering, for getting in touch with one's body-self, or for setting a context for the ritual activity (such as in preparation for a healing circle). Sometimes it is used as a route to commitment and action or to get answers to questions. Occasionally, it is to gain a sense of connectedness with the earth and with women around the world. Sometimes it is just for pleasure—to be in touch with beauty and with sounds, images, and feelings that are pleasurable. On occasion, there is hope for insight or for gifts, as one evening

---

66. Diane Stein, *Casting the Circle: A Women's Book of Ritual* (Freedom, Calif.: Crossing Press, 1990), p. 35.

when Marsha led a meditation focusing on receiving and knowing gifts of love, trust, faith, gratitude, and courage.

Part of that meditation dealt with trust, and the conversation afterward shows how unaccustomed women are to trusting themselves and others:

> Your Guide asks you if you are ready for the second gift. You say that you are, and again the mist surrounds you. When the mist disappears, you find that you are in Alaska sitting beside a fast-flowing river and surrounded by a meadow full of summer flowers. It is warm, and the sun shines on you as you look at the purple and yellow flowers. You look around and see a white she-wolf on a stone nearby. You look at her, and she looks at you. There is no fear. She lifts back her head and howls deeply, and you feel something within you, and you too lift back your head and howl . . . and you are a wolf, and you run and roll and play in the flowers with the she-wolf, and you delight in the play—and the wolf looks at you and says, "I give you the gift of trust," and you go back in your life, and you find all of the times you knew trust . . . and you feel the goodness of those times . . . and slowly the mist covers you, and you return to your body and bid the wolf farewell . . . and when the mist recedes, you are back with your higher self. She asks what you have, and you say, "I have trust."

Following the guided meditation, women talked about trust. "I was able to get into all of the gifts, except I had a really hard time with trust. I need to do some more thinking about what that means in my life." Several people agreed that trust had been very hard. "I got into being the wolf and I wanted to throw back my head and howl—but I did find it hard to feel the gift of trust." "I felt very desolate when you said to recall the times in your life when you had known trust—I did not find any at all, until I was sixteen, and I found another sixteen-year-old, whom I could trust. Later I found someone else, and as time went on, I found there were others, and as I have gotten older, there are more and more, and it feels great." Another added, "I could not find anyone that I ever trusted, and then I looked at myself and I realized that I had always trusted myself—and that was a real gift." So trust is very difficult for many; for others it is the means of survival.

There are pressures to be in touch only with patriarchal images of what one is supposed to be like—in terms of body size and shape, in terms of the level of intellectual capacity expected, in terms of relationships, and in terms of how one lives one's private and public life. A primary pressure is fear. Women who are afraid have trouble trusting themselves. Systems of domination are based on the perpetuation of fear and on keeping fear as the motivating factor in decisions and actions. If the people are filled with fear, they will not revolt, they will not form creative communities, they will not escape from fear.

There is no doubt that in our world, terror, acute fear, and dread are sensible responses. Blacks in South Africa can be imprisoned and tortured for a word, a look, a move. Latin American children frequently suffer from a state of psychotic dread from experiencing the disappearance of family members and the frequent raids and bombing of their homes. Canadian women on university campuses live now, not only with the fear of sexual violence that is frequently part of campus life, but, after Montreal, with fear for their lives. Fear as a way of life thus makes a great deal of sense in our world. Our hope lies in embracing fear, instead of being destroyed by it, and in finding our autonomy—that is, our capacity for inner self-direction in the company of others who are willing to support us on that journey.

For many women, much inner healing is needed in order to be able to embrace the fear and to trust themselves fully. But healing and trusting one's inner wisdom are essential if one is going to work for justice in the world. Pat talks about what this means in the Feminist Spiritual Community:

> A lot of the women who came to FSC are very needy. They have a lot of problems in their lives and are looking for support in getting their own lives together. This is important and has to happen in order for women to move toward justice work. I was there for a long time—trying to get my life sorted out, and as I have done that, I have been free to work in the Central American work and the peace work that I do.

Another woman says:

> I think we can be just with others when we are just with ourselves. We are doing justice to ourselves when we are being truthful with ourselves.
>
> Are you going to ask me why I am not active? I have some guilt for not doing more. But I have not been able to. I know women who were involved, so I was like a shadow. I have been healing myself, and I can't take on that much more responsibility.

Another woman talked about how, even when one learns to trust oneself, it is hard to share that with others: "I think it is very hard to ask in community for a personal ritual. It is a brave thing to put out a need or a celebration before the group and have that celebration honored. For example, when I had the ritual for my name changing, it was hard to ask and to have the community focus on me."

Despite the reality of fear and uncertainty about trust, several women talked about the importance of their own inner wisdom. Women find their inner wisdom is nourished through rituals.

> What happens to me in ritual, in community (or in that place of belonging, the holy holding, being fun), is that I honor, value, and know myself as a woman there. As the poem says, "I found God in myself, and I loved her fiercely." That happens to me in ritual. It is a magical thing. I want magic to come—so I make a place and wait. I believe that the earth wants to give us surprises and pleasure.

Along with group meditation, some women spend time with their meditations alone. One woman describes her personal meditations, which is a sample of the kinds of meditative time women choose when they are alone:

> My ritual life is different in the winter and summer. In the winter I do at least one hour per week of meditation and reflection. I rarely do that in the summer, but being out in the garden replaces that for me. I have to be in the garden at least one half-hour every day, or I feel that something is missing. Sometimes it is time for sorting out, but mostly I have no recollection afterward of having thought anything at all. I have such an active and curious mind that this time of not thinking is self-care. It is a time of centering, and it allows my head to clear.

Another gets in touch with inner wisdom through journaling. She said, "Another part of my personal ritual is journal writing. It is very integral to my self-understanding. It is where I share myself with myself."

Trusting one's self and one's own inner wisdom is part of feminist spirituality, but it is a part that is quite challenging for many women. Yet it is our hope. As the quotation at the beginning of this chapter says, "We always need to come back to our own inner selves where the heart of wisdom resides." It is within ourselves that we women will see beauty, find our identity and voice, gain shared visions in community, receive healing through trust and openness, gain strength for resistance, see choices where vulnerability would lead to new growth, and learn to trust our own inner wisdom.

· PART 3 ·

Digging Deeper

The third part of the feminist theological method on which this research was based is analysis. The intention of analysis is to pull together the definitions, categories, and concepts arising from the defining and naming of parts 1 and 2. Analysis asks questions about power and about personal and political implications. It involves digging deeper to look at what the categories mean in living situations.

The stage for analysis was set in the examination of patriarchy, feminism, justice, and ritual in part 1. This part elaborates on those concepts, using data from the research, and makes connections with the thealogical categories named in part 2. Further drawing together will take place in the concluding chapter.

Part 3 begins with some tools for analysis. Then it moves into an analysis of the data from several perspectives, starting with functions of ritual that have become obvious from the research. From there it explores and analyzes uses of symbols, forms of feminist spirituality that have emerged, and implications for structure and leadership.

Chapter 18

ANALYSIS

Many women struggle with what analysis means. Women in North America, especially white middle-class women, have been encouraged to focus their energies on home and family. We have been encouraged to see home and family as separate from politics, economic productivity, and decision-making that affect the community or world. We have been encouraged to believe that the feminization of poverty, the oppression of women, and violence against women happen to other, less-fortunate women. We have been encouraged to see things that are wrong in our lives and situations as our own fault, and to see politics and economics as beyond our understanding.

One woman used a metaphor from her reading of feminist psychology to describe this state:

> Anne Wilson Shaef at the beginning of her book [*Women's Reality*] says that the white male system is like a cloud of pollution. When it is all around you, you don't notice it. Unless women are able to separate themselves from it, they do not notice that they are caught in this veil of male pollution. In the pollution there are various women and men and minorities that do see the pollution.

To do social analysis requires changing our viewpoint to see the pollution. It demands recognition that home, family, politics, economics, and public decisions are interwoven. It requires that we examine the consequences of actions; that we question the implications of public policies; that we see the ways in which laws and economic practices of capitalist patriarchy affect our lives, our children's lives, and our communities. Analysis allows us to get a more accurate picture of what "reality" is than when we are surrounded by the cloud of pollution. It lets us see more than a narrow personal or individualistic view does. It empowers us to name our own experience in relation to the experience of others—both the similarities and the differences. Analysis helps us see that the public and private are not separate but make a strong impact on each other and that the political skills that women learn in child raising and in community activities are the same skills needed to be involved in the political spheres of school boards, government, or corporate boardrooms.

A description by Wendy Luttrell illustrates this interrelation, as some women tried to save the school in their area. They discovered that women organized budgets and found time between jobs, school, volunteer work, and kids, as well as figuring out what they needed to do and say in their meetings with the male-dominated school boards. They were enraged to discover that they did all the same things that the men on the school board did—but the men got paid and dealt only with each other, instead of having to deal with the lives of the children, families, and communities affected by their decisions. As Luttrell goes on to note:

> They also persistently pointed out that the very conditions that foster women's oppression—their multiple responsibilities as workers, wives, and mothers—were also conditions that enabled them to be more effective leaders. Their ability to change roles and to negotiate between the worlds of politics, community, and family grew directly from those multiple responsibilities. . . . Once they saw themselves as capable of participating in the public, political arena, the skills they had developed in the private realm of family and community, such as interpersonal communication and organization, translated nicely into leadership abilities. [1]

Analysis, then, is important to help us make connections and to empower us to act. As Marta Benavides's mother noted in chapter 3 above, "Justice requires not just action but reflective and responsible action." Analysis enables action to be reflective and responsible. It is the ground for eliminating patriarchy and creating a more humane society for all people, regardless of class, race, and sexual preference.

Thus, analysis allows us to see the personal and political consequences of choices and the implications of our own and others' actions, to make connections, to get a more complete picture of reality, to enable reflective and responsible action, and to build real change for women through elimination of patriarchy and creation of a humane society.

---

1. Wendy Luttrell, "The Edison School Struggle: The Reshaping of Working-Class Education and Women's Consciousness," in *Women and the Politics of Empowerment*, ed. Ann Bookman and Sandra Morgen (Philadelphia: Temple University Press, 1988), p. 145.

There are a variety of methods of analysis. As mentioned in the Introduction, analysis involves taking the data one step beyond naming and begins to interpret it in a broader context. Feminist analysis looks at the concrete historical conditions of women's lives, analyzes structures and the power relations caused by structures, and has a political agenda of serving the interests of women. In chapter 2 above, it was noted that feminism is a process—a way of approaching life and politics, a method of analysis. Any form of feminist analysis must dig into personal and political concerns, with an understanding that the process is as significant as the final solutions.

Charlotte Bunch and Nancy Hartsock propose two very simple tools that contain the essence of feminist analysis.[2] Both consist of a few questions that can be asked of any theory or proposed action. The tools are easy to use and are good measuring sticks for any emerging theory or for those who want to dig deeper or explore some areas more fully. An elaboration of some of the questions and a series of categories for analysis follow. Charlotte Bunch suggests five questions:

1. Does this reform materially improve the lives of women, and if so, which women, and how many?
2. Does it build an individual woman's self-respect, strength, and confidence?
3. Does it give women a sense of power, strength, and imagination as a group and help build structures for further change?
4. Does it educate women politically, enhancing their ability to criticize and challenge the system in the future?
5. Does it weaken patriarchal control of society's institutions and help women gain power over them?[3]

Hartsock's questions are similar but phrased and ordered in different ways:

1. How will it affect women's sense of self, and sense of our own collective power?
2. How will it make women aware of problems beyond questions of identity—that is, how will it politicize women?
3. How will the strategy work to build organizations that will increase both our strength and competence, and will give women

---

2. See the Conclusion for the application of the tools in theory testing.
3. Bunch, "Reform Tool Kit," in *Building Feminist Theory,* ed. Bunch et al. (New York: Longman, 1981), p. 196.

power to use (like money) to weaken the control and domination
of capitalism, patriarchy, and white supremacy?
4. How will the strategy weaken the links between these institutions?[4]

Both sets of questions emphasize women's sense of self, of confidence, and of self-respect. Chapters 7 and 8, "Embodiment" and
"Naming of Self and Experience," have opened up these areas and
some of the implications of asking these questions. We as women need
to find our voices and to be heard, to name ourselves and our experiences. Women need to know themselves as embodied persons and
to know the connections between personal and political dimensions of
sexuality, reproduction, and violence. Women need to name their own
needs and to choose how to care for others in relation to themselves
and the well-being of families and communities. We need to explore
the personal implications of our silences, our privilege, and our truth-
telling. Thus, in analysis of actions, situations, theories, and rituals,
questions around how they affect women's sense of self and well-being
must be asked.

Both Bunch and Hartsock also note the importance of the material
conditions of women's lives and of the ways in which women's lives
are affected by capitalism, patriarchy, and white supremacy. Chapter
1, on patriarchy, has elaborated on these conditions and on the interstructuring of gender, class, and race. This has also been discussed in
chapters 6 and 10 ("Survival and Safety" and "Diversity"). The phras-
ing of Bunch's question—"Does this reform materially improve the
lives of women, and if so, which women, and how many?"—serves as
a reminder that justice will not exist for any until it exists for all, and
that analysis must consider the effects of actions on those whose lives
bear no privilege.

Hartsock's question "How will it politicize women?" and Bunch's
"Does it educate women politically?" raise the quality of structural
analysis. One woman describes her politicization:

> At a personal level, in my own circle, I try to live as justly as I can.
> I am much more aware of being fair. I try to be aware that as a
> white woman, who I am creates injustice. It is both personal and
> global. For example, the class system. I was brought up to be class-
> ist. It is hard to swallow how classist I was and am. It used to be
> when I saw someone different, someone of a different socioeco-
> nomic class, I did not understand them and I thought them be-
> neath me. When I grew up, the real world was a surprise to me. I

---

4. Nancy Hartsock, "Political Change: Two Perspectives on Power," in *Building Feminist Theory,* pp. 16–17.

discovered that the fairy tale was not true. I had lived with the fairy tale that I was going to sail through life with no worry, no soil, just go through life. I saw no physical or sexual abuse until I grew up.

Movements for social change require that people look beyond their own happiness or their own individual solutions to problems. We also must examine systems and their interstructuring.

Joe Holland and Peter Henriot give a rather lengthy but useful description of what analyzing social systems means. Their description is followed by concrete examples from this research, showing how the elements that they describe can be used toward the politicization of women. They note that social analysis can focus on isolated issues (e.g., unemployment, inflation, hunger), on policies that address the issues (e.g., job training, monetary control, food aid programs), and on the structures of our economic, political, social, and cultural institutions that create the issues and policies. From another angle, social analysis focuses on systems—that is, the primary groups, local communities, and nation-states—that make up the world system. They suggest that we need to analyze systems in terms of time (historical analysis of how the system has changed through time) and space (structural analysis of how the system currently works). A final aspect of analysis is what Holland and Henriot call the objective and subjective dimensions of analysis. The objective dimension is made up of the organizations, behavior patterns, and institutions in society; the subjective dimensions relate to consciousness, values, and ideology.[5]

Holland and Henriot suggest beginning with issues. The feminization of poverty, the public-private dichotomy, violence, and individualism, as discussed in chapter 1, "Defining the Problem as Patriarchy," would be examples of analysis of specific issues. Who gets to name what beauty is, who benefits from sexual and spiritual closeting for safety and survival, whose experience is held as central, and who gains and who loses in situations of vulnerability emerge as issues from the categories named.

One woman gave a vivid example of the need for analysis of particular issues. In her case, the issue was educational curriculum, specifically, the failure of the American public school system to foster political awareness of the Holocaust. While studying in Austria, she went to visit Auschwitz.

I was horrified that in all my education I had never heard of Auschwitz, that I knew nothing about it from going to good American schools. I was in university at the time—and had never heard

---

5. Holland and Henriot, *Social Analysis*, pp. 14–15 (see n. 14 on p. 23 above).

of it. I became obsessed and had to learn everything and to work
to be sure it never happens again.

The second dimension of analysis that Henriot and Holland name
is creation of policies to address the issues. The visions of a just world,
articulated by various women in this project, show the policy directions that are needed. According to the women, policy changes might
involve overturned economies, reformed relationships and definitions
of families, participation in decision-making by those affected by the
decisions, power to choose in relation to options and responsibilities,
ethics of cooperation rather than competition, need for elimination
of potential for war (especially nuclear weapons), respect and honor
for people and the earth, priority on health and well-being, and valuing of differences.

All of these policy suggestions imply analysis of structures and systems as they currently operate. Capitalist patriarchy needs analysis.
The political and cultural implications of making a shift to the kind
of small-scale economies, participatory politics, and women-affirming
cultures desired also need analysis. Analysis of structures and systems
is discouraged in patriarchy by mystifying structure, by individualism,
and by horizontal violence. Thus, looking at structures is essential for
feminists to discover what the overt structures, as well as the covert
substructures, say about sex, race, class, and power. Examining structures in terms of who benefits and who pays the costs in the systems
is a powerful way of exposing a reality of the structures that patriarchy wants to keep invisible. Looking at the interconnectedness of
capitalism, patriarchy, and white supremacy, as Hartsock suggests, requires sharp analysis if a new social order is to be created.

A fourth dimension of analysis, according to Holland and Henriot,
involves the primary groups, local communities, nation-states, and global
systems of which we are a part. In feminism, this is especially important, according to the points made earlier about a woman-centered
politic and about diversity, as well as the understanding of the personal as political and the political as personal. It is important in this
analysis to see where women's voices are heard at every level. The
Canadian Advisory Council on the Status of Women indicates that
more women get involved in municipal politics than in provincial or
federal politics, partly because it is easier to gain access there. They
also suggest:

> Political involvement at the local level is also often easier to manage
> in relation to women's other responsibilities. It is difficult, but pos-
> sible, to combine a political career at the municipal level with the
> responsibilities of raising a family. Work for city councilors is often

part-time and does not involve as much separation from families as
travel to Ottawa or to a provincial capital might require.

Volunteer activity has also been a major pathway through which
women are recruited into municipal politics. Through work and
contacts in the voluntary sector, women develop knowledge about,
and interest in, municipal issues, experiences that may lead them to
consider running for municipal office.[6]

Municipal politics is thus a possibility for women. But what about
federal politics? Sue Findlay suggests that women's agendas have moved
more into the government sphere than they were before 1975, the
International Women's Year. With the more open stance of the federal government to hearing women's issues, feminists moved from the
strategies of rallies and demonstrations to trying to work with cabinet
ministers and civil servants to bring about legislative changes in the
status of women. In elections, candidates and parties made commitments to women, although equal pay for work of equal value, divorce
reform, child care, an end to battering of women, and reform to the
Indian Act for Native women to regain status were, or are, slow in
coming. The government has grown accustomed to making promises
to feminists in elections, but it has been less committed to the radical
structural changes that are needed than to the liberal feminist re-
quests for minor reforms within the system of structural inequalities.[7]

Women need to be central and occupy at least as much space as
men in governments, policy setting, and social and economic planning. But it is important that the quality of difference among women
involved in decision-making be maintained. In order for feminism to
be a movement toward the well-being of all women, race, class, age,
level of abilities/disabilities, sexual orientation, and geographic location all need to be considered. In order for justice for anyone to be
real, there must be justice for all. Thus the criteria in feminist analysis
is not what a particular action, policy, or decision will do for white,
middle-class, educationally privileged women, but what it will do for
the woman who has least and who is struggling for survival economically, racially, educationally, and reproductively.

The fifth area of analysis is historical—that is, looking at how systems have changed over time. The importance of naming patriarchy
as a historical creation has already been mentioned. What is based in
history is not a biological, natural, or ontological necessity. It is part

6. Canadian Advisory Council on the Status of Women, *Women in Politics: Becoming
Full Partners in the Political Process* (Ottawa, 1987).

7. See Sue Findlay, "Feminist Struggles with the Canadian State: 1966–1988," *Resources for Feminist Research* 17, no. 3 (September 1988), for more explanation of this
process and its implications for Canadian women.

of an organism, changing and adapting, to meet new circumstances. If patriarchy is not a historical necessity, it need not exist.

The problem of the historical amnesia of women has already been noted as well. Women must keep telling the stories of survival and resistance and of how the women's movement has functioned thus far. Even when patriarchal powers have erased all records and women have lost touch with past acts of resistance, hope, and survival, amnesia must not prevail. Remembering can give strength and courage and motivation for action.

More will be said about the objective dimensions (organizational and institutional structures) in chapter 22, "Leadership and Institutional Implications." The subjective dimensions (consciousness, values, and ideologies) will be explored in chapters 19 and 20, "Functions of Rituals" and "Symbols."

All of these elements, then, are important in keeping the concrete and material conditions of women's lives central and in serving feminism's political agenda of justice and well-being. Bunch's and Hartsock's questions are good beginning points for analysis and can be easily used in most situations. To go deeper into the areas for analysis suggested by Holland and Henriot is helpful. But what is most important is that women be politically conscious of the meaning of their lives in relation to the lives of other people, and aware also of possible choices and options that will contribute to justice and well-being for women in the world, including themselves. As Bunch and Hartsock show, analysis does not have to be complex—but it does have to be done.

Chapter 19

FUNCTIONS OF RITUALS

As indicated earlier, analysis leads to broader interpretations of data. It was also noted that rituals focus our energies, allow us to be renewed, help us bond, and inspire us toward action beyond the ritual. Rituals are symbolic actions that enable new visions of how things might be different and are a means of social and personal transformation. Thus, it is important to look more deeply at the data arising from the participant observation of rituals to see how this renewal, inspiration, and transformation can nurture and challenge feminists in their work for justice and well-being for women in the world. This analysis leads to a number of observations about the functions of ritual in feminist spirituality. Connecting the ordinary with the holy, keeping order in life, allowing for experiences that go beyond belief, linking the personal and political, taking one beyond oneself, bringing change, and providing a symbolic center of return are functions that grow out of the data and that are explored more fully in this chapter.

When I asked women what kinds of religious rituals are part of their lives, they often spoke about walks in natural surroundings, talking with their cats, making and eating meals with friends—the very ordinary aspects of their lives—as religious ritual. Women's rituals tell the truth about women's lives—about birth and menstruation; changing cycles of their bodies; double work days; social, physical, and economic needs; and love of nature. The first function of religious rituals, then, is to connect the ordinary experiences of women's lives, to notice daily life events in community and in the process of seeking meaning in one's life.

In a Christian congregation, one sermon addressed situations in the local setting of the church, especially in its mention of the housing problem in the area, the homeless, and the controversy over a proposal for a subsidized housing project near the church, which received opposition from area residents. In the service, people had an opportunity to name situations for which they wanted prayers. Included in the prayers were concerns for the people of Jamaica and Mexico whose lives were affected by Hurricane Gilbert, for Desmond Tutu in his work against apartheid in South Africa, "for those whose lives are filled with grief, who struggle with illness—whether the illness be mental, physical, or spiritual, for those who struggle with dependencies and other forms of evil that face them," and for children of the church and neighborhood.

The Feminist Spiritual Community begins its gatherings with announcements and a time of sharing what is going on in the participants' lives. One gathering included announcements about an upcoming convoy to Central America, a member's birthday party, the need for a friend for a seventeen-year-old pregnant woman whose husband is in prison, the NOW march on Washington in April for women's equality, and the University of Southern Maine women's week events. The naming circle also provided opportunity for many women to speak of the concrete situations in their lives, including child custody suits, far-away daughters, illnesses among relatives, incest survivor's work, concerns about jobs, and need for energy.

One individual named Sarah spoke of her rituals and how they connect with her daily life. She talked about personal, seasonal, community, and family rituals. Regarding personal rituals, she began:

> I live on a farm with lots of fields and hardwood trees. I like to walk to clear the chatter. As I walk away, I get in touch with my body, a moving meditation. By the time I get to where I am going and turn around to come back, I am ready to stop being inside and move outside, and on the way home I notice the trees, birds, and things in nature.
>
> The seasonal rituals involve putting in the garden in the spring and gathering apples in the fall. It is such an exquisite feeling to be out with the abundance of nature.
>
> Community rituals involve friends and people that I share ideas and sensibilities with. I am part of a Women's Deep Mysteries group that does rituals. Then on Sundays a group of women, men, and children gather and do rituals to the goddess, have potlucks and sweats.
>
> Family rituals are the times when all of the family comes together—weddings, funerals, graduations, etc. We work to make these special occasions.

Rituals thus can take many forms, but the effective ones connect the ritual experience with ordinary living.

Another function of ritual is to keep order in one's life. Joyce says:

I never thought much about ritual. Now I see the way I live is a ritual. I am aware of what comes forward to me. Like an accordion, the folds of each day come in, and each morning is like a new opening of the accordion. My husband and I begin the day together. We look at the hibiscus, share our morning meal, say good-bye, and go out into the world. In the evening we come together again, eat, watch the sunset, and our accordion then closes.

Many women long for the sense of order and beauty that Joyce describes. For women to feel the kind of safety described earlier, some sense of order is needed, whether it be the rhythm of the days referred to by Joyce, regular time with friends or in meditation, or space that is known to be free from harm. Rituals often feel safe to women when they are done in safe space, when there is planning of the ritual by the participants (or at least when the leader or leaders describe what will be happening in the ritual) so there are no frightening surprises, and when there is an order or pattern that makes sense. For example, the rituals of the Feminist Spiritual Community usually follow the same pattern week by week with enfolding, naming circle, candle lighting, announcements, meditation, action/reflection, singing, and blessing. Likewise, Christian worship services generally follow an order that remains constant, although content changes week by week. This pattern helps us to order and reorder our lives. Even when we change the content of our rituals, we often follow similar patterns, or if we give up one ritual, we replace it with another. For example, one interviewee says: "I have let go of some things. I used to meditate. I also had a smoking ritual. I can see it now as taking on other rituals to replace smoking. I can substitute a new ritual—lighting a candle or something as a new ritual rather than trying to stop and leaving an empty space."

In considering the need for order, however, it is important to differentiate between order and control. Order can be a way of providing freedom within a framework, safety for creativity, new rituals to fill empty spaces. Control means an external authority that imposes rules that one must follow and that seeks obedience rather than freedom, safety, and creativity.

Another of the functions of ritual is to enable people to deepen experiences and to experience elements of life that would not be known through rational living and knowledge of facts only. In the Feminist Spiritual Community, there are deeply shared experiences, with little emphasis on instilling particular beliefs. Little time is spent articulating beliefs, although there is some opportunity to do so in educational courses. At rituals, there often are statements of experience, without pushing further into what belief systems might make up the experiences. Sometimes women view the same event with very different eyes. For example, in a meditation on peace, as one person envisions a peaceful day in her own life, another may be envisioning walking safely and freely down the streets of her community, and another will see a planet where there is no more war and violence.

One of the significant differences between the Feminist Spiritual Community and the Saskatchewan Christian Feminist Network is in the area of articulation of beliefs. Network events are primarily educational in nature, with community building, support, ritual, and play as secondary (although essential) elements. *The Unbeaten Path* is full of information about theological issues and debates, current issues in Saskatchewan and globally, feminist theory, and inspirational sections. It rarely incorporates rituals or writings about ritual. Rituals at events connect with the theme of the event, and efforts are made to ensure that the content of the ritual fits with the program theme and is consistent with the values and processes of the event. The network tends toward ritual with interpretations; as two of the interviewees said, "The rituals have to make sense."

The Feminist Spiritual Community, on the other hand, is more inclined in the direction elucidated by David Kertzer, namely, that "rites are not simply stylized statements of belief. . . . Socially and politically speaking, we are what we do, not what we think."[8] But members both of the network and of the community would agree with Mary Douglas, who says that through the ritual, our perceptions are changed, and we experience things differently. She points out that rituals are not like visual aids or instruction sheets. If they were, they would always follow experiences. However, ritual can permit knowledge that would otherwise not be gained. Ritual also can modify experience through expressing it in structured form.[9]

Thus, while rituals embody the beliefs of the community, they do so in ways that allow for new experiences and for new expression as well as enabling us to live out those beliefs, articulated or not.

Another function of ritual is to link the personal and political. In the Feminist Spiritual Community, one of the political acts is to live in ways that show that "the personal is the political." Personal healing and global healing are not separated. Rituals allow for the personal healing and nurture that is needed by many for survival in daily living, while also seeing the interconnectedness of our lives with the lives of animals, trees, dolphins, and birds. Some of the rituals enable personal life events (a birthday, a name change) to become opportunities

---

8. David Kertzer, *Ritual, Politics, and Power* (New Haven: Yale University Press, 1988), pp. 67–68.

9. Douglas, *Purity and Danger*, p. 64.

for all of the community to reflect on those elements in our lives. In describing the personal and political link, one member said:

> For me the guided meditations evoke personal things. They give meaning on a personal level. But Community is a political level. The candle lighting and the naming circle are political. They are about making the connections and remind us that we are all involved in a common struggle and with a common vision.

While FSC is not an overtly activist group, it does allow the participants to be activists by creating an environment where a different vision of society can be explored, where an ethic for life for the planet is encouraged, and where ideas for actions can be birthed. Of course there are overt political actions by individual members of FSC and by FSC itself (such as Beth's going on a women's convoy to Central America, members' going to Washington for a March for Women's Lives, and women's carrying the FSC banner in the Portland Gay Pride march).

The Saskatchewan Christian Feminist Network also engages in rituals that link the personal and the political. One example of such a ritual comes from a gathering in Saskatoon focusing on women and work. The ritual began with singing, readings, and chants. Then women were invited to stand in a circle facing outward and to call out things they wanted to banish from women's lives. Sentences poured out: "You did that almost as good as a man." "She just needs a good lay." "What do you expect from the kid with a mother like that?" "We thought you would be able to change our son when you married him." "She shouldn't have been jogging on the river trail." "You're too old for that." "You are too young." "Don't you know what a woman's good for?" The words were banished from the circle by repeating a phrase three times, to cast them from the circle and the world.

The women then turned and faced inward to name joys, inspirations, and women's hopes, repeating forcefully after each, *"We celebrate . . . ":* "I celebrate my friend in Nicaragua who worked to unionize women there and was killed." *"We celebrate* your friend from Nicaragua. . . . "* "I celebrate women who are in the political struggle to make Canada a better place. I celebrate two women from our network who have tried to enter the political field—Pat Krug and Laura Balas." "I celebrate women who work for unions." "I celebrate the dreamers and the visionaries who think about what life could be like." "I celebrate all of you. I came as a stranger, and now I have new friends." "I celebrate the Native women who are speaking out about their lives."

Then, after a period of silence, women began to speak of commitments they wanted to make: "I recommit myself to speaking out at work and to trying to bring a feminist model to my work environment." "I just registered for a drug and alcohol counselor course, and I commit myself to following my dream. I will put my business card on the altar as a sign of doing what I need to do now to survive so that I can work toward my long-term goal." "I said this morning that there needed to be social, political, and economic changes, so I am going to go to the N.D.P. nomination meeting in my local constituency and do everything I can to keep the worst of the assholes out of office." "I commit myself to getting to know two people at Friendship Inn, where I do some volunteer work. I have done enough analysis of the systems, and now I need to become friends with some people." "I commit myself to the kids on the West Side for at least two more years. So many of them have so little and need so much."

In interviews, several women also spoke about what the personal as political means to them as they live toward justice and a political spirituality. Two samples show the significance. A woman deeply concerned about the environment says:

> Our politics and our spirituality are one. One flows from the other. Spirituality is basic. My political action is often personal—I write letters very well and respond well to things that affect me personally.
>
> I see social change like a snowball moving from the individual to the global. But it is more than individual change. When we think environmentally, there is the potential for violent change.
>
> One of my struggles is how to keep from being hopeless in the midst of the potential for destruction of the world by nuclear war or environmental breakdown. I feel we are being given an opportunity to make changes in ourselves and our small environment just where we are.

A Christian feminist sees spirituality and politics being linked together institutionally through the church:

> They come together in the institutional church, where we take stands for or against particular things, when we do things that enable people to do analysis and reflection on what is happening around us. In working with groups in and out of the church, I am working against injustice and violence. Whenever I am engaged in groups that are trying to empower one another and to be freed from things that oppress us, it feels like I am working toward the vision. Whenever we are taking each other's experience seriously and hearing one another, it feels like some healing is going on and that there is some movement toward wholeness. Whenever people are allowed

to speak the truth that may have been dangerous in their settings, that is a move toward wholeness and health.

Rituals also have the capacity to take one beyond oneself through, and to, community. Or in a transcendent way, rituals connect with reality-defining meanings and life-enhancing powers. One of the women interviewed says:

> When I was trying to be a Christian for about three or four years, I was involved in a prayer group. I liked it a lot—it used meditation and directing of light energy to family members and relationships that needed healing for whatever reason, and it held up and visualized people for healing. A lot of the meditations took us into stories from the Bible, and you imagined that you were there in the story and talking to Jesus. I liked it because there weren't any rules— you could just have the conversation with Jesus. There was group praying. We would name the needs and pray for the person out loud. It was good for me. It helped me to focus my energy and to open myself to others, even if God and Jesus did not mean that much to me. I had a real sense of grace—not grace as through the Son to the Father—but grace in the sense of definitely being connected to something greater than myself and of abandonment of myself to that power of grace.

Rituals have the power to help people find solutions to their problems. Often they give women space to think about things that are troubling, to hear principles for action, and to gain perspective by moving outside one's own limited interests and viewpoints.

Ritual can also act as a change-agent and as a forum for transformation. Barbara Lyon says, "After a ritual there is a sharing of the deep down knowing that we all have options and responsibility for the transformation of society."[10] Kay Turner also notes that rituals are one way of renewing commitments to societal transformation. She claims that transforming the symbols of power is of equal importance to transforming the political sources of power. Doing rituals that create psychic and spiritual changes for women is as important as working for reproductive choice, having domestic freedom, and establishing women's businesses. Lasting change for women will come only when both the symbols and the realities are changed.[11]

One woman elaborates on the transforming effect of ritual and its ethical effect:

---

10. Barbara Lyon, *Dance toward Wholeness* (Austin: The Sharing Company, 1981), pp. 68–69.

11. Kay Turner, "Contemporary Feminist Rituals," in *The Politics of Women's Spirituality*, ed. Charlene Spretnak (Garden City, N.Y.: Anchor, 1982), pp. 227, 222.

Ritual at times can have a transformative effect. In rituals we have often talked about the horrendous things that are going on in the world. We come quite laden down by those things. When we do banishing and calling forth, it makes us feel better. But it goes beyond that to renew and strengthen our energy. It gives me the courage to do the little things that I do. I feel not so crazy and alone.

I do little things. This week I phoned the school principal regarding the Teen Aid program. I wanted him to have a good critique at the upcoming town meeting about the Teen Aid program. The school board has agreed to meet with parents who want the program in the schools. He is not keen on it, and I wanted to point him to some resources that point out the problems with the program so that at least the right questions can be raised at the meeting. He wanted me to come, but I am not a parent. He says that does not matter. I am not sure if I will go, but I at least did call him. I don't feel very brave about political action. But I do more than I did a few years ago.

David Kertzer suggests that ritual can be even stronger than transformation, that it can in fact be used as a revolutionary strategy. He says that rituals help revolutionary political stances and organizations through providing legitimacy, creating solidarity, and leading people to understand their political universe in certain ways. Rituals also help people give up old habits and worldviews. [12] Through the creation of ritual and symbols, the powerless can often gain an identity and worldview other than that encouraged by the elite. Clearly this aim is central to the purpose of the feminist spirituality movement. The Women-Church movement, described in chapters 13 and 21, "Resistance and Undermining" and "Feminist Spiritualities," with the WATER's Easter rituals in Washington, shows one side of this radical strategy for creating change at a deep ideological level. To claim selves as church, and then to use the church's rituals as models of justice in the world, gives political identity and impetus to the Women-Church movement.

In ritual, we may come face to face with what race, class, gender, and sexual orientation mean in our lives as we hear from women who are different from us. For those of us who have privilege, this knowledge may mean changing our ways and our actions in the world. For those of us who experience double and triple oppressions and discrimination, ritual may provide occasions for autonomy and for being central, rather than marginal, and thus may give new options for actions in the world.

---

12. Kertzer, *Ritual, Politics, and Power*, p. 153.

Finally, Kay Turner suggests that rituals are important because "ritual acts maintain a symbolic center of which all the participants are aware. This center is a place to which one can return for support and comfort long after the ceremony has ended."[13] This function is especially important for women who live in a survival mode. To be able to call on the spirits of those with whom one has done rituals often helps one through the desolate circumstances of life. Being able to remember that flowers can grow in mud, that other ways of being are possible, and that other women care are spiritual resources that continue after the ritual itself ends. Rural women, who feel loneliness at being the only feminist for miles around, often find that the mementos of rituals and events and the knowledge that there will be other gatherings tide them through some of the loneliness. Rituals of solidarity, where there is a sharing of selves or involvement in actions for social change, create strong bonds that can be life transforming and can inspire others to new actions, locally and globally. Rituals filled with laughter also create strong centers and memories to hold after the ritual. Linda's ritual of recalling the women to whom she holds herself accountable as an activist, as described in chapter 9, "Community and Relationships," is another way of returning to the symbolic center many times. These allow women to make and make again.

These functions of ritual—to notice the everyday in the process of seeking meaning in life, to keep order in one's life, to allow for experience that goes beyond beliefs, to link the personal and political, to take one beyond oneself, to act as agent of change and forum of transformation, and to serve as a symbolic center of return—are what keeps women's rituals grounded. These functions help women dig deeper into the "subjective dimension of analysis" described by Henriot and Holland. Through them, women can analyze and explore the values and consciousnesses that undergird rituals and can assist movement toward the political agenda of the elimination of patriarchy and the creation of a more humane society. This analysis keeps women's rituals clear, concrete, and intentional and serves as a monitor for assessing whether feminists' rituals are taking seriously women's quest for well-being and justice, for challenge and nurture. Thus analysis of rituals enables a clearer view of how rituals function in society and, more specifically, within feminism.

---

13. Turner, "Contemporary Feminist Rituals," p. 226.

Chapter 20

SYMBOLS

A third implication arising from the redefinition of thealogical categories involves symbols. Symbols, rituals, and ideologies are closely linked together and are also part of what Holland and Henriot called the subjective dimension of analysis. Any hope for moving away from the ideology of patriarchy requires an examination of symbols. Any hope of moving toward a feminist ideology of justice and well-being for women in the world also means shifting old symbols and creating new ones. This chapter begins to explore the implications, including the social and political consequences of shifting symbols, through analyzing the meanings of symbols and their functions in rituals.

One of the interviewees describes the power of symbolism in ritual for her:

> I have an instant defensiveness against ritual. I would rather have a group that grapples with something. That is so important to me. I suppose I am also defensive because there is so much symbolic meaning that it envelops me. Often I am tired and don't want to expend that much energy. But I guess I grudgingly have to admit that I am glad to be part of the rituals—tears and all. The rituals are so incredibly meaningful that they are sometimes sad. Maybe they are so powerful because there is so much awful symbolism out there. But in ritual we catch sight of wholeness, which is central to meaningfulness. There is so much that is awful out there.

Another woman describes ritual in symbolic terms: "I think about personal ritual as vitamin supplements for my spirit. In the cold, cruel winter of sexist society, I need such supplements against spiritual malnutrition, a disease from which many women suffer."[14]

---

14. Norma Clifford, review of *Women-Church: Theology and Practice*, by Rosemary Radford Ruether, *Women's Concerns* 33 (Winter 1987): 21.

But what are symbols and symbolic terms? Symbols are shorthand ways of expressing a deep meaning, for particular groups, in particular contexts. Symbols represent something. They are not necessarily like what they represent in any way, but they have the power to evoke memories, feelings, and understandings that bring to mind what they represent, as well as the power to convey meaning. Joel Charon cryptically states, "Symbols are social objects used to represent (or 'stand in for,' 'take the place of') whatever people agree they shall represent." [15] He adds that symbols are social, significant, intentional, and for communication. Their meaning is social, whether they are words, physical objects, or ideas.

David Kertzer names some of the qualities of symbols after saying that he has "defined ritual as action wrapped in a web of symbolism." [16] He says that symbols involve condensation (i.e., synthesizing many meanings into one symbol), multivocality (i.e., the same symbols being understood by different people in different ways), and ambiguity (i.e., the symbol's lacking a single precise meaning). [17] The ambiguity of symbols means that sometimes they contradict each other or at least do not fit well together.

The qualities and power of symbols are closely tied to the functions of symbols. Certainly, the primary function of symbols is to communicate. The use of words and certain actions allows us to eliminate a lot of manual and bodily actions that would be needed without verbalization. Ideas and worldviews are shared, communicated through words and other symbols. Symbols thus are time and energy savers, shorthand means of communicating.

Language, although it is a complex symbol system, is one of the primary means of communicating. Much energy has been, and continues to be, spent in the United Church of Canada, and many other liberal denominations, on inclusive language, that is, shifting language to make it inclusive of the experiences of women and men, and to have the deity represented in feminine as well as masculine terms. Language that says what we really want it to say is exceedingly important, since it is through language that we acquire knowledge. Beverly Harrison talks about the importance of clear language:

> Language is not merely an "external" feature of reality. Appropriation of language either reproduces or reshapes our social relations. The potential of language, then, is either to expand human possibility or to function as a transmitter of the subtle, and not so subtle,

---

15. Joel Charon, *Symbolic Interactionism*, 2d ed. (Englewood Cliffs, N.J.: Prentice-Hall, 1985), p. 39.

16. Kertzer, *Ritual, Power, and Politics*, p. 9.

17. Ibid., p. 11.

> patterns of human oppression and domination. Language is through
> and through political, for it transmits the past to our present. . . .
> We have a moral obligation not to replicate language patterns that
> reinforce unjust social relations. [18]

Theological/thealogical language, as already noted, has the power
to convey strong messages about the divine, about meaning and power
in human relationships, and about values. The function of the symbol
system of language—to communicate meaning and insight—is critical
for justice for all.

Carol Christ adds another dimension to the discussion of the functions of symbols:

> Religion fulfills deep psychic needs by providing symbols and rit-
> uals that enable people to cope with crisis situations in human life
> (death, evil, suffering) and to pass through life's important transi-
> tions (birth, sexuality, death). . . . Symbol systems cannot simply be
> rejected; they must be replaced. Where there is no replacement, the
> mind will revert to familiar structures at times of crisis, bafflement
> or defeat. [19]

We thus need some kinds of symbols and rituals to help us through
crises and transitions. As mentioned in chapter 15, "Loss," one woman
talked about having rejected patriarchal religion and many of the
symbols of Christianity. She then felt bereft and frightened at the
time of her mother's death because she had no symbols to replace
those of traditional Christianity. Women's descriptions of loss and
vulnerability identify the need for new symbol systems to assist women
through these difficult times. Communities and relationships of support likewise assist in crises and transitions.

An example of using symbols at times of transition is a ritual led by
Willow to celebrate her fortieth birthday.

> Willow talked about the meaning of the full moon—the mother as-
> pect of the moon full of potential for new birth and new life. She
> related this to her fortieth birthday and the potential for a new
> decade of life. In a candle holder there were four candles—three
> blue and one rainbow colored. She lit a candle for each decade of
> her life and talked about experiences she had had in that decade.
> After each decade of her life she allowed a time for reflection, guid-
> ing us to think about those decades in our lives silently. After the

---

18. Beverly Wildung Harrison, *Making the Connections*, ed. Carol Robb (Boston: Beacon, 1985), p. 24.

19. Carol P. Christ, "Why Women Need the Goddess," in *The Politics of Women's
Spirituality*, ed. Charlene Spretnak (Garden City, N.Y.: Anchor, 1982), p. 118.

fourth candle Willow led a meditation on fullness and on the potential for growth in our lives. Following the meditation a mirror and
bowl of salt water were passed around. The mirror was held so that
the woman could see herself and see the reflection of the goddess
[herself] as she washed her hands in salt water. Each woman could
say what fullness she wanted in her life, what she is giving birth to.

Symbols help to locate us, to find our place in the cosmos in crisis
and transition, as well as helping us to communicate with one another
in the ordinary times. We need symbols!

Another function of symbols is to create ethos. Clifford Geertz says
that within ritual, we use sacred symbols to develop the tone and
character of people's lives, "its moral and aesthetic style and mood—
their world view—the picture they have of the way things in sheer
actuality are, their most comprehensive ideas of order."[20]

For example, the symbols in the logo of the Feminist Spiritual
Community as described in the member's handbook give a sense of
its ethos and what it is:

The logo of the Community is a circle of women singing with hands
clasped the way we do on Monday night. The [four] candles are the
candles we light each Monday. The star represents the four directions.

The logo was designed by Jane Cunningham, a member of the
Community who died of cancer. It is a special gift from her to the
rest of us and also a symbol of her presence with us.

The symbols reflect the ethos, including the ongoing care for a now-
deceased member. The circle represents the political commitment to
equality; the candles reflect the ethos of care about new members,
women who are not present but would like to be, and the gathered
women; it also shows the connection with the women of their sister
village in El Salvador.

A different kind of ethos is the personal ethos by which one wants
to live. One woman talks about the way she dresses as a symbol of
what she wants to say about herself, or, to put it another way, as the
ethos she wants to create in her life.

Our ways of dressing are symbols. I dress differently now than I
used to. I dress comfortably and for me. I adorn myself for me,
and if others enjoy it, fine. But I do not dress to attract others. I
started wearing jewelry again a while ago—for me. And painted

---

20. Clifford Geertz, "Religion as a Culture System," in *Reader in Comparative Religion:
An Anthropological Approach*, 2d ed., ed. William Lessa and Evon Vogt (New York: Harper and Row, 1965), p. 209.

toenails are a kind of symbol. I got a peacock feather and a scarf with peacocks on it—just to show myself off.

Rituals are also done to create results. Mary Douglas points out that "ritualism is most highly developed where symbolic action is held to be most certainly efficacious."[21] Raymond Firth adds, "It is assumed that symbols communicate meaning at levels of reality not accessible through immediate experience or conceptual thought—hence it is argued, that in some sense they are revelatory."[22]

One woman talked about the symbols of the tarot as a means of revelation about important things in her life:

> In the more traditional spiritual dimension, I do meditation and reading of tarot cards. I never have a tarot reading that does not hit me right between the eyes. I know that sounds like the old-fashioned Christian who picks up the Bible and opens it and says that any old verse that the person reads is just what they need. I have to keep brushing that old tape away as I do the tarot. It is not that I see, out of the blue, messages sent specifically directed to me—but rather that what comes up, comes out of my deepest concentration and is the focus of my deepest concern—which I might be aware of consciously or not. But in the tarot reading it comes to the surface in the form of an image. I am amazed that something I need to think about or feel comes out in the image. It helps me to be in touch with myself. I see this in the wider context of the goddess, a wider context of spirituality. It is not just like going to the telephone and dialing a number—but rather the image is a piece of the whole that I need to work with today.

Circles for healing and meditations for conjuring up new images are other examples.

So we use symbols as a means of communicating with, gaining grace or favor from, and receiving revelation of God/gods/goddess. The symbol creates something at a deeper level, taking us beyond the concrete into another realm—the realm of grace, of communication with one another and with God, of holy space. In and of themselves, symbols have no necessary purpose. Insofar as symbols represent something else, however, they can become efficacious or revelatory.

Historically, symbols have also been used to objectify roles. According to Abner Cohen, "Symbols also objectify roles and give to them a reality which is separate from the individual personalities of their incumbents. . . . By objectifying roles and relations, symbolism achieves

---

21. Mary Douglas, *Natural Symbols* (London: Barrie and Rockliff, 1970), p. 8.
22. Raymond Firth, *Symbols: Public and Private* (Ithica: Cornell University Press, 1975), p. 49.

a measure of stability and continuity without which social life cannot exist."[23] For example, the role of the prime minister, the queen, a minister/priest, a teacher, or student are all defined so that people know what to expect. One of the challenges of feminism is to break down dualism and stereotypes, and so this function of ritual needs clarification in feminism. The role needs to be seen as a role to enable the group to function, not a role vested in one particular person. The role of the ritual leader(s) or of the meeting convener(s) or of the educator(s) can change from person to person, but whoever is filling the role needs to know what functions need to be carried out for the well-being of the group. Symbolic roles, then, are shared, and the leader holds only the power ascribed by the group for the particular function and for the limited time in which she bears that responsibility in the group.

A different dimension of the question of roles is raised by the creation of symbolic roles for what might be called "affirmative action purposes." One example of this is the role of crone in many feminist communities. Older women in North American society are devalued, and so for feminist communities to offer a ceremony of respect and to honor the wisdom of the elders contributes to the personal well-being of the crone and to the revisioning of the value of aging women in society. In the Feminist Spiritual Community, a croning ritual is held yearly for all the women who have turned fifty-six that year, and they keep the "crone stones" for a year. In the Saskatchewan Christian Feminist Network, parties with rituals, gifts, and hilarity are often held for women in the network who turn fifty. At network events, the crones often entertain through story-telling or outrageous acts and skits to pass on their wisdom and love of living radically to the younger women of the network.

Crone wisdom also helps in maintaining continuity in the groups. The telling of the group's stories and the remembering of the purposes of the group in its formation and ongoing life are vitally important.

David Kertzer points out that a function of symbolism is to provide continuity in groups. Kertzer claims that it is through symbolism that people gain their impressions and ideas about an organization. Since, in most organizations, people (including leaders) change, "it is only through symbols that we think of organizations as being the same."[24]

The use of the logo of the Christian Feminist Network would be such a symbol. No matter who is in the network or what particular

---

23. Abner Cohen, "Political Anthropology: The Analysis of Symbolism of Power Relations," *Man* 4 (1969): 220.
24. Kertzer, *Ritual, Power, and Politics,* pp. 16, 18.

activities are going on, the logo remains the same. As Joan McMurtry describes it:

> The logo, created the first year by member Gayle Tufts, is of a butterfly with two women with outstretched hands silhouetted on the wings. A cross stands in the centre of the butterfly. Tufts describes the symbolism. "A butterfly represents our emergence and freedom as women. Two women symbolize our sisterhood with arms outstretched in openness and celebration. The cross: we centre on Christianity, knowing Jesus acknowledged and treated women as equals to men." This logo appears on all Network mailings, brochures and newsletters. [25]

Symbols also help set boundaries and keep control. Group symbols help one recognize belonging. An interesting example of this function was at the March for Equality for Women's Lives in Washington in April 1989, where FSC women carried a large banner with FSC's name and logo. Many women from all over the country came up to the banner carriers and said, "I once was a part of the community." The symbols and banner allowed them to identify with the group.

But symbols can do more than set positive boundaries by identifying a group. They can also be used to control others. As a means of control, symbols are used in three ways—appealing to a symbol as a repository of value or to justify an action (e.g., using the Bible as a justification for saying that women should be silent in church and thus should not be ordained or provide leadership); manipulating of symbols by a powerful person or group (e.g., the advertising campaigns after World War II to send women back to the home so that men could have the jobs available when they returned from the services); and inner transformation, or shifting the subjective understanding and intellectual framework for the symbol (e.g., the anti-choice strategy of imaging fetuses as independent beings separate from and endangered by the women in whose bodies they are growing). [26]

Nelle Morton urges clarity in understanding how symbols work to control women:

> We must make it our business to know step by step how religious images create political and social structures. It is equally important to work from the other direction, to see how customs, etiquette, manners, structures, and other forms of social and political ritual provide compulsory external norms that lead to internalized assent,

---

25. Joan McMurtry, "Education for Change: 'The Saskatchewan Christian Feminist Network'" (Major paper for Master of Education degree, University of British Columbia, March 1990), p. 16.
26. Firth, *Symbols*, pp. 83–85.

commitment and feelings. Trace these outer forms to their images
and symbols and see how their origin was designed to keep women
in line. [27]

One of the functions of feminist spirituality is to break patriarchal
control of symbol systems so that women can be namers and shapers
of well-being in the world.

A final function of symbols is to connect us with the world around
us, especially the natural world. Several women spoke of natural symbols. A Canadian woman talks of the trees in her life:

> It is also important for me to be near trees. I love dancing with
> trees. It feels like I am connecting with the universe. Their long
> roots go into the ground, and likewise there are many roots going
> down from me to provide sustenance and survival. I often fancy
> myself as a tree. Trees have been important to me as long as I can
> remember. Trees give beauty, delight, strength, courage—they are
> just a beautiful thing.

A Puerto Rican woman living in the States talks about the full moon.

> At the full moon ritual we do it for world peace. The moon con-
> nects us all—and not just people but all of nature too. It gives a
> sense of cosmic harmony. It strengthens the harmony of the nations
> when we do rituals with the moon. It is a harmony that is more
> than just an absence of war. It connects individuals to each other,
> to nature, and to the past and the future. Sometimes the rituals are
> for people, but sometimes they are for the other things connected
> to the moon—the ozone and the oceans. Nature connects us all.
> Sometimes when I feel the wind, I feel that connectedness to life
> and to my country.

Another woman describes Christian symbols that connect her with
nature: "There is an outdoor service on the pastoral charge every
year. It is a Communion service. For Communion we use a loaf of
bread and grapes. Outdoors it feels strongly connected with nature. I
feel the presence of God in nature. I feel it in growing things, but in
wildlife even more so."

In summary, symbols are things that represent something else and
that have the power to evoke memories, feelings, and understandings. They are ways of condensing meanings, of permitting different
understandings without making difference divisive, and of upholding ambiguity for particular purposes. Purposes and functions of sym-

27. Morton, *Journey Is Home*, p. xxiii.

bols were described, with examples from feminist rituals and from individuals to clarify. It was noted that symbols are understood to communicate, to aid transitions, to create ethos, to procure results or revelations, to set roles, to provide continuity in groups, to control, and to connect with the natural world.

These functions of symbols, while not exhaustive, do represent ways in which symbols are used and the importance and power of symbols and symbolic actions in creating and maintaining ideological positions. They show the significance of examining symbols as part of analysis. The examples of symbols important to the women in this project also give a sense of the evocative nature of symbols and of the ways that they can be used in creating a feminist culture and a world where women's well-being and justice are taken seriously.

Chapter 21

FEMINIST SPIRITUALITIES

Besides examining the functions of ritual in women's lives, analysis means looking at the ideologies and belief systems that underlie and grow out of the rituals. Analysis involves connecting the specific data from this research to the broader contexts of feminist spirituality, exploring differences among the women and groups in the project, and analyzing the theology/thealogy that emerges from the rituals.

The women in this study are making choices about how to live out their spiritual lives and about which theologies/thealogies they will accept. They long for a spirituality that will truly nourish them. One woman says: "I am where I am. I don't feel finished. I am not comfortable where I am at. I don't know where I am—so I don't want to stop. I need to be exposed, challenged, renewed. I need something to help me be nurtured so that I am not stuck in an unhelpful spot."

Women seek ways to live out their spiritual lives that are consistent with their feminist political views and nurturing to their spirits. All struggle with what faith means, who the divine is, what female sexuality has to do with spirituality, and how to live lives based in ethics of just and mutual relationships with each other and all of the created universe.

As with political views, the spiritual views of the women in this project do not fall easily into categories and classifications. However, four main streams of feminist spirituality show some of the choices contemporary women are making and provide ideological and theological background for some of the concerns women express in their rituals. The four primary groups are Christian feminism (growing primarily from liberal Protestant Christians), Women-Church (consisting primarily of women from the Roman Catholic tradition), goddess spirituality, and other emerging feminist spirituality groups. As already stated, I address this range of spiritual expressions from the point of view that diversity is good and that ethical considerations of working for justice for women in the world are more important than doctrinal difference. There is much pressure for the different groups to be separate, instead of working together respectfully, for justice. Patriarchy prefers separation. As Rosemary Radford Ruether notes:

> Much as heterosexual feminists were pressured to repudiate their lesbian sisters in order to protect themselves from the charge that "all feminists are lesbians," so biblical feminists will be pressured to repudiate their sisters in the Wicca movement to protect themselves from the charge that "all feminists are witches."[28]

The challenge, then, is to work together with freedom, integrity, and hope to enable the diversity of expressions that will allow women to work for, and receive, justice and nurture in the world.

Christian Feminism

Many of the women interviewed came to feminism through their Christian faith and their experiences as part of liberal churches. They grew up with theologies that claim all people are made in the image of God, that value all people equally, that work to transform situations of evil to goodness, and that believe in justice for all people everywhere. These feminists challenge the church to be true to its roots—to seek liberation, work for justice for the poor and oppressed, and speak out for the rights of the weakest and poorest in society. Within their churches, the women work for the participation of women in representative and decision-making roles, job and pay equity for women, language and imagery that includes the experience of women and more adequately describes the nature of God in feminine and neuter/inanimate images (instead of using only masculine terms such as Father, Son, Lord, and King), and consideration of ethical questions and moral values that will take seriously the realities of women's lives, including abortion, birth control, lesbian existence, varying lifestyles, and economic survival.

Many of the women who identified themselves as Christian feminists have a strong global awareness and work for global justice for women. Several of the Christian women have spent time in Asia, primarily in South Korea and the Philippines. One of the women I talked with spoke of her experiences in Asia:

> The South Korean people choose to be Christians. They choose to be different rather than being born into Christianity as most of us

---

28. Rosemary Radford Ruether, "Female Symbols, Values, and Context," *Christianity and Crisis* 46, no. 19 (January 12, 1987): 2.

are. It is one choice out of many for them. So it is very different, and they display a very strong zeal and commitment. The South Koreans are very involved in political action, especially the women. Their demonstrations are often broken up with apple bombs, which shatter in a million pieces in the body, but they are willing to stand up for their faith—that is, that justice must be had, that democracy must exist, that there will be no poor, that there will be an end to militarism and torture. They always are being taken in by the police, and they go to jail and they pray and they are released and they go back on the streets and they are arrested and jailed and pray together again and again. It is amazing. They do this because they are Christians. I had never seen anything like it. I had never seen *my* faith acted out like this with such positive zealous fervor.

The women link this high level of commitment to global justice with a belief that it is through human work for just, mutual, and loving relationships and systems that God can be made known in the world. Feminists who choose to be in the church believe that the church can and will reform itself (by the power and grace of God) in order to take women, women's experience, and spirituality seriously. These women believe that the patriarchy of the church and of the Scriptures must be confronted, that women must be recognized fully at every level of church systems and in all theological/thealogical discussion and constructs, and that women's spirituality and experience must be fully integrated into the life of the church and its mission for justice in the world—if the church is to call itself a faithful witness to God's love and intention for creation. The kinds of thealogical categories and ritual understandings presented in chapter 8, "Naming of Self and Experience," must be integrated into church life.

Worship—the primary ritual of the Christian church—is important in the lives of Christian feminists. Several women talked about its significance. One says:

> For myself, if I do not participate in a worship service at least once a week, I feel lost—not just on Sunday but for the whole week. Worship feeds me. It speaks to me about how I am living my life, what changes I am needing to make, what is life-giving that needs to be celebrated. It helps me to remember that in the coming week nothing will separate me from the love of God—no matter how I feel or what happens. God is there—as well as other people who are supporting me.

A second states:

> I have gone to church in the United Church all of my life. That is important to me. I like it that it is almost the same every Sunday—

we say the same prayers, sing the same songs. But it is important to go to church and then to coffee after. It is so important to be together and to talk about the sermon over coffee. Sometimes the sermon really touches me. Especially when it says that we are a blessing to each other. I grew up on fall-redemption theology that strongly emphasized that we are all sinners. It is only recently that I realized we are all blessings. I could not understand why, if God was so great, we were all sinners. This new understanding makes God a lot better.

These women are nurtured by the rituals of their faith. Christian feminists also struggle with the aspects of Christianity that have male biases or embodiments. They deal with the sexism of Scripture in differing ways, and they struggle with the dilemma presented by having a male person, Jesus, as the central focus of Christianity.

SCFN member Jamie Bushell names her dilemma around Jesus in a poem:

what to do with jesus

> i never knew you well
> and now
> no longer able
> even
> to call you Lord
> i find myself
> sort of stuck—
>
> like when you see
> an old lover for the first time
>   again
> without the love.
>
> what to do with you
>   intimate stranger?
>
> and yet, with the old god dead
> can you step out from behind
> your lambs and thorns
>
> maybe be for the first time
> someone i can care about
> for being
>   no more/no less god
> than me?

In struggling with the same question, Rita Nakashima Brock indicates that "Jesus Christ need not be the authoritative centre of a feminist Christian faith." She suggests that, over the centuries, understandings of Jesus as Christ have shifted greatly with the social and political demands of the context.[29] Brock says that it is Jesus' life as prophet, healer, teacher, and friend that matters, that provides the symbol base for Christians. The emphasis, then, for many Christian feminists is on Jesus' life, on his having lived, rather than on a theology of the cross or of atonement. Or as one interviewee says: "Jesus is important and made important discoveries and did important things—but so did lots of other people. I am eternally thankful for what Jesus did though—it makes justice work a lot easier for us."

Even more important than the theology of the church, the women talked about the sense of belonging that they know through the church. A SCFN member elaborates:

> I stay in the church because it is a place of belonging. I have had good experiences in the church and have met a lot of wonderful women through the church. At this point I have more freedom to do what I want to do in the church than I would anywhere else, so I can't think of why to leave. The church is where we meet others of common interest. It is the place where people in small towns go if they have any spiritual interests and questions. So it is important to stay connected to the church.

Christian feminists thus have theologies based in the gospel call to liberation, in global justice, in worship, and in reinterpretation of the meaning of Jesus and of the Scriptures. They value the sense of belonging and community that they experience in the church.

Women-Church

While none of the women interviewed identified with the Women-Church movement directly, many of the Christian feminists did identify with the political and theological/thealogical intention of Women-Church. I have identified them separately because of the different locus of origin and the strategy of becoming a parachurch organization, rather than integrating themselves into the church as many Protestant Christian feminists have chosen to do. The sentiment of one interviewee expresses the political basis for the formation of Women-Church:

---

29. Rita Nakashima Brock, "The Feminist Redemption of Christ," in *Christian Feminism,* ed. Judith Weidman (San Francisco: Harper and Row, 1984), p. 68.

I feel robbed. I understood that the community of faith was supposed to nurture me, but the rituals of their community never
touched me. I never felt nourished by Christian rituals, and that
has been my community of faith. I never felt understood in the
expression of rituals or the discussion of rituals. I have a deep level
of resentment about that loss and feel that the kind of rituals that
have been meaningful to me have been despised and devalued by
the religious community that claimed to nurture me. I resent that
they were destroying and denying access to a whole lot of people
inside and outside that community.

One of the values in feminist spirituality is that all people must be
able to participate freely and publicly in the making of decisions that
affect their lives. There is often deep sorrow, pain, or disillusionment
that women have not been able to shape the spheres and institutions
in which their spiritual lives are being lived.

The participants in the Women-Church movement, primarily women
of Roman Catholic tradition, have chosen to move from this sorrow
and disillusionment. They now name themselves as church—as people of faith living out their spiritual lives. Having spent time trying to
get the institutional church to move away from practices based in hierarchy, clericalism, and patriarchy, Women-Church communities said
that it was time to be part of spiritually nurturing communities faithful to the call of God to inclusiveness, mutuality, nurture, and justice.
Women-Church is both a political strategy and a spiritual resource.

Mary Hunt defines Women-Church as "a global, ecumenical movement made up of local feminist base communities of justice-seeking
friends who engage in sacrament and solidarity."[30] Women-Church
is composed of small groups that gather in each others' homes for
worship, social change, and community building and that are linked
to other base communities through formal and informal networks.
They use only the parts of Christian tradition that take women seriously, and they also choose to connect with spiritual groups from other
traditions. Women-Church stresses equality of all participants, both
self-identified women and women-identified men. It is important to
note that Women-Church does not see itself as a new denomination,
nor does it demand exclusive allegiance. According to Rosemary Radford Ruether:

The call for new communities of faith and ritual assumes that existing institutional churches do not have a monopoly on the words
of truth or the power of salvation, indeed that their words for women
are so ambivalent, their power so negative, that attendance at their

---

30. Mary Hunt, "Defining 'Women-Church,'" *Water Wheel* 3, no. 2 (Summer 1990): 1.

fonts poisons our souls. They have become all too often occasions of sin rather than redemption, places where we leave angry and frustrated rather than enlightened and healed. We do not form new communities lightly, but only because the crisis has grown so acute and the efforts to effect change so unpromising that we often cannot even continue to communicate within these traditional church institutions unless we have an alternative community of reference that nurtures and supports our being. . . . I would contend today that we as women can indeed speak as Church, do speak as Church, not in exile from the Church, but rather that the Church is in exile with us, awaiting with us a wholeness that we are in the process of revealing.[31]

Elisabeth Schüssler-Fiorenza makes the same point: "As the *ekklesia of women* we claim the centre of Christian faith and community. We do not relinquish our biblical roots and communal ecclesial heritage, but we call the patriarchal church to conversion."[32]

These theopolitical strategies and commitments within Women-Church are important in feminist spirituality and connect strongly with the thealogical categories identified in the chapter titles "Naming of Self and Experience," "Trusting Our Own Inner Wisdom," "Resistance and Undermining" and "Community and Relationships." They are, and can be, the basis for new communities of women that gather for ritual and renewal and for social action projects.

Goddess Spirituality

Goddess spirituality comes in a variety of forms, according to the women of this project. Rituals of the Feminist Spiritual Community often involved learning about, and encountering, the goddess. The introduction to one ritual included the following statement:

This month we are focusing on goddess traditions. There are many different understandings of what that means in different cultures and eras and among different groups of women. When I think of the goddess, I think of the power that is known when women unite, the knowledge that we can go beyond our finite selves to something more, the wisdom that lies deep within women's hearts, the pleasure that we experience concretely day by day through our bodies, our connectedness to all that lives and shares in the wholeness of the universe, to all that is connected to the cycles of birth, life and death.

---

31. Ruether, *Women-Church*, pp. 5, 69.
32. Elisabeth Schüssler Fiorenza, "A Feminist Critical Interpretation for Liberation," *Religion and Intellectual Life* 111, no. 2 (Winter 1986): 22.

Other rituals involved connections with particular goddesses—Aphrodite (the goddess of love), Artemis (the archer and goddess of courage), Brigid (goddess of smithcraft, poetry, and healing), and Persephone and Demeter (mother and daughter). One woman spoke of her experience of ritual in a small group: "There is freedom and trust to be creative. We can ritualize on the spot. There is a sense of the goddess speaking through us or somehow letting us tap into the inner spiritual being of life that we are part of."

Starhawk is one of the most popular authors among the goddess-centered women with whom I spoke. She describes her understanding of the goddess in ways that would be consistent with most of the goddess-centered women interviewed:

> The Goddess does not rule the world; She *is* the world. Manifest in each of us, She can be known internally by every individual, in all her magnificent diversity. She does not legitimize the rule of either sex by the other and lends no authority to rulers of temporal hierarchies. In Witchcraft, each of us must reveal our own truth.[33]

Most of the women interviewed connect witchcraft/wicca with their goddess spirituality in the way Starhawk does here. Some goddess-centered women would call themselves witches; others would choose different ways of naming themselves spiritually. But they would probably agree with Starhawk when she says:

> The importance of the Goddess symbol for women cannot be overstressed. The image of the Goddess inspires women to see ourselves as divine, our bodies as sacred, the changing phases of our lives as holy, our aggression as healthy, our anger as purifying, and our power to nurture and create, but also to limit and destroy when necessary, as the very force that sustains life. Through the Goddess, we can discover our strength, enlighten our minds, own our bodies, and celebrate our emotions. We can move beyond narrow, constricting roles and become whole.[34]

The symbol of the goddess is the moon. One woman told of a ritual she had been part of that connected the moon and the goddess.

> A ritual I liked was at a cottage where we were dancing under the full moon. It was as if we became some other creatures—nymphs of the goddess. Dancing under the full moon gave us such freedom of expression. I was free to be myself, and others also had that

---

33. Starhawk, *The Spiral Dance* (New York: Harper and Row, 1979), p. 9.
34. Starhawk, "Witchcraft as Goddess Religion," in *The Politics of Women's Spirituality*, ed. Charlene Spretnak (Garden City, N.Y.: Anchor, 1982), p. 51.

freedom. We were free to be the goddess that we are, to do our own dance, or to come together, however the goddess spirit moved us.

The moon's three aspects reflect three stages of women's lives, and its cycles of waxing and waning coincide with women's menstrual cycles. The significance of this connection was already noted in chapter 7, "Embodiment." The new moon is the maiden, the woman belonging to herself alone, the wild child, free and untamed. White is her color; spring is her season. She brings laughter, flowers, songs, and play.

As the full moon, the goddess is the mature woman, the sexual being, the mother and nurturer, giver of life, fertility, grain, joy, the arts of civilization and healing. Her colors are the red of blood and the green of growth. Her time is summer.

As the waning, or dark, moon, she is the old woman, past menopause, the hag or crone who is ripe with wisdom, patroness of secrets, prophecy, divination, inspiration, and power. She contains the terrible, the destructive, the fearsome. Her color is the black of night; her times, autumn and winter. She brings dark secrets and wisdom. White, red, and black candles are often used at cronings to express the fullness of the crone's life.

To be a goddess-centered woman is to recognize the goddess within— to awaken her symbols and imagery in our minds and to draw from her the power to act. Nelle Morton says, "When I consider myself a goddess woman, I am not interested in a Goddess as an object of worship. But she is part of my present and I am nurtured by her."[35] At an FSC ritual on new life, one woman lit a candle, saying, "I light this candle for the goddess in every woman here [turning around to look in the eyes of each woman in the circle], and may we always recognize her presence there."

There are no external authorities in goddess spirituality. The standard for deciding whether to adopt or reject a given practice in a ritual is, "If it works for you, do it as long as it harms no one."

Feminist Spirituality Growing from Consciousness-Raising Groups

The final dimension of women's spirituality that emerged is from those groups that began as consciousness-raising groups, groups of women that came together to tell their stories. In consciousness-raising groups, women "heard one another into speech," to use Nelle Morton's

---

35. Morton, *The Journey Is Home*, p. 150.

phrase.[36] Women got in touch with themselves as women, discovered the pain and suffering and anger in their lives, spoke (often for the first time) of their experiences and feelings, and discovered that those feelings were shared by other women. Consciousness-raising groups have been an essential part of the feminist movement, but most feminists move from the initial consciousness raising to new aspects of feminist expression and need ongoing small groups for political action, support, ritual, and/or theology/thealogy/spirituality. One woman who has a highly integrated spirituality involving political action, ritual, community, and personal meditation describes a consciousness-raising group from her past.

> When I was in Rochester, the women's consciousness-raising group, in a sense, provided the ritual for me (although I would have turned around and run away if anyone had said that to me then). But there was a check-in time for all the women and a pattern of the groups. We all gained lots of insights, and some of my oldest ongoing friendships were started in those groups.

Another describes a group that has changed and developed over seven or eight years: "It is one place where regular ritual happens. That is important because it is not something that I create or look for on my own. Also it is a very safe space to talk about the innermost fears and dreams in a way that I do with five more easily than I could in a large group."

This spirituality arises out of feminist community. It is not based on a return to the goddess, the practice of wicca, or holy writings and revelation. It comes from shared experience—both the inner depths and the outer actions. Several of the small groups that women from this research belong to would fall into this category—groups that gather for study of feminist theology/thealogy, for rituals that are created from the group rather than out of any tradition, for support and healing, and for nurturing actions to resist patriarchy. A typical comment of women who are part of this kind of group would be, "What is most meaningful is circle rituals—not goddess rituals but rituals that include elements of women's ways of knowing holiness among us. These are important to me." One woman started a group with a few women. They went for a walk together and then came back to the house of one of them and discussed articles they had read or listened to poetry they had written. The Regina Book Club is another example of this kind of group. Another group alternates by visiting one time and doing rituals the next. Some choose the route of exorcising the patriarchal demons and searching for positive affirmations.

---

36. Ibid., p. 55.

All these different forms of feminist spirituality are present among contemporary feminist women in and beyond this project. They are an example of the diversity that is present among women and of the positive choices toward life-giving spirituality that women are making. They show the ways in which women are naming their experiences of the holy and seeking meaning in their lives. They are one example of the resourcefulness of women described earlier: "The women I know on the prairie are very resourceful women. They have the strength that comes from saying so often that yes, it can be done." The women here are saying yes, it can be done—women can name their needs and can create and discover spiritualities that are nurturing and challenging and that lead to justice and well-being for women.

Chapter 22

LEADERSHIP AND INSTITUTIONAL IMPLICATIONS

Shifting the theological/thealogical content of religious life means shifting the forms and structures of religious life. Holland and Henriot describe this factor as the objective dimension of analysis.

Not surprisingly, the structure of groups and the question of whether they involve hierarchy emerged as an issue throughout this research. One of the principles of feminism is that all participants should have the opportunity to be involved in the naming and shaping of the common good. In hierarchical groups, some people have more power than others and therefore can influence decisions in stronger ways than others. Thus, hierarchial groups are seen as inappropriate in feminist circles. In circles everyone has a voice; everyone speaks with authority and power. Discussions in both the Feminist Spiritual Community and the Saskatchewan Christian Feminist Network took place about how to eliminate hierarchy and asked whether attempts to work in non-hierarchial ways can succeed.

For some years, the Feminist Spiritual Community employed a staff member. Eventually it was decided that a staff member inevitably had more power in the group than ordinary members, and so the FSC eliminated this position. All members and participants are structurally equal. Anyone can participate in the business meetings, in leadership of rituals, and in any of the activities of the community or can bring things forward at the community for a decision regarding community involvement (e.g., cosponsoring events). Thus, the community structure itself avoids hierarchy. But a discussion among three members shows that the formal structure and the informal reality are sometimes in tension.

X: There is hierarchy in FSC, but it is undesignated. Some women have more respect in Community than some others. The hier-

archy may be through length of time in community or experience.

Y: Some have earned respect. That seems to me better than respect that comes simply because you have a title.

Z: It is difficult because of the world we live in. We cannot expect
ourselves to be devoid of hierarchical thinking.

X: It is there. There is a positive hierarchy. These women have
been around for years.

Z: Positive hierarchy is a contradiction in terms. Hierarchy is inherent layering. It is a way of distributing power.

X: But the root of hierarchy is "hier"—here, not higher.

Z: There are appropriate uses for hierarchy. It is a descriptive term.
But in forming a group of people and in establishing leadership,
it is never appropriate. It is a way of organizing power. It is a
struggle in FSC, but it is not appropriate for anyone to have
more power than anyone else.

In the Christian Feminist Network, the issue of hierarchy is raised
in a variety of ways. From time to time, women ask whether having
COG (Consultative Overview Group) is hierarchical. Members are
elected to COG on suggestion from the network membership. The
purpose of COG is to do some of the administrative work of the network, to have a view of the whole, since there are many parts, and to
envision ways in which the network can be proactive in meeting the
needs of feminists in Saskatchewan. Its intent is to be a "cog" in the
wheel of the network along with the other parts, including gatherings, events, *The Unbeaten Path,* and action groups. However, the women
on COG are active members of the network and do initiate activities
within the network. Thus, sometimes the question is raised whether
having such a group is hierarchical.

The network also struggles with what hierarchy means in some of
its gatherings, most notably the annual November event. Each year, a
different planning team plans the event, different resource people
lead the educational components, and different women attend. But
there is always some tension between old-timers and newcomers at
the event. It is usually stated at the beginning that this is a new event,
and so everybody is to work together with the planning team and
resource people to make it what is wanted. The strong friendship
bonds among women who see each other rarely because of geographic distances and the expectations brought by women mean that
there is often a perception of hierarchy, or of an in-group, despite
the intent for it to be an educational event with sharing and access to
power by all. Being schooled in patriarchal modes of operating means

that even structures of equality and consensus do not guarantee that hierarchy will not emerge or be perceived.

One of the possibilities in avoiding hierarchy is to avoid designated leadership. Some would suggest that if people are clear about the purpose and what needs to be done, they do not need a leader. Starhawk indicates that leaderlessness works well in small, intimate groups where people are relatively equal in experience and commitment, know each other well, and have time to develop trust. In these groups, all share power and responsibility, making the groups "leaderful" rather than leaderless. Starhawk also notes that:

> Leaderlessness also works well in direct actions. The law enforcement authorities often attempt to identify and remove leaders of civil disobedience, expecting groups to be rendered incapable of making decisions. . . . Leaderlessness may serve us less well in larger organizations, when levels of skill, experience, and commitment vary.[37]

Starhawk's concept of leaderful seems important when one considers the group needs. For women to feel at home in a group, they need to feel safe, they need to feel that they are listened to and respected and that their personal needs as well as their capacity to contribute to the goals of the group will be taken seriously. Thus, it is important in feminist groups not to deny that leadership gifts are present, and it is equally important for women not to hold back simply because they do not want to be perceived to be seeking power. Leader-filled groups recognize the skills and gifts that different people bring or want to develop, and they use such assets for the well-being of the whole. Thus, practices of shared leadership, rotating leadership, and having different people be responsible for different aspects of group life at different times are as likely to limit hierarchy as is trying to be leaderless. Room for emerging leaders and for people who have not had leadership experience to practice and acquire the needed skills is important. Joan McMurtry notes that for the Saskatchewan Christian Feminist Network:

> The frequency and annual nature of events provides the time, space, and continuity to learn, to create, and to reinforce the underlying values and principles of the network. The shared leadership within the events allows for members to experience and practice leadership and planning skills, and to learn from a diversity of members' own experiences and styles of leadership.[38]

---

37. Starhawk, *Truth or Dare*, pp. 269–70.
38. McMurtry, "Education for Change," p. 71.

Starhawk raises a caution concerning these dimensions of leadership that is worth noting:

> When leadership cannot be acknowledged, but nevertheless exists, a difficult burden is placed on those who exercise it. In order to make their skills and knowledge available to the group, they must somehow pretend not to be influencing the group. . . . When the group pretends that its leaders are not leaders, it cannot hold them accountable for their actions and decisions. Nor can they be expected to exercise leadership with any consistency. Others who might want to gain influence in the group cannot see how this is done. Power is concealed and no one feels safe.[39]

Besides hierarchy, a second important consideration in groups is that different structures and different needs of groups determine the kind of leadership needed. All of the different feminist groups described in the preceding chapter have structures that invite certain kinds of leadership. For example, wicca uses small groups and leadership from within the group. Another example, from Christian feminism, would be that formal Sunday liturgy may have varied leadership, but often the ordained or paid-accountable minister provides much of the leadership or the continuity in leadership.

In less-formal groups or groups that have nonhierarchical structures, the leadership is likely to be shared or rotated. One of the women comments on what she likes in rituals:

> I want them to be life-affirming! Circular, with shared leadership.
> I like rituals where we feel joined, where we create community.
> Rituals where leadership is not authoritarian but encourages equal participation of everyone help us to see the domineering model that is usually used in our society.

Another factor in assessing group structure and leadership is to note who does, and does not, participate in rituals. Who speaks, and who does not? Do only articulate people have power? Who decides when, how, and where ritual will be? Whose interests does the ritual serve? Who moves? Who sits? Who indicates it is time to begin and to end? Who makes connections in the group? Are the decisions based in concrete material conditions of the women's lives? Who functions to keep the group nurturing to women, and who functions to keep it radical? What are the rewards and benefits for each? What values get upheld?

For example, in the Feminist Spiritual Community, shared leader-

---

39. Starhawk, *Truth or Dare*, p. 155.

ship is more important than perfect rituals and quality control. In the Christian Feminist Network, geographic location is often a key factor in determining planning groups for events. Since participation in decision-making by those who will bear the consequences of the decisions is a high value in feminist groups, these analytical questions around the meaning of participation are essential.

Class issues can also be involved in the way leadership takes place in groups. I had a conversation with two women—one middle class and the other working class—about a particular situation in which conflict existed. What the middle-class woman described as personality conflicts, the working-class woman described as issues of power and process. The bottom line for the working-class woman was a fierce loyalty to family; for the middle-class woman the task was most important. The working-class woman wanted resolution by confrontation; the middle-class woman wanted to negotiate.

When there are such different perceptions of a situation, it is hard to have equal participation and shared values in a ritual. This is also true in groups with members of different cultural heritages, different worldviews, and different concepts of the purpose of ritual.

What to do with demanding members is also a concern in feminist groups. Often there are women who are very needy and who demand great amounts of the group's attention. If they are not accustomed to operating in a direct manner (which, as we have seen, includes many women), then subverting the group process is a way of getting the attention of the group. Leaders of groups whose agenda includes support and nurture often find it hard to determine when to limit one person for the sake of the group and when to affirm that what the individual is saying is critical to the group's life. It helps if all group members can take responsibility for the process and for calling each other when behaviors are not helpful in the group, rather than expecting the leader(s) or facilitator(s) alone to do so. Using check-in, where everyone gets to say what is going on for them as the group begins, passing a talking stick so that only the woman holding the stick can speak, giving direct and specific feedback about behavior, and having time and space for each woman to be heard and for conflict to be open in the group often allows women's individual needs to be met and frees them to participate more appropriately toward the group goals. Oftentimes simple truth-telling brings change.

One of the other elements that came up in the research was the capacity of leaders for autonomy. This topic directly connects with the earlier chapters "Naming of Self and Experience" and "Trusting One's Own Inner Wisdom." Frequently, when leaders were secure in themselves and certain in the role of leader, the group flowed with some ease. Often, when leaders were unsure of themselves or of what they were doing, or were distracted by personal problems, the process would be more difficult. One of the women interviewed talked about how she has gained skill and a sense of personal autonomy through the women's movement:

> The women's movement was major for my understanding of leadership. It helped me to name empowerment and name being a facilitator. It has become more of a way of being than a style of leadership. It has had all kinds of influences in all kinds of areas of my life. For example, it has been key in parenting. Finding that balance with kids, of what they are able to be responsible for, at whatever stage they are at, is a challenge. It is to seek interdependency at every stage. They are not just dependent and then one day they have to have independence. It is much more fluid.

A final issue is leadership in rural areas. Often we hear stories about the friendliness of the prairies and of how people help each other out. In small towns, everybody gathers at the times of deaths, marriages, fires, or other significant or crisis moments. But the fact that many farms have been foreclosed because of the economic policies of the government and banks has led to drastic depopulation and the loss of many communities. Another interviewee describes the impact on her and her family.

> Now we shop for groceries at Co-op stores wherever we travel. We drive 17 km to our post office, 38 km in the opposite direction for our doctor and hospital, and 16 km for church. We deliver grain to these communities or others within a 20-km radius. We are now part of many communities, and yet our energies are concentrated on none.[40]

Gordon Hendrickson, a rural pastor, describes what this problem means for leadership in Saskatchewan, stating that in the past four years, over one hundred people he has known personally have moved or died. This population decline limits potential leadership in church and community and means that those available are overworked. It also increases the financial burden on those left to keep the small community alive.[41]

One of the other problems in areas of small population is the relationship between local and regional leadership. Often, people who are competent local leaders are recruited to work regionally or na-

---

40. Pat Krug, "Drastic Change," *The Unbeaten Path* 27 (June 1989): 6.
41. Gordon Hendrickson, "Impact of Population Decline," *Practice of Ministry in Canada* 5, no. 2 (May 1988): 27.

tionally in their organizations. This policy frequently leaves a vacuum at the local level because leadership is not broadly enough based in those communities.

The problems of rural depopulation, of community disintegration, and of local leaders' becoming involved in provincial and national leadership do affect the women's movement in Saskatchewan. Many rural women feel alone and isolated as feminists in their own areas and need the connections with other feminist women. It is hard to have support groups and groups committed to feminist actions for justice in small towns because of the intensity of living, the struggle of many small-town and farm people to maintain a viable living, the need to be involved in established community activities that contribute to the community as a whole, and the pressure of conformity that is sometimes exerted. Thus, rural women often find their primary connections with women from other locations, such as through events of the Saskatchewan Christian Feminist Network. But returning to rural communities and trying to live peaceably with a raised consciousness or trying to form supportive groups is not an easy task. Thus, some feminist women become quite active beyond their own communities for their own sense of well-being, a decision that can leave a leadership void in the community. This is one of the dilemmas that face feminists in provinces with small population bases and high rural populations. It is difficult to develop feminist activity and to keep feminist leadership active in rural areas.

Issues of structure and leadership in feminist groups thus involve struggling with how to eliminate hierarchy, seeking consistency between the structure of the group and the way leadership is exercised, assessing who does and does not participate in rituals, clarifying perceptions across differences such as classes and cultures, finding strategies for equalizing participation when some members are needy or dominating, developing autonomy in leaders, and looking at the implications of feminism for rural women and communities. Analysis of all of these aspects is needed for women's spirituality and feminist thealogy to be rich, vibrant, and empowering in women's lives.

·PART 4·

Living Out Feminist Thealogy in Ritual and Justice

In the method outlined in the Introduction, it was noted that action is an important part of any feminist theological method or theory. Action is the intent of feminist research, since the goal of feminism is to bring about social, economic, political, and cultural change through elimination of patriarchy and to advance women-centered cultures with just structures and material conditions that foster the well-being of all.

This part deals with action. First, it outlines some criteria for developing and choosing actions, theories, and thealogies consistent with feminist ritual thealogy named in the second part of the study. Second, it explores criteria for rituals and the implications of these criteria for justice-making rituals and political spirituality. Third, it advocates fuller implementation of women's culture, especially through women's artistry. Finally, a few specific strategies and actions provide ideas for potential activities that will contribute to the long-haul process toward justice and well-being for women.

Chapter 23

CRITERIA FOR FEMINIST THEORY, THEALOGY, AND ACTION

In determining whether feminist theories, theologies/thealogies, and actions are going to promote women's well-being and structural justice in the world, it seems helpful to have some criteria on which to base considerations. In this chapter, a range of criteria growing out of the emerging thealogical categories of this project will be named.

In relation to the category of *beauty*, criteria begin with the concept of beauty as a need in women's lives, as a means of exposing injustice, as an element of life cycles, as a way to show originality and truth, and as a form of hospitality. The criteria growing from these aspects of beauty might be:

1. The theory, thealogy, or action should lead to sufficiency. The Centre for Vision and Policy describes sufficiency as occurring when "all have enough to live well. Food, shelter, clothing, art and science, music and literature, healing and caring services, friends and families, private and public space are available to all in the quantity and quality necessary to live with integrity and grow toward excellence."[1] Sufficiency would enable women to live with adequate resources so that there is enough for both bread and roses, for the necessities for physical survival, and for the nurture of the spirit and of relationships.

2. The theory, thealogy, or action must invite renewal. The cycles of life and of birth-to-death-to-birth, as described by the women, are based in cycles and circles, in renewable forms of technology, life, and systems.

3. Balance between humans and nature should be sought, and beauty should be defined in that context, rather than a context of domination of the earth by humanity.

---

1. Centre for Vision and Policy, "Ethics and Economic Justice" (Draft document for discussion, Winter 1989, Portland, Maine), p. 6.

4. The theory, thealogy, or action needs to set a mood or context of hospitality—the action needs to be inclusive by nature and must show beauty through its exposure of life in its fullness, in contrast with life in its horrors.

Criteria related to *survival and safety* grow out of the concepts of survival as a spiritual resource for women, out of the realities that make women's lives difficult, and out of women's need for safe space. Criteria emerging are:

1. The belief system needs to acknowledge patriarchy as a systemic evil that oppresses women. There must be social, economic, and political analysis of power and its use and of the concrete material conditions of women's lives in the world. The beliefs developed must not be sexist, racist, heterosexist, classist, or productivity-centered, so that all women are free to live fully without worry about survival and safety.

2. Issues of basic human rights, global concerns, and structural injustice need attention by all women in every situation. Laws based in substantive justice and laws that give realistic and adequate protection to the vulnerable must be central agendas.

3. Feminist theory, thealogy, and action must be based on the real material needs of women. For example, women with disabilities need certain conditions met for survival and safety. Often, these conditions would be of benefit to everyone but are not implemented because able-bodied people do not need them for survival and safety. Rosentraub and Gilderbloom ask:

> Why do we not build our facilities to meet the needs of people with some limitations? The usual response is that it costs too much. It is our contention, however, that we are socialized not to think about people with limitations. . . . In many cases, disability is not so much a function of an individual's physical limitation as a function of the ability of social and physical environments to meet the needs of all people. Wheelchair users, for instance, are only disabled if their environment is not conducive to use of a wheelchair.[2]

4. Feminists will work for global and interpersonal peace wherever possible. The safety of the planet requires an end to war. Personal safety for women means an end to violence in the streets and homes of every nation.

Embodiment is the third category named and is based in concepts of knowing ourselves in and through our bodies, despite the patriarchal

---

2. Mark Rosentraub and John Gilderbloom, "The Invisible Jail," *Social Policy* 20, no. 1 (Summer 1989): 31, 32.

patterns of dualism, which creates cultural expectations of what women's bodies should look like and do, and patterns of violence against women.

1. A primary criterion is that feminist theory, thealogy, and action must be affirming of women's body-selves. They can invite listening to one's body to learn feelings, options, and wisdom. They affirm and acknowledge women's sexuality and capacities to bear and not bear children. As one woman puts it:

> I believe the Creator gave us a strong will for life in ourselves and for children. But I also believe we are given, by that same Creator, a *strong* intuitive sense when we are ready to become the loving parent that every child deserves. Only the woman herself can assess her own readiness; no one should deny her options.

2. The body and the material world are not separated from the spiritual. Women have the right to control their lives, including their bodies.

3. Relationships are also known through our body-selves. It is important to have theories and thealogies that affirm relationships that are respectful and that are life-giving.

4. One of the interviewees suggests the basis for another criterion when she says, "Various types of work would be divided up, so the same person would not always have to do the same chores and tasks. Everybody would have some of the sustaining, drudging, and creative chores to do." This would mean that all people were respected and that all would share in the tasks that contribute to the well-being of the whole. None would have to do demeaning tasks all of the time, or in ways that led to the valuing of some persons over others.

Naming of self and experience calls women to assert their identities and to name their own needs in relation to the needs of others. They need to find their own voices and speak about what their lives are really like in personal and political terms.

1. A most important criterion for feminist theory, thealogy, and action is that it allows women to speak in their own voices, out of their own experiences.

2. All theories, thealogies, and actions should lead to greater self-respect for women.

3. All theories, thealogies, and actions should uphold a variety of women's life experiences so that, as discussed in part 3, the question of whether something will lead to improvements in women's lives also asks which women, and how many.

Community and relationships were named as central in women's theal-ogy—through friendships, through the community of saints, through global solidarity, in pain, in empowerment, and through friendship with the natural world. Criteria for feminist theory, thealogies, and actions arising from the category of relationships are the following:

1. Relationships that are valued and upheld are ones that are acces-sible to all people. This means that friendship, rather than heterosex-ual marriage, would be a normative relationship in feminist theory, thealogy, and action.

2. Feminist spirituality is based in community. Rather than being individualistic, it involves shared wisdom and insight, sharing our lives, prayers, and actions for justice in the world. Community involves re-spect for, or honoring of, people. Acting together is important.

3. Accountability is critical. There must be thought about who will pay the costs and reap the benefits of any actions and theories. Hav-ing answered such questions to the best of one's ability, then it needs to be decided to whom one will hold oneself accountable—poor women, Native women, women with disabilities, middle-class women.

4. A broad and dynamic range of relationships must also be con-sidered, including relationships among people, between human and nonhuman life forms, and involving mutuality and shared power, goods, and services.

Much has already been said about the category of *diversity* and of the importance of recognizing and valuing difference as part of fem-inist theory, thealogy, and action. Specifically this means:

1. The limits to pluralism are ethical rather than doctrinal. The ethic of working toward a world where substantive justice exists for all people and all of the creation is the bottom line. Judgments about forms of spirituality should be based on whether they support justice, mutual well-being, and right relations among all humanity, more than on the specific doctrine, beliefs, and resources.

2. One's own experience needs to be compared and contrasted with others, especially with others whose lives are very different from one's own.

3. Being aware of global implications of one's decisions, as named by Kwok Pui-lan, is also significant:

> Students here [in the United States] know too little of the unspeak-able suffering of women in other parts of the world. Our hearts have not been touched, our minds have not been challenged and our eyes have not seen the numerous ways that our lives are inter-twined with others. Women living in other contexts are not vivid human beings for us, for we know too little about their stories, their songs, their religions, and their dreams. Feminist scholarship is dis-

embodied if it focuses on the spiritual quest of Western women without paying heed to the daily rice of Third World women. Without a deepening of our religious vision, our scholarship will speak only half of the truth.[3]

It has already been stated that much *healing* is needed in women's lives both personally and structurally. Some criteria were already stated in chapter 11 for rituals related to healing. Along with those criteria, a few others need mentioning.

1. It is important to see social change as an ongoing process—partly because the earth and humanity are alive and the interconnections of the elements are always changing, shifting, and seeking balance, and partly because the patriarchal practice of so many years will not change without reaction. Carter Heyward suggests that every move has a countermove, so those who expect fast progress will end up in disillusionment and despair. Liberation is not an achievement, victory, or carefree state of being. It is the long-term process of change.[4] Thus, intentionality for the long haul is an important criterion.

2. Feminist thealogy, theory, and action are not separate and isolated from the multifaceted realities of women's lives. As Mary Hunt helpfully notes:

> *Feminist theology never stands alone, but always in the good company of ethics and ritual.* No action-reflection model will be adequate that does not put real life questions to the fore. Nor can there be any adequate expression of feminist insights without the aid of the arts, prayer, movement, and silence. Thus we see theology as intimately connected with ethics and ritual so that to describe it in isolation is already to have violated our process.[5]

For healing to be real, there must be integration of life. Wholeness is thus another criterion.

3. A third criterion is that inclusion of all people, regardless of their physical abilities/disabilities, illnesses, age, or proximity to death, is essential for the well-being of the whole of society.

Play and humor invite the ordinary and traumatic moments of life to be experienced in light of all of life, the stories to be told, the inconsequential happenings to be given meaning through laughter in community, and the demanded order of patriarchy to be disrupted through disorder and creativity. From the section on play, two criteria arise:

---

3. Kwok Pui-lan, "A Vision of Feminist Religious Scholarship," *Journal of Feminist Studies in Religion* 3, no. 1 (Spring 1987): 102.

4. Heyward, *Our Passion for Justice,* p. 180.

5. Mary Hunt, "On Feminist Methodology," *Journal of Feminist Studies in Religion* 1, no. 2 (Fall 1985): 86.

1. Laughter should never be at the expense of someone else, nor should it degrade or demean another.

2. Play and laughter should be mixed with seriousness.

The chapter on *resistance and undermining* discussed how patriarchy attempts to destroy feminism and showed some of the ways feminism resists and undermines patriarchy—by naming it as historical, knowing histories of resistance, choosing political and systemic resistance, buycotting, changing legislation, carrying out acts of civil disobedience, creating chaos out of order, and participating in rituals. Criteria arising out of these understandings are:

1. Learn history, including the changes in patriarchal practice and the ways in which women have resisted and survived. This can be done in a variety of ways. For example, Louise tells of a ritual at her church:

> In the Unitarian Universalist Sunday service one of the important rituals is lighting of the chalice. It is a symbol of beginning, gathering, and getting involved. Usually the person who is lighting the candle says something. For example, this past week was Susan B. Anthony's birthday, so a woman dressed up as Susan B. and read a prayer that Susan had written about work and women's involvement in it and the equality of women and men. The candle in the chalice is very beautiful, and it helps people to reflect.

2. Choose actions carefully in light of the analysis of the context and the impact of those actions on women's material conditions. A Christian woman who has lived in Korea talks about a criterion of willingness to suffer for one's beliefs:

> There is a willingness to suffer for one's faith. I went to Korea with a superior sense, thinking that everyone had to own their own faith. But in their culture if your father had been martyred for his faith, then you follow that faith.
>
> Canadian Christians are apathetic. They have not struggled. They take for granted that Christianity is the only way. They feel like they were born right, and so God is going to honor them.
>
> While I was in Korea, I had to work with others who had to resist cultural pressures in order to become Christians. They knew something about the cost of discipleship.

Making clear choices about one's faith, about what would be beneficial to women, and about what constitutes justice, in concrete terms, means that one will live with consequences and sometimes with suffering because of the analysis and choices for belief and action one makes.

3. Follow a principle named by Carter Heyward: "We must make no peace with any oppression—our own or that of others."[6]

4. Know the difference between charity and justice, and choose theories, thealogies, and actions that are just in nature. One woman with a physical disability describes what this means to her:

> My increasing disability means that I always understand the difference between justice and charity in new ways. I get insights that go beyond the disability. Charity too much involves the unmutual interchange that is patronizing and demeaning of the person. Justice means that it does not matter if you like the person, that they are entitled to your respect and are given some access to responsibilities. Much of our attitude toward the disabled has been charity. But I refuse to spend my life being grateful!
>
> Equal access does not mean treating everyone the same but in allowing everyone access to the resources that they need to live. Affirmative action is based in that—and so is seen by many as unfair. They cannot see that to be equal some people need to be given accessibility.

5. Be aware of the facts, and have enough knowledge in a given area to be able to know what is going on and what strategies are likely to be effective.

Vulnerability is experienced by women in personal, spiritual, sexual, and conflictual ways. Women need both freedom and protection in these areas of vulnerability. Criteria for theor.cs, thealogies, and actions that involve vulnerability are:

1. The person who is going to experience the consequences of the action should be able to participate in making the decisions involved, so that vulnerability is as far as possible chosen, rather than enforced. A woman talked about what accountability meant to her in her work and about the dilemma caused by feeling accountable to the women's movement but being in a government job where she was vulnerable.

> I was conscious as a federal government employee that if I did or said anything that it would be picked up. I needed to protect my job. What got me going, though, was the abortion issue. When the Borowski case was on, I rationalized that this had nothing to do with Employment and Immigration. So I snuck out at noons and went to the marches and rallies.
>
> Retirement is wonderful. I can do *whatever* I want. I am still very interested in the abortion issue and in ethical issues regarding reproductive technology. I got to develop a submission to the Royal Commission on Reproductive Technology. I am involved in letter

---

6. Heyward, *Our Passion for Justice*, p. 5.

writing and in telegrams to Mulroney, especially lately over the proposed new abortion legislation. I do this as part of the Feminist
Network Action Group.

2. Feminist theories and thealogies must lead to and involve actions.
It is not always easy to act. As one woman confesses: "My involvement
in the women's movement had been local and not very extensive. I
thought I was involved until I moved here. Then I discovered that I
had just hung around with women who were involved and that I had
not really done much myself." Charlotte Bunch pushes on this point
of action, especially as it applies to global justice. Class, racial, and
cultural analysis is critical in international work with women. It is also
important that North American women do not simply feel guilty or
apologize for their existence as Americans. Women in other parts of
the world

> are not interested in guilt or shame, but *in our actions*, and how we
> can have a genuine interaction about both our similarities and our
> differences. This quality of interaction comes from being clear about
> who we are and what our politics are, and then being able to listen
> to others without assuming everyone else is going to be the same.[7]
> (emphasis added)

3. What is not said must also be addressed. Consideration of omis-
sions, as well as actions, must be part of the criteria:

> While white obviously racist individuals are avoided, the elements
> of everyday life—family forms, food, sport, etc.—are shot through
> with racism. Non-white people associating with them will/do feel
> oppressed by their very way of "being" rather than by what they do
> or say "politically." These white progressive activists may have dealt
> with the overtly political, ideological dimensions of their own rac-
> ism, but not with their common sense racism. It is perhaps for this
> very reason that the racism of the left feminists is almost always of
> omission rather than that of comission.[8]

4. We need to acknowledge that sometimes there are no positive
choices available, that all we can do is minimize harm.

The thealogical category of *loss* is a reminder of the depth of losses
in women's lives, of the lack of spiritual resources in patriarchal religion, and, in transitional times, of the need to assist women as they
search for meaning in their losses. The image of crone, the image of

---

7. Connie Griffin and Linda Roach, "International Feminism, 'A Passionate Politics,'"
Woman of Power 7 (Summer 1987): 7 (interview with Charlotte Bunch).
8. Himani Bannerji, "Introducing Racism: Notes toward an Anti-Racist Feminism,"
Resources for Feminist Research 16, no. 1 (March 1987): 11.

women mourning together, and an image of sadness provide the potential for new theories and thealogies and actions around loss. The primary criteria are:

1. The loss must be acknowledged and allowed to exist as a reality in women's lives.

2. For spiritual integrity, we must have connections with the past and the future, creating a faith rich enough to pass on to our children. The spiritual resources we embrace need to be rich and to incorporate the realities of women's lives and spiritual dilemmas so that loss is not equated with failure and so that our children can know better ways of embodying loss than our religious heritage has provided for us.

Feminist theory, thealogy, and actions are all enriched by *vision*. Visionary communities imagine and create new ways of being in the world and give concrete focus to dreams of what a just and sustainable world might look like.

1. The primary criterion growing out of visioning is that feminist spirituality needs to enable participation by all affected in the naming and shaping of the common good. Those with least power should be enabled to have equal access to decision-making with the powerful; they need equal say in what actions would enable justice, mutuality, and well-being.

2. A second criterion is to promote empowerment through shared leadership, strong group processes, good communication skills, and development of strong self-esteem.

The final theological category suggested was that of *trusting our own inner wisdom*—to know what is good for oneself, to move from fear and lack of trust toward healing. Criteria in this category for the building of feminist theory, thealogy, and action are:

1. Listen to oneself, paying attention to one's inner voice, dreams, and intuitions.

2. Practice mutuality—that is, trusting one's own inner wisdom and respecting and listening to the inner wisdom of others.

Obviously there is much overlap in the criteria suggested among the different categories in the development of feminist theory, thealogies, and actions. Because they grow out of grounded experience in women's lives, many of them seem quite ordinary and based in common sense. Thus, while the list is long, it is not complex. It would be easy for a group to choose a few criteria and then to assess where they stand in relation to them, as they talk about their beliefs, rituals, thealogies/spiritualities, and actions.

Chapter 24

CRITERIA FOR
FEMINIST RITUALS

Living in a world where feminist values are not the norm, where patriarchal practice occupies the foreground, and where there is little affirmation for women's wisdom and spirituality means that there must be some spaces for the renewing of the core values of feminism and for affirming women as whole, sane, and healthy beings. This chapter shows how feminist rituals can assist that process of renewal and affirmation. It builds on the criteria for feminist theory, thealogy, and actions laid out in the previous chapter and looks specifically at criteria for feminist rituals that contribute to justice and well-being for women.

The first criterion for positive feminist rituals is that *they must have careful preparation.* To be prepared means to have considered the environment, the mood, and the ways in which the ritual will be carried out. Feminist ritual thrives in environments that uphold the elements of beauty, safety, and sacred space. The way in which seating space is arranged, the colors, the objects, the central focus space, the accessibility, and the lighting all affect the environment that is created for the ritual. Equally as important as the physical environment is the psychological environment, or the mood, that is to be created for the ritual. Linda Clark, Marion Ronan, and Eleanor Walker suggest that in preparation for leading rituals, women should "get in touch with the deepest, most authentic meaning of the event for the celebrating community. . . . Get in touch with the feelings you or others may have about the event, so that they can be taken into account in designing the action."[9] If the people planning the ritual are in touch

---

9. Linda Clark, Marion Ronan, and Eleanor Walker, *Image-Breaking, Image-Building: A Handbook for Creative Worship with Women of Christian Tradition* (New York: Pilgrim, 1981), p. 37.

with this depth, then there is more likelihood of having meaningful rituals and also of having rituals that do not twist in unexpected and painful ways. A mood of invitation, rather than demand, and a sense of hospitality help women feel at home as they gather for rituals. Gathering in a circle, where everyone can see everyone else, often helps create a mood of inclusion.

Preparation for rituals also involves thinking through how the ritual will work. Rituals should be simple and clear. According to Clark, Ronan, and Walker, "The best rituals are the most economical in their use of words and gestures in relation to the meaning they are intended to express."[10] There should not need to be explanations of what is going on during the ritual. Any instructions to help participants feel comfortable can be given at the beginning of the ritual. The ritual itself should be short and have easy transitions.

A second criterion for effective rituals is that *everyone needs to be clear about the intention of the ritual.* As women talk about what rituals do for them, one says, "When I am involved in rituals, I am grounded and centered. I know where my energy is, and where I want to put it. I feel less dispersed. It helps me be centered so that I can do the work for justice." Thus, it is helpful to ask, What is hoped for from the ritual? What effect do you want to elicit and invite? What actions will embody that intent? What words, readings, and music will support the actions? What symbols are meaningful to the community and understood by everyone that will contribute to this end? How can these symbols be arranged so that they will engage everyone's attention?

A third criterion regarding rituals that grows out of this project is an understanding that *rituals must be inherently just.* Rituals themselves must embody justice, as well as pointing toward justice in the world. One woman describes it this way:

> Virtually all of the rituals that I am involved in are rooted in a commitment to justice, and the rituals are an activity of justice making and are done with a vision toward global well-being. [By "justice making," I mean] two things: 1. In the rituals that I have been part of and in the rituals I create, I try to be just. I try to be conscious in the process of making the rituals. 2. In the naming, strengthening, visioning, and sealing of the vision, there is a commitment to justice making. Ritual in and of itself helps to move the struggle along. It is a way of keeping clear.

Rituals must be an opportunity to practice living in just ways. From a specifically Christian perspective, Mark Searle notes that "celebrat-

---

10. Ibid.

ing the liturgy should train us to recognize justice and injustice when we see it. It serves as a basis for social criticism by giving us a criterion by which to evaluate the events and structures of the world."[11] Through our rituals, we should be able to know deeply the difference between structures of good and evil and to live our way into new alternatives that present positive visions of social arrangements. In the church, rich and poor, employer and employee, women and men, heterosexuals and homosexuals, persons of various colors, ages, physical and mental abilities—all people are wholly acceptable and are, by their very existence, to be afforded respect and just treatment.

Rituals also give opportunity to envision justice in those places where it does not yet exist. Lisa talks about her dreams for life and the hope she gains through spirituality:

> I want to effect change. I have been moved by things I have experienced and read, and I want to pass it on. I feel like I need a discipline to do that. I need regularity in some meditation or ritual to keep myself going in order to pass it on. I need to feel connected to others. I think through spirituality we gain a sense of responsibility and that our spirituality needs to be acted out in our lives.
>
> I have read a lot and had personal encounters that have taught me a lot. I learned that I have more choices than I ever thought I had. I want now to help others see that they have more choices too. I want people to be awake and alert rather than living in a slumber of consumerism and television. I want people to have meaning in their lives—I want meaning for myself and meaning for others.

Rituals, then, can be models for justice, can strengthen and seal the vision toward justice in women's lives.

Consideration of the appropriate processes and structures for participation and leadership is a fourth criterion in the creation of effective feminist rituals. Rituals should involve all of the participants in meaningful and authentic ways. For people to feel comfortable in rituals, they need to know who is who; where they fit in; what is expected of them; what kinds of safety, options, and accessibility are built in; and what the intent of the ritual is. They also want to know that the ritual will have some depth to it; will give them courage to face the hard issues in their lives; will invite them into insight, community, and compassion. The structures for participation can be built on these elements.

As was noted in chapters 9 and 22, justice-making rituals are those in which everyone has opportunity for participation and involvement. In fact, one interviewee defined whether or not an event was a ritual by the level of participation:

---

11. Searle, "Serving the Lord with Justice," p. 29.

[A particular celebration] felt incomplete to me because there was no ritual. The group there was never a group. One person did it; no one else had anything to do with it. Even if two people had had a conversation, it would have made it OK, would have made it a ritual. But nothing got fed in. She did it herself—controlled the whole thing. I do believe that there is more energy in it if it comes out of the group—all of the group preferably, but at least more than one person. I have a deep belief that when two people are together, more than one plus one happens.

Leadership should be shared as widely as possible, while still maintaining a sense of direction and intentionality in the ritual.

This project also indicates that a primary criterion is that *rituals must arise from, and connect with, the ordinary events and experiences of women's lives.* Rituals become important to women when they link daily life with justice making and personal well-being. For example, one woman talks about rituals in relation to her work as a social worker. She is learning to bring rituals into her work.

I have been working on rituals on how to leave work without taking it home with me. I get so wrapped up in other people's stories of their pain and tend to be overly responsible. I want to be able to be there but not be overwhelmed. So I have begun to do rituals as I leave—saying something to myself or visualizing, imaging the cares of the day flowing out the exhaust as I drive home, or some other kind of symbolic letting go of the stuff I hear.

Or there was a death last year of a man that I had been working closely with, and I found it very hard, so I did a personal ritual around his death.

It is exciting for me how all of this fits into my workplace. I have been leading a group where there are lots of issues of anger. I had been telling one of the women I work with about the tactile things we did with the girls where I worked last year. She went out and got some Plasticine, and we gave it to the group. They could make images of people or whatever it was that caused them anger. There was a lot of pounding and throwing against the wall. The room was filled with a lot of energy as the people talked and made their figures. I was not quite sure what we were going to do, since I did not want to send people away with all of that energy. One of the women in the group suggested that we say a little phrase—something about letting all go and keeping it here. Being involved in the rituals that I have meant that I was aware of the power of ritual. I suggested that we take up the phrase and say it three times. It worked. People let go and were able to leave it all there.

Another talks about the different view of money she has when she is feeling centered versus when she is frazzled.

> I am not so anxious about money. I don't worry so much, if I make
> a donation, whether I will have enough to last me to the end of the
> month. I can't give the kind of time I would like to to a lot of
> organizations, so I choose to give financially. It doesn't happen with
> such a sense of duty if I am really centered.
>
> I also have less of a feeling that I have to be doing all the time
> and be at all places. I am more able to delegate and to write letters
> of support. I am more gentle with myself and with others.

Thus, rituals that allow women to be centered and to connect their
spiritual strength to everyday aspects of life and work are important.

A sixth criterion for effective feminist rituals is that *the rituals should
lift up shared myths and stories*. They retell the myth of community in
ways consistent with beliefs of the community. For example, feminist
rituals can acknowledge the skills and value of women's survival, can
allow for searching for meaning in the midst of loss and vulnerability,
or can act in visionary ways. Rituals can validate each woman as holy
and good and powerful. Rituals can tell truths about women's lives
that need to be addressed for justice for women to happen. For example, SCFN member Joan McMurtry describes a series of sermons
she preached on Phyllis Trible's book *Texts of Terror*, a book that delves
into four scriptural stories of terrible violation of women. Knowing
that many women in the congregation had been victims of violence
and sexual assault, she decided to name the truths of women's lives,
with the hope that there could be redemption in the telling and through
the experience of community. The Scripture stories are stark and bitter, but Joan nonetheless believes that God loves women and all who
are victims in society. She describes what happened:

> People listened intently. Some squirmed. Others did not return for
> the second tale. Often, when we left for home, people were quieter
> than usual. Tapes of the services were left at the back of the church.
> Two just disappeared. Within weeks of the series I became involved
> with two families where incest had occurred. On the other hand,
> some don't remember the series at all.
>
> I'm not sure that I would have the spiritual courage to tell these
> tales every week. Some weeks I'm happy to conduct weddings, visit
> with the committees, and play with the children. It's frightening to
> know such evil. This past week I've counselled a couple who beat
> each other, a woman who was raped at fifteen and is still fright-
> ened, grandparents whose granddaughter is in a psychiatric ward
> as a result of sexual abuse in the home, and I have been trying
> desperately to know how to help another incest victim learn to be a
> healthy and happy adult.
>
> I can understand why these texts of terror are never told! I am
> tired and worn out from them. Nevertheless, my courage will come

from the lives of the victims—those found in scripture and those discovered today.[12]

Truth-telling about the realities of women's lives, then, is a criterion—creating the myths and telling the stories that let women know they are not alone.

One of the important affirmations in this project was the way in which women linked their personal and political lives. This *capacity to link personal and political* is a seventh criterion for creation of rituals that contribute to justice and well-being for women. Political work is often seen as very demanding, and so the rituals are a significant factor in keeping women going in that work. Jane's response offers a relevant insight:

> Some part of me often goes back during the week to the meditation from Monday night. It is integrated into my work and my being. For example, the meditation that Gilda did on the tree of life—when there was all kinds of shit going on at work, I thought of that and of the need to keep my roots firmly planted like the tree—able to be flexible and bend but to have those roots firmly planted.
>
> Lots of people ask me how I can keep going on the Central American stuff. How can you keep on when all those people keep dying? I have to stay centered so that I can work at it. I always have to have that vision of global harmony before me so that I can keep at the hard everyday work to bring peace about.
>
> I can't tell if spirituality is the motivator for my work for justice, or if justice is the motivator for my ritual and spirituality. For me there is no separation of the personal and the political.

A ritual in the Feminist Spiritual Community that linked the personal and political was one created to send Beth Koehler on a women's convoy to Central America. The theme of the convoy was "Between Women There Are No Boundaries." The ritual began with the statement:

> Between women there are no boundaries. This is a statement of faith. While in fact there may be no boundaries between us, as all major religious traditions attest, we have created boundaries—political, economic, social, even within ourselves we have barriers as we split off parts of us that do not "fit in." So we make this claim that "Between Women There Are No Boundaries," and we commission Beth to be part of this message of hope. All utopian social systems have emphasized this, but as women we have been conditioned to

12. Joan McMurtry, "Redemptive Storytelling: Biblical Texts of Terror," *Women's Concerns* 33 (Fall 1986).

ideas of competition and scarcity, whether between women of different racial or social groups, or economic classes or levels of formal education. So to do what we do in this is an act of defiance to the created construction of reality that says there are boundaries.

In ritual, we live out the capacity to vision a world of human and global interconnectedness and to live as if that world of just personal and political relations were in place already.

An eighth criterion is that *feminist rituals must contain elements of healing, change, or transformation.* A woman who worked in Nicaragua describes gaining a sense of transformation from the Mass there.

> When I was in Nicaragua living in the barrios, I went to the Mass there every week. It was—I don't know how to say it in English—a living Mass. People came from all over, dressed in their cleanest rags. The handshake and the kiss of peace would take hours. The old would cry, and everyone had lost some family member or someone they knew and loved to the war. They were so poor. There was nothing in the country: the economy was so bad. But they gathered for the Mass, which was very radical and peace-oriented, and they would sing, "We shall overcome." It was a very *powerful* experience! People there live their religion.

Another example of rituals for healing and change are gatherings that happened for many Canadian women who sought out opportunities to be together to deal with their horror after the Montreal massacre in December 1989. An SCFN participant, barb janes, spoke at a memorial held in Saskatoon for the murdered women. janes notes the sensational headlines, the relentless alarmist newscasts, and the feelings of fear evoked by simply being a woman in a society of hate. She adds:

> I felt it could have been me. And I was afraid and angry.
>
> As the week went on, I was angry not only at Marc Lepine, not only at a culture that encouraged and supports violence against women, not only at the male students in that classroom who seemed to have done nothing to stop the violence, more than that I was angry at the voices who said, "Let's not panic. Let's not get all paranoid. Let's not get our tea-towels in a tangle. After all, this is an isolated incident."
>
> This is, by the killer's own admission, a political act and we should be enraged. We should be outraged by any attempt to soften that harsh reality. It is not enough that we gather here to mark the lives of 14 women. It is not enough that we make these women into martyrs for the feminist cause. It is not enough that we vent our anger and our tears, important as that is.

It will be enough when we use our rage as the fuel for change. It will be enough when we stand up to woman-hating, no matter how or where or when we encounter it. It will be enough when we stand together, holding each other up and just plain holding each other.

This is a day of pain, a day of fear, but it is also a day of pride. It is a day to take pride in being a feminist. It is a day to be proud of what we stand for and to know what we stand for is right and just and true. It is a day to know, as civil rights workers in Alabama know, as lesbian and gay liberationists in Vancouver know, as AIDS activists in Montreal know, as the Lubicon in Alberta and the Innu in Labrador know, as welfare recipients in Saskatoon know, as feminists everywhere know: Evil will not have the last word, because we are right.

We are right and we will keep on keeping on. You can't kill the spirit. Keep on keeping on. [13]

Deborah Marshall writes about the same event and suggests that as a ritual, women gather and pass a spool of red thread. Each woman is invited to tie a red thread around her wrist until violence ends. The red represents the blood of women. The tying represents the solidarity in our insistence that this suffering must cease and that we must do something to help end the bloodshed. [14]

These rituals show how women can be empowered for action and for living their daily lives, even in unfriendly environments. The strength gained from the rituals—and from communities where sorrows are shared, evil is named, joy is spoken, and freedom is sought—is a valuable resource as women seek to name the thealogical categories that make sense in their spirituality and to work politically for justice in the world. The rituals create environments and moods that invite justice; they connect with the real experiences in women's lives, contain diversity, and call for transformation, thus meeting many of the criteria outlined above.

Inclusiveness is also an important criterion. Words and music need to be free of racist, sexist, heterosexist, and classist language. Rituals can use many different languages and cultural expressions to add to the experience. Inclusiveness means that rituals should respect difference and should allow for the diversity of experiences within, and beyond, the group to influence what happens in the ritual.

Diann Neu recognizes the importance of *embodiment* in rituals:

Body Expression is included through movement, gesture or touch. Invite people to stand in a circle, arms on shoulders, and sway dur-

---

13. Rev. barb janes, "Rage Must Be Channelled to Fuel Societal Change," *Star-Phoenix*, December 15, 1989 (by permission of author).
14. Marshall, "Ministry of Women," p. 43 (see n. 17 on p. 25 above).

ing a song. Encourage warm embraces during greetings of peace. And, of course, if you have dancers in your group, invite them to do a solo dance and/or choreograph simple movements to music or readings for the community. When blessing bread, pouring wine, washing hands, use dramatic gestures that can be seen by all. [15]

Actions that affirm women's body-selves and allow women to feel positive about their bodies are vital. This also means showing care regarding accessibility for persons with disabilities and providing options for people who are, for whatever reason, not comfortable with certain kinds of touch or movement. In rituals, a mix of the dramatic and ordinary, of the serious and playful, can often be strengthened through the use of movements, various senses, and the arts.

Criteria for the creation of rituals that lead to justice and well-being for feminists, then, include careful preparation through creation of environment, mood, and process; determining the intent of the ritual; structuring the ritual to be just by nature; creating processes of involving all participants and sharing leadership; connecting ordinary events and experiences from women's lives with spirituality; sharing stories that tell the truth about women's lives; connecting personal and political aspects of life; using elements of healing, change, and transformation; inclusiveness; and embodiment. Following these criteria can challenge and nurture women in their work for justice and well-being in the world.

---

15. Diann Neu, "Guide for Planning Feminist Liturgies," in *Women-Church Celebrations: Feminist Liturgies for the Lenten Season* (Silver Springs, Md.: WATER, March 1985), p. 4.

Chapter 25

CREATION OF WOMEN'S CULTURE THROUGH ARTS

Patriarchy manifests itself in concrete and material forms, and as already stated, feminism seeks to change the material conditions of women's lives in specific and concrete ways. Much has already been said about the pervasiveness of patriarchal culture. One way of shifting from patriarchal culture is by the development of women's culture, that is, development and interpretation of a feminist framework, ideology, and way of being in the world that deal with economic, social, artistic, and spiritual factors. The categories in part 2 were the beginning of naming a new framework. This chapter will look at two aspects of the creation of a women's culture: (1) the theoretical and (2) the meaning of the arts in this transformation.

Culture is "the way of life of a group of people, the configuration of all of the more or less stereotyped patterns of learned behavior which are handed down from one generation to the next through means of language and imitation."[16] More specifically, culture is the basic social organization, the patterns of economic, social, spiritual, and kinship structure and infrastructure. Culture also gives representation and attributes meaning to the structures. Culture is not just a given; it is not a biological necessity but a construct of humans based on survival and on what is important to them. Culture contains both structure (i.e., the way food is produced, society is governed, people are educated) and ethos (i.e., the beliefs, assumptions, values, and expectations arising from and validating the structure).[17] It represents the worldview of the group or community through its myths, its patterns of communication, and its symbols.

---

16. Victor Barnouw, *An Introduction to Anthropology: Ethnography* (Homewood, Ill.: Dorsey Press, 1971), p. 11.

17. Centre for Vision and Policy, "Ethics and Economic Justice," p. 24.

Gerda Lerner describes woman's culture as "the ground upon which women stand in resistance to patriarchal domination and their assertion of their own creativity in shaping society." It includes the familial and friendship networks of women, their affective ties, and their rituals. Lerner goes on to claim that in light of the number of women in the world, women's culture is never a subculture: "Women live a duality—as members of the general culture and as partakers of woman's culture." [18]

Mary Daly puts it a little differently:

> As Survivors know, the media-created Lie that *the women's movement* "died" has hidden the fact from many of our sisters that Spinners/ Spinsters have been spinning works of genesis and demise in our concealed workshops. Feminists have been creating a rich culture, creating new forms of writing, singing, celebrating, cerebrating, searching. We have been developing new strategies and tactics for organizing—for economic, physical, and psychological survival. [19]

Mary Daly suggests a separatist society of women—that is, that women should choose to live separately from men and from the practices of the world steeped in patriarchy, as much as is possible. Rosemary Radford Ruether suggests that, rather than the creation of separatist societies of women, some separation is important for the development of women's culture. However, she does not see it as the long-term solution for global justice. Rather, the need for time apart from men and for communicating separately in women-only groups is essential. She notes that other repressed and dominated groups (e.g., ethnic groups) have often retained remnants of their own culture and may have developed subcultures of resistance (e.g., modes of talk, songs, and dances). This unity as a subculture has not been possible for women because they have been isolated by the patriarchal family structure, colonized by their education, and defined as inferior. Thus, there has not been the needed separate space for the development of a critical culture. [20]

Creation of women's culture involves women's being together and trying out new economic patterns, new ways of organizing, new senses of autonomy, and new symbol systems. Several of these elements have been discussed elsewhere, so the focus of the creation of women's culture through the arts will be primary here.

Chapter 20, "Symbols," noted the importance of having symbols in order to create and live out ideologies. Symbol systems create just or

---

18. Lerner, *Creation of Patriarchy*, p. 242.
19. Daly, *Gyn/Ecology*, p. xv.
20. Ruether, *Women-Church*, p. 59.

unjust structures, giving them meaning, reinforcement, and cultural values. Thus, women who are impassioned by feminist politics, spirituality, thealogy, and activism need symbol systems to support their beliefs, positions, and actions. Carol Christ accordingly asserts:

> The creation of new symbolisms in art, literature, music, religion, and ritual will make feminist goals easier to achieve. Instead of a discontinuity between symbols in the deep mind and desired social change, there will be a continuity and reciprocal reinforcement. If a feminist symbol system were created, then feminists might be able to overcome the feeling we sometimes have that we are struggling against the tide of nature and history, against, as it were, the "general order of existence." Instead of being devalued in songs, stories, rituals, and symbols, feminist moods and motivations would be reinforced by cultural symbol systems. Instead of remaining unarticulated, feminist conceptions of an order of existence could be expressed.[21]

This new "order of existence" is beginning to be formulated and articulated through feminist artistic expressions. Women's newsletters, journals, films, videos, music, and bookstores are becoming more common, especially in larger urban areas. And women are excited about these new creations. One woman says: "Discovering women's music was like Christmas when I was four years old. I can't describe the power it has. It is a really deep need, touching the wounds, knowing that there is someone who feels like I do." Another adds: "Music is both survival and subversiveness. When I found women's music, it was like a whole counterculture. Women's music helped me say the things I was thinking. It helped woman me. The humor has done a lot for me. It is good to be able to laugh with something."

Being an artist, however, is not necessarily easy. The problems raised in chapters 8 and 17, "Naming of Self and Experience" and "Trusting Our Own Inner Wisdom," are real for artists. Artists need to listen to their inner voices in order to create. They need to believe in themselves and believe that they have something important to create and communicate.

Rural women have an added difficulty in being artists. Pam Patterson notes that while rural women are traditionally seen as hardworking and responsible family supporters, they also have to cope with isolation, financial hardships, little day care, and few support networks. For artists, these stresses are multiplied.

---

21. Carol Christ, *Laughter of Aphrodite* (San Francisco: Harper and Row, 1987), p. 139.

Simply being unable to run off to a film or an art show can unnerve the newly arrived rural woman. Winter can be especially traumatic and, as contact with other artists becomes minimal, occasional visits to urban art events begin to feel like trips to another planet.

Materials, supplies, books are difficult and expensive to acquire. Advanced workshops and classes are often found only in larger centres. If you are able to get a gallery show, you will have to cope with the expense of crating and shipping your work since funding from the arts councils doesn't always cover the cost of transporting and insuring the artwork, or of the artist's travel, accommodation or other expenses involved in just leaving home for a few days.[22]

Despite this difficulty of women's finding themselves and their own voices that can be expressed in the arts, and despite the challenges faced by rural artists, many women are actively involved in artistic endeavors. Many of them would see themselves as social-change agents, or as pointing to the problems in society and the need for its transformation.

Feminist spirituality is done collectively, and therefore it is often expressed through art forms, rather than through formal statements of belief. Thus, it is often through examination of the arts that we begin to get an understanding of feminist spirituality. Particular arts have the capacity to bring us into touch with the holy, with ourselves, and with society in different ways, as we seek justice and well-being in society.

Art that breaks down hierarchy can lead toward justice. While patriarchal practices seek justification for hierarchies, it is to the advantage of women, and all who are dominated, to seek surprises and reversal of power structures. Historically, the circle dance was used to bring people of all classes and ranks together. Dance was an equalizer that broke down barriers between clergy and laity, old and young, Christians and non-Christians, but it was considered too radical and was banned by the church.[23] Barbara Lyon notes that "moving is not the usual intellectual choice. . . . Starting a circle, hierarchy is broken down. All are included. No one is hidden from another. Holding hands, everyone in the circle is touching."[24]

One ritual of the Feminist Spiritual Community that used dance was particularly powerful for many of the participants:

The meditation moved easily from the cave of women's power and mystery to the dance, with everyone holding hands and moving to

---

22. Pam Patterson, "Let's Not Forget Our Kin in the Country," *Women's Education des Femmes* 6, no. 2 (Spring 1988): 36.

23. Doug Adams, *Congregational Dancing in Christian Worship* (Austin: The Sharing Company, 1984), see chap. 2 and pp. 35 and 48.

24. Lyon, *Dance toward Wholeness*, p. 45.

the songs we were singing. Kate then let go of Beth's hand, and the circle became a line, and a spiral was created going around and around tighter and tighter. Eventually the pattern reversed, and Beth and I held spruce boughs in an arch–birth canal, and the women went through in a line that became a circle and then went through and around in a figured pattern, slowing and speeding as the drums, tambourine, and rattles carried the beat and the singing rose and fell. The energy was high; the circle took on a life of its own. Debbie and Elly took the boughs from Beth and me, and we joined the circle/line. After a time the music slowed, and the line moved into a large circle. Singing continued.

The arts have great power to move us to places that our intellectual choices might not take us. The arts have the power to open us, to challenge us, to give us new eyes to see, to touch our emotions, to heal, and to create beauty.

Sometimes the holy is known in works of beauty—in the way in which the artist is able to capture a mood, a moment, or an image that takes our breath away or stirs something deep inside. We are nurtured, strengthened, and comforted by the creation. Sometimes we know the holy in works that challenge or criticize—that name truth in its raw forms, warn us of impending doom if a course continues, or bring to focus amorphous anxieties. The creation makes us disturbed, horrified, and motivated to action toward change.

Martha Ann Kirk, a Roman Catholic nun who works by day with illegal immigrants and refugees fleeing from Central America and who lives at night in a household with battered women and children, elaborates:

> Good Christian ritual should be sensitive to the power of the lovely to bind up the wounds of those who come to service after a week of dealing with the practical which so often is stripped of beauty. Ritual should allow persons to center themselves, to regain eyes and ears to see, beauty they may have missed. Ritual should lead persons to celebrate this beauty not just in their souls but in their whole bodies.[25]

Art in rituals, then, intends to bring us to awareness of the presence of the holy and to restore us to life and beauty.

The arts are evocative and allow us to be in touch with the depth of ourselves and our emotions. One woman describes as follows the emotional impact of reading: "Sometimes I read to relieve anger. Other

25. Martha Ann Kirk, *Dancing with Creation* (Saratoga, Calif.: Resource Publications, 1983), p. 93.

times it is to empower me. Or I like to bawl a lot—get it all out. I don't always know, at the start of the book, which of the emotions it will be, but reading helps me that way." Jane describes the relation of music and mood for her:

> Music and mood are closely tied together for me. I also connect music and landscape and mood. I am delighted when I hit the right music with the right landscape. When I go on long drives, I often plan the music to suit what the landscape is going to be. One time when I was driving over the Rockies, the sun was going down in the sky, and I had on a tape of Mozart's Clarinet Quartet. It was just the right music. Other times I have taken long drives on the prairies in summer and autumn when the fields are ripening. Carolyn McDade's words fit so often with their wonderful landscape images in them.

Holly Near adds that music is a significant art form as women begin to discover the wonders of their lives.

> There are millions of songs to be written about our growth and failures. Songs that help us weep away grief, loss, sadness. Songs that help us scream our rage, our fears, our nightmares. Songs that support loving and tenderness. Songs that illuminate our differences, that teach us to acknowledge our bigotries and encourage change. Songs that celebrate our rebirth, our spirituality, our power, our politics, our insight, our instincts, and our vision. Women's music has served to bring some of us together in one place so we can get to know ourselves and each other.[26]

Several women at a Christian Feminist Network event talked about how music helps us know ourselves and brings people together, especially women and children.

> Music makes me want to connect with others. If I hear music that speaks to me, I can believe that someone else somewhere is able to share that emotion that I am feeling. There is a sense of "Oh good, somebody knows."

> Music is connected to the nurture of my body. To be without music is like to be without food. It is essential—like drinking water. I find myself humming or singing a particular song, and when I bring it to consciousness, it helps me recognize the mood I am in.

---

26. Holly Near, "Singing for a New Day," in *In Her Own Image: Women Working in the Arts*, ed. Elaine Hedges and Ingrid Wendt (Old Westbury, N.Y.: Feminist Press, 1980), p. 272.

I feel really safe with my daughter when we make up songs and sing them together. She sings herself to sleep at night, just makes up songs with whatever comes into her head and sings away. I like it a lot and feel so safe with her then.

One of the most special times I have with my kids is in the car, where we sing and sing and sing. They are old enough now that they would be embarrassed to do it anywhere else, but there is something about doing it in a closed space where no one else can hear. I don't know how long they will want to do it, but they still do now.

Mary adds a different kind of relationship:

Another kind of music that I love is the music of the loons, the owls, and the wolves. They have such beautiful music, and when we are at the cottage and go canoeing at night or just sit out, I can hear the sounds of the birds and animals, which is a sort of music. We are all interconnected, and we have to work for them. They have to be part of our understanding of justice.

Poetry also adds to one's sense of the presence of the holy and of our capacity for injustice and justice. C. P. Mudd claims that poets unveil things and give us eyes to see and senses to feel the joy, pain, excitement, or sadness of any given moment so that we may take hold of a fundamental truth of life. Mudd suggests brevity in poems, an economy of words in poetry.[27] Loraine MacKenzie Shepherd's poem "Empowerment" shows the impact of this ideal.

Empowerment

Rush through,
　　roaring in surging billows,

　　　　　　　　　　　　r
　　　　　　　　　　　a d
　　　　　　　　　w
　　　　　　　p
　　　　swirling me u
　　Empowered beyond the fetters,

BURST THROUGH

I A M !

Riding abreast of the tumbling waves,
　　spilling around and around,

---

27. C. P. Mudd, "Arts Come Home," *Modern Liturgy* 8, no. 5 (1981): 29.

through and through
Surging through,
SURGING THROUGH

I A M !

Story and myth are still another of the arts that are used in ritual and in justice work. One woman says:

> Reading for me is a spiritual experience. Because it connects stuff for me, it meets my needs, feeds me, challenges my way of thinking and being, and broadens my thinking. It tells me that all relationships are not the same. I always have a sense of well-being after a good read. Reading is essential to me. I could not *not* read. I could not pray, not go to church. There are a lot of things I could give up, but I could not *not* read.

Fontaine Maury Belford puts literature into a broad context, suggesting that "literature makes us aware of the invisible posing as the inevitable and thereby opens the way for change to occur." She goes on to say that literature helps to determine culture, through converting the reader. "One is moved; one's being is relocated in such a way that the world is never quite the same again. This movement takes place beneath the level of sentiment or pleasure. It occurs, rather, at the center of being from which all creation, all action springs."[28]

One of the members of the Regina Book Club talks about the connection between reading and ritual for her.

> My favorite reading is from a magazine, *Saskatchewan History and Folklore*. On Mother's Day, I am going to take my tape recorder over to my mother's place and get her to tell stories from her past. She tells such interesting stories, and I want to get some of them down, especially because I want to be able to tell them to my grandchildren. I like reading the stories in the magazine because they are so ordinary. They are good stories. The women don't come through as hard put by, and yet as I read about these pioneer women on the prairies, I think that they are most amazing women. The men write about machinery and horses, but the women write about interesting things. One I read recently was about a woman who was at home with the kids when a prairie fire was coming and she had to figure out what to do. They were feminists, although they did not even know it.
>
> I was telling some of the women at work about these stories, and

---

28. Fontaine Maury Belford, "Leadership, Literature, and the Uses of the Imagination," *The Network* 9, no. 3 (Spring 1990): 16.

a lot of them did not even know their grandmother's name. I thought about all of the times at PCTC when we have said, "I am _____, daughter of _____, granddaughter of _____." In a sense we have done our research through our rituals.

Myth, a form of story, is also a bearer and creator of culture. Bronislaw Malinowski describes myth (which he defines as sacred story) in terms of its functions. He says a myth is a story that establishes beliefs, defines rituals, and determines social and moral behavior. Although the myth may be set in the community's past, it is told for the purpose of the present community's governance, order, and action. [29]

Mary Daly, in her usual skeptical manner, adds a feminist critique to the anthropologist's view:

> Patriarchy perpetuates its deception through myth. . . . Myths are said [by scholars] to be stories that express intuitive insights and relate the activities of the gods. The mythical figures are symbols. These, it is said, open up depths of reality otherwise closed to "us." It is not usually suggested that they close off depths of reality which would otherwise be open to us. [30]

Part of the creation of women's culture, then, is the creation of new myths that name women as heras and that tell the stories of our lives in new and insightful ways.

Television is a contemporary creator of myths and stories that can also give insight into ourselves and into the nature of the holy. As Maureen says:

> I love to watch "Magnum PI" on TV. He's like me, loyal to a fault, accidentally solves problems.
>
> A verse in the Bible that has always meant so much to me is one that even in the last days, even the elect (the righteous) will have trouble knowing Christ. So I have always kept one eye open so that I can see the Christ. I always look for that little bit of grain, always see everybody's good side. It started with fear—that I might miss Christ, and that would be dreadful—but it has been a thread that has kept me connected through the years. It is what has allowed me to see God in the mundane and in human situations.
>
> I feel like a detective. I love to watch "Magnum PI," "Miss Marple," and all of those shows. They are my role models. I think God is a detective, and I love the mystery! And I always am looking for the clues and trying to put the pieces together.

---

29. Bronislaw Malinowski, *Sex, Culture, and Myth* (New York: Harcourt, Brace and World, 1962), pp. 249, 247.
30. Daly, *Gyn/Ecology*, p. 44.

Myths retell and enliven the story of the community. Cast into feminist contexts, myths provide role models, explain women's festivals, and tell how heras and ordinary women have coped with the existential crises of life and have transformed patriarchal contexts to women-centered visions. Myths give hope and courage to women and allow for healing and honoring of women's selves.

The arts invite us to name and embody the truths in society, to engage with all of our senses and capacities, to enter the presence of the holy, and to create new possibilities. The arts call us to wholeness and to community. They open doors for women's culture with its emphasis on women's symbols, experiences, relationships, music, dance, poetry, stories, and myths. The arts are one avenue to gain new insight into women's self-definitions and cultural expression and to move toward the elimination of patriarchy and the creation of a feminist vision of justice and well-being.

Chapter 26

ACTIONS AND STRATEGIES

Donna Hawxhurst and Sue Morrow assert that "the most important resources that exist in any feminist community are women acting. It is one thing to create a vision of a better world; it is another to act on that vision, to find ways to begin living it out and building on it. Effective change requires both vision and action."[31] One of the women interviewed in this study also says: "Every year I have come to love the background strategizing more, especially talking to people and trying to get things going. It is still important for me to accomplish things and not just talk about them, to do concrete things."

Women do want to act—and need to act if a world of justice is to come into being. A range of actions is needed, and different women will choose to engage in different ways in the long, slow process of change from a patriarchal world to one where women experience justice and well-being. As we ready ourselves for actions, it seems important to begin with concrete actions that will allow us to have hope. Small signs of change give us hope and courage for the larger projects.

One place to begin is to know who our neighbors are—those like us and those different from us. We live in a global village, and many of us live in local communities where there is opportunity to acquaint ourselves with the homeless, with street kids, with those trying to make ends meet on social assistance, with gay and lesbian people, with people from other countries and cultures, with Native people, with francophones, and with those whose worldviews differ from our own—not as audiences for charity or evangelization, but in mutuality, with openness to being challenged deeply by these neighbors about what love and justice mean.

Another strategy for change is through raising children to be just

---

31. Hawxhurst and Morrow, *Living Our Visions*, p. 134.

and caring people. A media image portrays feminists as being against motherhood—but in fact, feminists make the best mothers. They raise children aware of themselves and the world, of options and values, of what justice means and how to work toward it, and of how to be self-critical and self-respecting. One woman says that she wants to pass on to her daughter "a sense of a loving God, a God who is faithful, a God who is for justice and for peace. I don't care if she memorizes verses from the Bible if she knows what it is to love and be just to others." But it is not easy to live with all of the pressures of mothering, employment, and volunteer activity.

Another woman talks of the choices she has made:

> I had a big involvement in Amnesty until my younger child was born. I put a lot of energy into Amnesty in Saskatchewan, in writing to prisoners of conscience, in coordinating the refugee program, trying to get local lawyers involved, and helping people through the refugee process.
>
> Having children has changed all of that. Now I do not have much energy to put into political work. I enjoy political action groups but am not able to schedule them regularly at this point in my life. I wish I had more time and energy for this kind of thing.

A rural woman notes:

> [My husband] and I agree that we will do 50–50 in housework and in parenting—but I notice the housework before he does. I was taught to notice and he wasn't, and it is often easier to do it than to ask him to do it.
>
> Our relationship is vastly different than most of the relationships here. But it is a pain that he doesn't do more. Men get all kinds of praise for doing what they do—any little bit of housework or child care—but no one notices if we women do it. There is still a long way to go!

In a just society, women would be free to make whatever decisions they needed to, for however long they needed to, in relation to political action in the public and the private sphere. All people would participate in the decision-making, and women would be supported in their decisions rather than, as sometimes happens, made to feel guilty for not doing enough or not valued for what they do.

Another action strategy is to live as if justice and equality already exist. We can work to achieve mutuality, fairness, and love in the intimate day-by-day relationships in our homes and spheres of friendship. We can make decisions in our workplaces and political activities that emphasize justice, ecological stability, and adequate resources for all. We can envision a world where all people live with dignity, suffi- ciency, and just human relationships. This is not to suggest living in a naive state. It is to suggest that practicing living as if the world shared these values is one way of beginning the process of change and of testing whether our ideas are workable. It is helpful if we can have communities of like-minded people to support us as we attempt to live with values contrary to those of the dominant society, but even small actions and signs alone are significant.

One rural woman in ministry talked about what living her values as a feminist means to her. She spoke about having gone to a workshop on domestic violence. On returning home, she raised the issue of do- mestic violence from the pulpit so that people would be more aware that it happens in rural areas, not just in big cities. Consequently, a woman talked to this minister about abuse in her childhood from her father. The minister was able to help her get to a support group in the closest city and was with her through the changes, growth, and confrontation of her father.

Some concrete actions thus are getting to know our neighbors, rais- ing our children respectfully, and living justly in our daily lives. It is important that we recognize that the actions in the private sphere and in the community are as "political" as actions in the public sphere. All actions have consequences, and they are interrelated in the creation of the common good and of social policies. In North America, peo- ple are taught to think of politics as the same thing as government, and thus they see their only possible political action as voting. Politics is not seen as part of everyday life; it is seen as something politi- cians do.

David Matthews suggests that "understanding connections, others, and consequences—all in the process of making a political choice or judgment—is what political thinking is about. . . . The reason we act in politics is to maximize something we hold to be valuable or worth something."[32] He says that we must know facts; more than facts, how- ever, we must know how to make connections, what the facts mean to others, especially those whose lives are different from ours, and the costs and consequences of the choices we make. And, he says, we must make choices together because the choices and decisions made to- gether will be much better than those any one person can make alone. This way of looking at politics—as involvement in decision-making and making connections in things we think important—allows for a grounded politic. It makes politics accessible to everyone and allows for all to participate in the shaping of the common good.

---

32. David Matthews, "The Political Community," *The Network* 10, no. 1 (Summer/Fall 1990): 18.

Some of the women interviewed have chosen actions in the public sphere of the electoral political process. Linda describes what being part of electoral politics has meant to her, reiterating Matthews's points about making connections and involvement. She joined the New Democratic Party because of their policies and because she believed that they look out for people who are disenfranchised. She was involved in various committees and especially in seeking justice regarding housing and women's work. In order to see what politics was like, she ran for city council. She liked the opportunity to speak with people and the way in which even very short conversations could be meaningful. She was praised for being "an honest politician." She continues:

> The second time I ran, I was cajoled and dragged in. I had a commitment to run a fair and honest campaign. It was amazing. Everyone became friends—some church people, some wiccan, some gay, lesbian, and straight, some working on Ph.D.s, some in feminist counseling, some postal workers. No one wanted the campaign committee to end. It created a spiritual community—a ritual of respect, a sense of honoring one another. I was the central focus to bring together friends from all these different focuses. My manager was a PWA [Person with AIDS]. It was very good for many people to connect with him. Some of the women were quite conservative but became NDP with the hope of getting me into the house. . . .
>
> What motivated and motivates me is to bring some sense of vision. I know a lot of people, and I want to bring them into the political process because I believe that they have something to offer. I am able to help people to see themselves as part of the political process. I am also motivated to be in politics because of the need for human rights in British Columbia and in Canada. If we have the gift to speak out for justice, then we have the ability to be in the political arena.

Linda also indicated that electoral politics is not an inviting place for women. Despite the hard work of campaigners, it is hard to get a nomination and hard to maintain one's own values and commitments if one does manage to win.

Pat, a Saskatchewan farmer and member of the SCFN, also describes what the electoral process was like for her.

> The myriad of details of over one year's work to gain the nomination and to run in the provincial election make it easy to, in a mind-boggling way, say nothing or babble a great deal.
>
> There are some realities—it costs a lot of money, it requires a single-mindedness and uses up all one's energy so that there is very little to give in supporting others. The ways others can help are by

offering to give gas and driving skills, by direct financial contributions, by checking with those running the campaign and doing some of the nitty gritty door-knocking, proof-reading, typing, pamphlet-setting-up, writing press releases, speech writing. . . .

This is no time to be looking to get support from a candidate—only time to *be with* and help organize—perhaps by writing comments on cards or whatever. The candidate needs to be able to hit the doorway, talk to folks and run on to the next. The pace is relentless and needs to be. 10,000 calls take up time and energy to make, and the more done the better. There's almost no time for speech preparation and one needs help to come up with something.[33]

Besides running for office, another strategy used by women to influence political change is lobbying governments. Lobbyists are people who seek to influence the political process. Lobby groups are usually short-term, frequently single issue, and concerned with ideological, social, and altruistic goals. They try to influence cabinet ministers, members of Parliament, and senators, although they rarely get access to the civil servants who actually write the bills.

Lobbyists also use coalitions in which a number of groups with a common basic concern band together to put pressure on governments. One effective coalition in Canada is the National Action Committee on the Status of Women (NAC). NAC comprises some 450 women's groups from across the country. Its purpose is to lobby governments for the interests of women and to bring a feminist analysis to government discussions.[34] The annual meeting is the forum for policy direction setting, and an executive board consisting of representatives from various interests and regions works through the year. This arrangement gives the stability, cohesion, and continuity needed to work effectively as an institutional pressure group. Many members of the Christian Feminist Network are also members of NAC-affiliated groups and give financial support to NAC.

Much of the lobbying done is by individuals at a local level and through letter writing. Betty talks about the kind of lobbying she does primarily through letter writing:

I do a lot of letter writing to members of Parliament. I usually get an answer. Sometimes it is a form letter, but I do keep writing.

I am really interested in world peace. I worry about the U.S. arsenal buildups. There is an article in *Christian Science Monitor* this

---

33. Pat Krug, "Reflections on a Provincial Campaign," *The Unbeaten Path* 8 (1983).
34. Christine Appelle, "The New Parliament of Women: A Study of the National Action Committee on the Status of Women" (M.A. thesis, Carleton University, Ottawa, April 1987), pp. 55, 69, 74.

edition that shows how the U.S. is replacing their old missiles and bombs with new nuclear warheads. It is ridiculous!

Fortunately the Canadian government is affected by letters. They got so many letters about the nuclear submarines that they did not buy them, and they took Perrin Beatty out of the minister of defense position. They should have written thank you letters to all of us for telling them not to do it! Think of how stupid they would look now if they had gone ahead and bought eight nuclear submarines just as Gorbachev is seeking peace and with all of the things that are going on in Eastern Europe.

I also am opposed to the testing of armaments over Labrador and the Native communities. They say they are not offensive weapons, but it is clear that they are. Why? What is the matter with Canada and the U.S.? Canada sends off all kinds of materials to Third World countries that can be used only for making wars. They need food, not weapons for civil wars or for fighting against their neighbors.

Another form of lobbying is protest rallies and marches. Feminists all over Canada participate regularly in protests—against the Gulf War, against the proposed abortion law, against violence against women, against environmental destruction, and against many other issues. David Kertzer argues that mass rallies are an effective means to demonstrate popular support for a cause. They are dramatic, show political strength, and publicize the lobby group's goals. Participants in rallies also increase their identification with the group and reinforce their opposition to the foes that are symbolically represented in the demonstration. Kertzer adds, "Such mass demonstrations gain their force through the careful manipulation of symbols, combined with the emotional impact of having so many people together for a common cause."[35]

Besides entry into party politics and lobbying, women also work to shift economic practices in their political endeavors. Starhawk envisions a more just economic system, based on the inherent value of all members of society and trusting and educating all to participate in decisions that affect their lives. Interdependence, and being sure all are nurtured and cared for, would be the economic basis. Small enterprises would be both innovative and sustainable, as well as being run by those who work in the businesses. Self-reliance for the necessities of life would be central, with agricultural land being used first to serve local food needs and only secondarily to create exports.[36]

Besides self-sufficiency, any redefinition of economics needs to include both formal and informal economies. Currently, the low-paid

---

35. Kertzer, *Ritual, Power, and Politics*, p. 119.
36. Starhawk, *Truth or Dare*, pp. 315, 330.

jobs of women and their unpaid labor at home and in the community are not seen as contributing to the gross national product. For women to be valued, there must be an integration of paid labor and social goals involving home and community work.

Several women in the project talked about economics—about the paid and unpaid work they do, about the lack of adequate and interesting employment opportunities, about their desire to work outside of the high pressure of capitalist patriarchy. During the time of the project, six of the thirty-six women interviewed started small businesses of their own, primarily to be able to work in different ways from the usual work patterns established in capitalist patriarchy. One woman, who was a few years into her new vocation, talked about what it has meant for her:

> Material things are not as important to me now. Money still worries me. I used to think that I had to have at least $1,000 in the bank; now I am lucky to have $25. Now I think of all the people who cannot ever afford to go to the dentist. I could. Even if I did not have the money, I could somehow get the resources to go to the dentist. But some really cannot.
>
> I have different priorities now than I did before.

So women are seeking to live with different visions of the economy and are risking much to do it.

A woman in ministry who uses a different strategy said, "I try to focus on education and consciousness raising. I believe they are a primary form of social change. Once people become aware of injustice, they do something about it." The final section of this book, the Study Guide, also serves this purpose of education as a means of social change.

Another way of bringing about social change is through changes in rituals. Ritual change is symbolic change, but it can lead to direct action or to ideological change, so it can be an important element in strategizing for change.

One way of causing change is to re-form or alter the system. This involves recognizing that we are part of the system and that the system is dependent on feedback from its parts to keep it in balance, which means that we have the capacity to change. A start is to bring people of different life situations together. Economics are a major factor in everyone's life, but women bear particularly heavy loads. Our rituals can alter the system by allowing people who do not have money to donate (or money for dressing up, for bringing food, or for covering child care costs) to participate as freely as those who do have money. But reforming the system across economic class-lines means not just making things free; it also means addressing different perspectives and different worldviews created by the economic circumstances of people's lives.

Another route is reappropriation of the rituals of dominant groups. This strategy is used frequently by oppressed groups—the oppressor's format is used, but the levels of meaning in the content are shifted. For example, the black church in United States under slavery used liturgies and music that gave visions of freedom. WATER, a part of the Women-Church movement, suggests that "being church is the best revenge." WATER, as already indicated, is a parachurch group not officially sanctioned by the Roman Catholic church but made up of people who continue to name themselves Catholic. They embody one stream of Catholic theology to live as church, using Christian (and other) resources to nurture their faith, to shift power relations, and "to live in permanent rebellion against social injustice"—that is, to be church.[37]

Rituals can also be used for the recovery and preservation of "dangerous memories."[38] Knowing that there is more than one interpretation of past events, knowing that we are not the first to seek change, and re-membering ourselves through the integration of a usable past are strategies for change. This is supposed to be part of what Scripture reading does in Christian liturgy, but unfortunately the lectionary of weekly readings suggested by the church subjugates many of the dangerous memories. It leaves out stories of Mahlah and her sisters demanding of Moses that their father's land be left to them, since they had no brothers; it leaves out the sections of Acts where diversity and chaos are upheld, rather than unity and order, in the young church.

Another strategy of change through rituals is that of resistance, of making clear choices to do other than that which is expected or accepted. For example, one can refuse to participate in songs, hymns, meditations, or prayers that promote sexism, racism, or imperialism. Resistance also involves naming what is wrong in systems, being overt about that which is often hidden or ignored, and telling the truth about what is going on.

Resistance can also be expressed through the creation of rituals of protest. The call by the Canadian churches to have a day of prayer for peace after the 1991 Gulf War had begun was an act of resistance against the Canadian government's decision to enter the war. Other examples and ideas are found in chapter 13, "Resistance and Undermining."

---

37. Hunt, "Being Church Means Loving Well" (Event at Prarie Christian Training Centre, March 9–11, 1990).

38. This term is used by Sharon Welch in *Communities of Solidarity and Resistance* (Maryknoll, N.Y.: Orbis, 1985).

It is important to recognize that not all women will choose to act in the large structures of society. While it is hoped that all women will act toward justice, still electoral politics, lobbying, and revising the economic system may not be the spheres in which some women exert their energy. Ritual actions, raising children to be just and caring people, living in just ways in intimate and community relationships, and modeling different patterns and values are political actions to change patriarchal ideology. The choices of what spheres to devote energy to are important to honor. The constraints on women's lives—when they are disabled, when they are dealing with past traumas, when they are raising young children, and when they are doing the many other things expected of women in our society—mean that women need to make choices that will allow them to live with integrity and well-being.

A number of different options for actions have been presented here. They are intended to spark the imagination for action, rather than to limit. What is important are women's choices to act in concrete ways in every circumstance, to know our neighbors, to raise children to be caring people, to live as if justice exists, to be just in personal relationships, and to live in the community in ways that model the values of justice and well-being for women and all of creation.

Conclusion

WOMEN AS NAMERS AND SHAPERS OF THE COMMON GOOD

Theory in Feminist Theological/Thealogical Method

The focus of this project has been the question, How can and do religious rituals nurture and challenge feminists in their work for justice and well-being in the world? The question has been addressed through a process using a variety of women's experiences and participant observation of rituals, doing so in grounded feminist theological/thealogical method. This work has moved through the stages of the method, with the Introduction looking at why the subject is important. Part 1 provided definitions and characteristics of the component parts of the subject area. Part 2 named categories of feminist ritual thealogy arising from the data. Part 3 discussed tools for analysis and emerging understandings of the functions of ritual and symbols, forms of feminist spirituality, and patterns of leadership and structure. Part 4 focused on actions with criteria for theories, thealogies, actions, and rituals, ideas for women's arts and culture, and strategies for action. This final portion of the method draws together the data from the previous sections to gain theoretical insights into the fundamental question, How can and do religious rituals challenge and nurture feminists in their work for justice and well-being in the world?

As was noted in the Introduction in discussing methods, the theories developed through this feminist theological method are theories created in the active struggle toward the elimination of patriarchy and the implementation of feminist values for a world where justice and well-being for women exist. They are not value-neutral or made from spectator knowledge. Rather, they involve a holistic approach to women's life experience and a political agenda of increased justice and well-being for women. Theories emerging are to be substantive (i.e., must contribute to the knowledge base in a particular area), being specific enough to be grounded and general enough to be usable. Theories should be strong and integrated enough to withstand the questions for analysis by Bunch and Hartsock, as outlined in chapter 18, "Analysis," and should conform to the criteria listed in chapters 23 and 24. It was also noted that this feminist theological/thealogical method is ongoing—the theoretical insights presented here are not the final insights to be gained in this area. They are stepping-stones from some white Canadian and American women's experiences of rituals, faith, nurturance, and activism. The insights are an invitation to further study, conversation, and theories.

The primary areas of theoretical insight are in the quest for a non-sexist god/dess, in an emerging shape of justice, and in feminist ritual thealogy. After elaboration of these three areas, some analytical testing of the theories will be explored. Finally, I will return to the initial question—How can and do religious rituals challenge and nurture feminists in their work for justice and well-being in the world?

The Quest for a Nonsexist God/dess

We began with Nelle Morton's question, "What if we remove the sexism from God and there is nothing left?" and with the vision that God is not simply a patriarch or patriarchal construct. In the Introduction I said:

> I write with the hope that . . . the integration of women's experiences of the holy will help us to know something more of God than we currently know, and that knowing more of the holy will lead us to a sustainable world order where justice and peace create a kindom of well-being for all humanity and the world in which we live.

The voices of the women heard in this project have, I believe, contributed to broadening understandings of the holy and have named the holy in ways that are not dependent on sexism for their existence. This chapter looks at some of the insights about the holy that have emerged.

The first insight is that for women, God/goddess is concrete. The divine is not an abstract ideal or separate from our daily material existence. As Eleanor Haney said, the candles, the smells, the flowers "are not just metaphors. They're it." The earth, air, water, and fire are it. The holy is the natural cycle of birth-to-death-to-birth in human life and the natural world. God/dess is sunsets, being in touch with the ground, bread for a common meal, bridges across diversity, women's stories being told, loving relationships, yearnings, stones in the pocket as the presence of power, the passion to make and make again. God/dess is concrete and earthy.

Goddess/God is the concrete acts of justice, the challenges to systems that oppress or deny human rights, the improved material conditions of women, the quality of sufficiency. As quoted earlier, Carter Heyward claims, "For some feminists, god is the source of justice; for others, the maker of justice; for others, justice itself: god *is* justice." Or to use one of the examples from chapter 13, "Resistance and Undermining," god/dess is the least coin, given to improve the living conditions of the least woman in the eyes of society.

Feminists would say that a patriarchal god based in the power and material conditions of male rulership on earth and the head of a great patriarchal hierarchy is neither necessary nor helpful to women's spiritual needs. A god that embodies language and the shaping of reality in ways that reinforce sexism, racism, heterosexism, ageism, classism, able-bodyism, and militarism is a god created by patriarchy. A god that holds history and humanity over nature, dividing the world into dualisms, is no god at all. As one interviewee said, "I grew up on fall-redemption theology that strongly emphasized we are all sinners. It is only recently that I realized we are all blessings. I could not understand why, if God was so great, we were all sinners. This new understanding makes God a lot better." We need a better god/dess than the one created in the image of the patriarchs.

The god/dess described here is a diversity and invites diversity. The holy grows, changes, is organic, and is manifest in many ways. She invites bridging and connecting. What is different is not "other" but is related. God/dess is eyes that see and wisdom that knows contrast— the bread and roses, the trouble and beauty, the flowers in slaves' gardens, the alabaster oil poured on Jesus' head, the beauty and injustice.

So the holy is concrete—in the material conditions and "stuff" of our lives, in just systems and action, in blessings, and in diversity.

The holy is also in ourselves and in each other. The Scripture story of Jephthah's daughter makes clear that the God of Abraham and Isaac cannot be counted on to rescue women. The women have only each other and their mourning. They must be each other's god/dess, since the god of Abraham and Isaac does them no good. There are many daughters of Jephthah still here today—daughters of a legacy of needless deaths through physical and sexual violence, through poverty, and through devastation and devaluation. Still today, women have only each other and their mourning. Our hope is in women who have internal resources and whose silent strength is the will to survive. Our hope is in our survival and in our own inner wisdom, in our ability to trust ourselves and each other to know what is right and good and life-giving and sustaining. Our hope is in holding up the mirror to ourselves and saying, "Behold the goddess!" Our hope is in knowing that god/dess is in ourselves, in our longings for peace and wholeness and justice and joy. Our hope is that god/dess gets her identity from us and that we hear each other into speech. Our hope is that she loves to hear, and be, our voices as we are involved in conscious truth-telling about our lives and the lives of women in the world.

The nature of the holy is known in our nature and in our embodied selves. It is as our embodied selves that we participate in the divine. Our consciousness of ourselves, of others, of immanence, and of transcendence is through bodies and senses. In this way, we, as women, can know ourselves in the image of God or of many different goddesses. Our bodies show diversity of god/dess through the many sizes, shapes, colors, forms, and life stages our bodies take. Women know goddess through body cycles and our capacity for reproduction. Women know the holy through laughter that bubbles up from inside and lets us be ourselves, lets us be divine.

The nature and being of the divine is also in friendships—in relationships of mutuality, in care, in looking to the well-being of the other, in connectedness with others here and now and beyond time and space, in mutuality with nature, in just actions between people, and in intense conversations. In relationships of these kinds, we experience the holy in concrete ways.

So the holy is in ourselves and in relationships of mutuality and justice.

One of the strongest images of god/dess that comes from the women in this research is that god/dess is a survivor. It was noted in chapter 6, "Survival and Safety," that the holy is in "spiritual nurturance needed for healing and for becoming a healthy person who has survived an unhealthy situation." The world as we know it, under the ideology and practice of patriarchy, is unhealthy—and yet women have survived. Women have survived violence and violation, economic and material suffering, farm foreclosures, job losses, desertion, death of children, and a million other kinds of losses. It was noted already that survival and safety are the places many women can look to see the divine in themselves and to love her with tenacious tenderness. Has god/dess survived patriarchy in the same way as women have? Is god/dess also damaged and in need of healing but able to be named a survivor?

Can the crone be recovered as a positive image of the holy—as one who has survived through losses, one who knows loss as natural and inevitable and as part of the life cycle of the universe, one who is the bringer of death and destruction, one who grieves and rages freely, one who sees survival as a principle of moral action toward integrity, dignity, and security?

The identity of the holy is cyclic and transitory, according to the understandings of the women here. God/dess is the flower of the field, the meal prepared and shared in love, the stormy sky, the moment of communing laughter, the capacity to make and make again. The divine is transformer, transforming, adapting, and resilient to survive. In many ways it does not even matter what god/dess is like. There is playfulness in women's spirituality. Women dare to say that everything may not have ultimate significance. And if it does not really matter in some cosmic scheme of things, then we might as well live fully, laugh loudly, love deeply, create just and life-giving structures—because they and each other are enough.

Maureen's delightful image of God reflects these ideas of God as transitory, playful, and adaptive: "I love to watch 'Magnum PI,' 'Miss Marple,' and all of those shows. They are my role models. I think God is a detective, and I love the mystery! And I always am looking for the clues and trying to put the pieces together." Her way of naming God as the detective indicates that God is not the eternal, unchanging, omnipotent one. Rather, God, like humanity, is searching for the clues for meaning, loving the mystery, changing strategies as more pieces are discovered. As survivor and detective, god/dess is searching for healing from patriarchy—searching for ways to be a nonsexist god/dess, to be justice, to be within, to live relationally, to dwell amid trouble and beauty, to create sufficiency and well-being for all the world. The divine is searching for meaning in loss, looking for clues to a framework for naming and living fully into women's experiences. As detective,

> she calls us
> into chaos
> meets us
> in chaos.

She asks,

> are you frightened?
> are you free?

The image of divine that emerges from this study also indicates that the divine has needs. The divine, like women, needs to be heard into speech—allowed to speak in her own voice from her own wisdom within. The divine needs our care giving. As quoted earlier from Elizabeth Dodson Gray: "Male religion has always stated *from a child's point of view* its central image of God-the-Father as caregiver" and sees care only as receiving. She says no theology has been imaged and written by those who give care. What if god/dess were the receiver of care— if we were to know God in the care we give to the environment, the earth, and each other? At this point in history, it would mean that we have to be the healers of the holy. Distorted and damaged by patriarchy, the holy needs support and healing to be whole. Like us, the divine needs safety and hospitality for healing to occur and for her dreams to be fulfilled.

We can remove the sexism from God as we participate in her healing—and there will be something left. There will be something known in the concrete experiences of women's lives; something known in justice, in blessings, in diversity, in ourselves and each other; in knowing that the holy is in us and our decisions and truth-telling, in our bodies, in our relationships of justice and mutuality. We will know that there is no external rescuer but, rather, a survivor, a crone, a transitory and changing one, a detective in the mystery, one who, like us, needs to be heard, needs care, healing, and hospitality. We can remove the sexism from God/dess, and with our holy action there will be a sustainable world order where justice and peace create a kindom of well-being for all humanity and the world in which we live.

The Shape of Justice

As with feminist thealogy, so the shape of justice is just beginning to emerge. The feminist movement has appropriately focused much energy on analysis of patriarchy and on concrete actions to lessen the effects of or to eliminate patriarchy. Less time and energy have been focused on the long-term dreams of what a just and sustainable society would look like. This section weaves together some of the visions of the women interviewed in this project. It is called the shape of justice because it is a shape—it is not a platform of strategies to achieve an end to patriarchy and the creation of global justice in five years. It is, instead, some patterns and visions that call for small groups to gather and own and refine and re-create them, to mold them into workable plans for local actions toward justice and well-being. It is a shape, not a form or a product.

Some principles that lead toward justice have emerged from the research. First, women must be involved in naming and shaping of the common good. Second, justice must be expressed in concrete and specific terms, since oppression is known concretely and specifically. Third, justice means recognizing that everything has political implications. Fourth, questions of power must always be on the agenda. As already stated, the primary criterion in feminist analysis is not what a given action, policy, or decision will do for white, middle-class, educationally privileged women, but what it will do for the woman who has least and is struggling for survival economically, racially, educationally, and reproductively. Fifth, substantive justice involving transformation of social, political, economic, cultural, physical, and personal systems is the goal of feminism.

The content of the visions is rich and inviting. The elements of a just world, described by the women interviewed, are in six dimensions.

First, *social* changes are needed to shift from a world of patriarchal values and practices to one of justice and well-being. The foundation stones include understanding and respect, cooperation, and shared social power. Marginalized people would be valued as much as white middle-class heterosexual men. We would take notice of who speaks, who does not, and what power articulate people possess. We would recognize that all have special skills. Gardeners and farmers would be valued as much as doctors. There would be "no crime and lots of fat happy ladies." Life-supporting actions and speech would be the norm. Although there would be conflict, there would be respect for our social and spiritual environment. Interactions in families, friendships, and other relationships would be mutual and supportive. No one model of family relationships would be privileged. Various kinds of groupings and kin structures would be affirmed. People would choose whether or not to accept sexual monogamy in their mutual and primary relationships. There would be more emphasis on community and less on individualistic approaches. People would be able to make real choices in relationships. Children would be cared for and valued in the community.

In the *political* sphere, women's visions involve shared power and structures that value people and that let people and groups be self-determining, shaping their common future. Privilege and oppression would be eliminated. Actions and decisions would be based on the question, Is this good for our world? Questions would be asked about who gets to name what beauty is, who benefits from sexual and spiritual closeting for survival and safety, whose experience is held as central, who gains and loses in situations of vulnerability. Consistency and integrity would be seen as inherent in choices. Shared political power would mean that all are empowered, and there would be concrete world equality, reflective and responsible action, peace, and autonomy for all members of the human family of nations. People would be able to make choices about their own lives and not be overrun by some other government. Countries would assist each other for health, peace, and living conditions conducive to developing intellectual, artistic, and spiritual life. All would work together to preserve and enhance life and to bring safety, harmony, and peace. There would be more women leaders, including more women in Parliament and more women judges. Politics would be participatory.

Economics would be revised in major ways. All would have a place to live, ability to grow something, and food to eat. There would be no poverty, ignorance, disease, prejudice, or war; all would have constructive, enjoyable, and interesting employment, occupations, and pastimes. Multinationals would be eliminated. Small-scale economics would be valued, and there would be equal pay for work of equal value, elimination of the feminization of poverty, public-private dichotomies, violence, and individualism—including an end to economic dependence of women on men individually and collectively. We would question whether decisions are based in the concrete material conditions of women's lives, and which women, and how many; question what class analysis happens, and by whom, and whether people of differing classes interpret events differently and have equal power. Resources would be shared, giving similar resources and privileges to all. Attention would focus on the poor of the Third World, and there would be global concern. Farm land, agriculture, homemakers' pension plans, and housing would come ahead of military expenditures. Taxation would come from top incomes, not bottom, so that taxes such as the Goods and Services Tax would not be allowed to increase the feminization of poverty. Shared economic power would mean that people were not obsessed with money and would have much leisure. We would honor earth, air, and water.

Culturally, there would be diversity. All would learn from each other, and education would be structured differently. All races, genders, and age groups would be valued and honored; we would do a better job of living with difference. Creativity, imagination, and intuition would have larger roles in the ordering of society; difference would be valued as the source of enrichment, rather than as a basis of oppression. It would be a woman-affirming culture. We would always question what overt, and covert, structures and substructures say about sex, race, class, and power.

In the *physical* area, a just world would mean elimination of violence, fear of violence, and war; accessible health care and medical assistance; health and rejuvenation, little short of immortality.

Women's *personal* visions of justice involved a world with self-esteem for women, men in touch with feelings, respect for emotional environments, bliss for everyone, development of human potential, and acceptance of people.

Interestingly, none of the visions described by the women was based in self-fulfillment, in gaining personal power, or in one group's having power at the expense of others. Instead, the interviewees talked about the elimination of social, economic, military, and other patriarchal problems, and about living in a world of valued individuals, healthy and diverse relationships, economic and environmental sustainability, equality for all, and shared decision-making and power.

These various aspects of a vision of justice can be combined in the development of concrete policy plans for the creation of just social, political, economic, cultural, physical, and personal systems and relationships. They are the shape to be molded into forms of beauty, integrity, sustainability, sufficiency, and hope.

Feminist Ritual Thealogy

What is feminist ritual thealogy? First and foremost, it is a way to describe women's experience of the holy through ritual. It brings together ways of talking about spirituality, ways of describing what is true and real and meaningful in women's lives, and visions for justice that women have. It looks at ordinary human experiences—walks in nature, conversations with cats, making and eating meals with friends, birth, menstrual cycles, changing cycles of bodies, menopause, double workdays, economic needs, ordinary days, and life that opens and closes like an accordion—and creates rituals from the sacred in them. It creates rituals that invite deepening of experiences and allows for experiences not attainable just from facts. Feminist ritual thealogy links the personal and political and can take one beyond oneself in an experience of grace. It can be a change-agent with ethical implications and can provide a symbolic center to return to for support and comfort after the ceremony has ended.

In chapter 2 above I quoted Chris Smith as saying, "Our spiritual lives are in desperate need of rituals that weave the political and the religious together as one fabric. It is important that we give a new name to spiritual praxis." I believe that one of the "new names" that we can give to our spiritual praxis is feminist ritual thealogy. This study has shown how women weave the political and religious together—how they say: "I do not want political action and spirituality to be separate"; "Our politics and spirituality are one"; or:

> Whenever I am engaged in groups that are trying to empower one another and to be freed from things that oppress us, it feels like I am working toward the vision. Whenever we are taking each other's experience seriously and hearing one another, it feels like some healing is going on and that there is some movement toward wholeness. Whenever people are allowed to speak the truth that may have been dangerous in their settings, that is a move toward wholeness and health.

Feminist ritual thealogy attempts to bring together spirituality, politics, and feminism. It attempts to place the kind of thealogical insights about god/dess and visions of justice named in the sections above into the context of ritual.

At this point in time, feminist ritual thealogy is based in inarticulate yearnings. It has no words or concepts from patriarchal religions or reasoning to give it validity. To use Esther Broner's words, "There's no cartography. These ceremonies we make for the first time. We're snow angels—we make our own marks."[1] It is emerging, partly because as feminists, we cannot tolerate a ritual void. We need to replace the deadening rituals of patriarchy with positive, life-giving, woman-affirming rituals.

Feminist ritual thealogy is developing in the kind of personal rituals described—driving, swimming, praying, reflection, Scripture reading, tarot reading, peeling carrots, baking, gardening, and bathing. It is developing in activities "to be in touch with the ground, to have time alone . . . to integrate, to think through experiences and get ready for more." It is developing in group meditations to center, to see beauty within, to find identity and voice, to gain shared visions in community, to receive healing through trust and openness, to gain strength for resistance, to see choices where vulnerability would lead to new growth, and to learn to trust one's own inner wisdom. It is developing in resistance and proactive moves, joining in marches and rallies, lobbies, letter writing, and economic cooperation. It is developing in rituals for seasons, in communities, and in kin relationship groups. Feminist ritual thealogy is whatever helps us in our human longing for connection with the universe, with one another, and with the earth and in our longing to be at peace and have integrity within ourselves.

There are beginnings of frameworks and insights of what might be a feminist ritual thealogy emerging from this project, but they are only beginnings.

The frameworks for feminist ritual thealogy grow out of the key principles articulated by the women interviewed. First, all feminist thealogy must be biased toward inclusion of female experience in any theological/thealogical endeavor and must support actions toward justice, mutuality, and well-being of women in the world. As was stated, rituals can be models of justice and can strengthen and seal the vision toward justice in women's lives. Second, as noted in chapter 20, "Symbols," one of the functions of feminist spirituality is to break patriarchal control of symbol systems so that women can be namers and shapers of well-being in the world. Feminist rituals are based in the shaping of new symbol systems. Third, rituals allow women to stay clear, or centered, in themselves, in political activism, and in work; rituals can provide release so one can act in appropriate ways. Rituals

---

1. Esther Broner, "Half the Kingdom" (National Film Board of Canada video on Jewish feminism).

provide for the well-being and integration of individual women; as one woman put it, "I think spirituality is being me, my whole being, who I am."

Fourth, rituals must be real. They must be grounded in the concrete experiences of women's lives. They must speak to women's real experiences and must allow for the despair and joy that women face. They must address violence and violation; they must acknowledge the many different relationship configurations that exist; they must challenge racism, ageism, able-bodyism; they must engage the whole being. Rituals must be open to insights beyond the scope of the limited experience of one group and must engage with those whose lives are very different from our own. Fifth, feminist ritual thealogy breaks down hierarchy, allows participants to interpret images and moods, and evokes new understandings and depth and relationships through music, dance, poetry, story, and myth. Finally, feminist ritual thealogy challenges us as women to work together as biblical feminists and goddess/wicca feminists, with freedom, integrity, and hope, reminding ourselves that the goal is justice and well-being for women and that our diversity of beliefs can enrich our ethical practice toward justice and well-being.

The content of feminist ritual thealogy has already been detailed in part 3. Out of this particular research, the categories that emerged were beauty, survival and safety, embodiment, naming of self and experience, community and relationships, diversity, healing, play and humor, resistance and undermining, vulnerability, loss, vision, and trusting our own inner wisdom. In new groups, other content of feminist ritual thealogy might arise, and other ways of naming categories might emerge.

Along with these specific contents, we can list here a few other significant points about the content of feminist ritual thealogy.

First, feminist ritual thealogy is both historical and utopian. Earlier, it was pointed out that neopaganism is based on utopian vision, while Christian tradition is based in history. A spirituality that reaches across boundaries incorporates both of these elements into its rituals and thealogy. Feminist ritual thealogy is historical in that it is bound up with the ordinary and concrete material conditions of women's lives and grows out of the condition of the oppression of women in a patriarchal society. Feminist ritual thealogy is utopian in that it invents and works toward a vision of a just, peaceful, sustainable society for all humanity and the world.

Second, feminist ritual thealogy is collective. It is created in communities committed to the well-being of women through the integration of spirituality, politics, and feminism into dynamic forms. It is created through rituals and through embodiment of feminist values in community.

Third, because feminist ritual thealogy is prowoman, sometimes it chooses strategies of affirmative action. One example mentioned earlier was creation of the symbolic role of crone, to show value of and respect for older women and to allow older women to entertain with skits, story-telling, and outrageous acts in order to pass on wisdom and love of living radically in the groups' rituals.

Fourth, feminist ritual thealogy does not place history and nature in opposition but, rather, sees the connection between them as essential. The grounded conditions of our existence on this fragile planet mean that we must take care of the earth if we are to survive, if we are to have any history in the future. Thus, feminist ritual thealogy is based in symbols to connect us to the world around us—the moon, trees, sunsets, rocks, oceans, wide prairie horizons, and delicate spider's webs.

Feminist ritual thealogy matters because it is an articulation of women's spiritual experiences. It matters because it is a beginning for an ideological framework other than that of patriarchy. It matters because it demands improved material conditions for women whose lives are full of suffering, calling for justice and well-being so that women can be nurtured and challenged in the sacred dimensions of their ordinary days. It matters because our lives are rooted in transformation.

Testing the Theories

The feminist theological method used in this project requires that the theories developed be able to stand up to testing. One process for testing the theories is to examine them in light of Bunch and Hartsock's questions posed in chapter 18, "Analysis."

The first question is, "How will it affect women's sense of self, and sense of our own collective power?" or "Does it build an individual's sense of self-respect, strength, and self-confidence?" I believe that women's sense of self and self-esteem is strengthened when we see god/dess in ourselves and can therefore trust our inner wisdom and our capacity for just relations. Our sense of self is also increased when we know ourselves, as women, to be embodiments of god/dess. Women's self-confidence is strengthened when we name god/dess as survivor of patriarchy and all of its destructive forces. Our self-esteem is increased as we see god/dess as one who wants us in mutuality and relationship and who needs our help in her healing. The idea of the shape of justice also focuses on increased self-esteem, respect, and acceptance and on the development of human potential as part of the content of a just world. The insistence of feminist ritual thealogy on rituals addressing the realities of women's lives lets women be affirmed in themselves and confirmed in their perceptions of what is happening to them and around them. Feminist ritual thealogy is based in the ordinary—and so women's self-esteem is enhanced because their spirituality is respected and is not seen as lesser for being concrete and ordinary, instead of being based in an unattainable piety, idealism, or dualism. The validation of diversity means that women can know the holy in conversations with their cats, in Christian worship and prayer, and in dancing goddess circles. It lets women be themselves—a critical component of self-esteem and self-confidence.

The next of Bunch's and Hartsock's questions is, "Does this reform materially improve the lives of women, and if so, which women, and how many?" Because god/dess is understood as justice in concrete forms, the question of improvements in the material conditions of women's lives is always present as a primary theological/thealogical question. It means that improvements are always tested by checking them for ways in which they might be sexist, racist, heterosexist, classist, ageist, pro-able-bodied people, or imperialist in their content or form. If domination of any is going to be increased or reinforced, then it is not in the interests of any women or of god/dess as justice. The understanding of god/dess as diversity requires respect for difference, but difference in ways that embody mutuality rather than domination. Substantive justice improves the living conditions of women who are experiencing suffering of any kind. It requires economic and political change and an end to violence. Justice replaces capitalist patriarchy with shared resources, power, and decision-making as well as with freedom from fear of violence. It asks questions about the politics and power relationships of everything. Feminist ritual thealogy also acts as a change-agent toward justice by exposing injustices, by connecting the personal and political, by grounding rituals in the real-life experiences of women, and by providing safety, beauty, and diversity.

The third of the questions for Bunch and Hartsock is, "How will it make women aware of problems beyond questions of identity—that is, how will it politicize women?" or "Does it educate women politically, enhancing their ability to criticize and challenge the system in the future?" According to the theoretical understandings, god/dess is understood as concrete and historical or, in other words, is changeable in ways that have political consequence. Earlier, Catherine Madsen pointed out that the biblical story of Jacob wrestling with the angel is important for women because it shows that women can argue with God and win. It means we do not have to accept a god who reinforces patriarchy but that we can push for god to change and to grow to deeper comprehension and compassion. These understandings of god/dess also encourage women to trust in their inner wisdom and to accept the fact that women know more than external authorities give them credit for. The Edison School example shows that when women become politically involved, they discover that they know more than the male politicians they encounter because of the many different worlds they inhabit. Women are politicized by knowing that god/dess is within and that they can trust their inner knowledge. Visioning what can be is also a political act. Utopian visions normally grow out of what currently exists and out of the hope for changes in the current social order.

The visions of justice presented here focus on tax reforms and pensions for women because these are inadequate in the present systems of politics and economics. The principles for justice also note that women need to recognize that everything has political implications and that power relations must always be questioned. Feminist ritual thealogy links spirituality, politics, justice, and well-being and designs intentional rituals for change. Most important, feminist ritual thealogy gives critique and creates symbol systems and ideological underpinnings of decisions, symbols, religious practice, and politics. Thus, it politicizes women.

Bunch and Hartsock then ask, "Does it give women a sense of power, strength, and imagination as a group and help build structures for further change?" and "How will the strategy work to build organizations that will increase both our strength and competence, and will it give women power to use (like money) to weaken the control and domination of capitalism, patriarchy, and white supremacy?" One of the thealogical insights, important in response to this question, is that god/dess is not omnipotent. God/dess is transitory and changing, not above it all and controlling everything. This fact greatly weakens the power of patriarchy because it breaks the pyramid of power, the chain of command in which white, heterosexual, educationally privileged men are closer to god than poor, Native, or lesbian women. Patriarchy is also challenged by the diversity of images of god/dess that feminist thealogy evokes, including feminine forms and manifestations of the deity.

Another threat to capitalism, patriarchy, and white supremacy is the realization that there will be no rescuer. What happens depends on us. This knowledge encourages women to join in collective, reflective, and responsible action instead of exercising only passive obedience or waiting for a knight in white armor or other superhuman rescuer. God/dess is the detective looking for clues to the mystery of justice and wholeness, just as we are. The visions of justice proposed by the women in this project involved an end to hierarchies and articulated the idea that all involved in life-affecting decisions should be part of the decision-making and of the naming and shaping of the common good. The women held visions of affirmations for the many kinds of mutual relationship and family configurations that exist, and might exist, instead of the one, privileged nuclear family of capitalist patriarchy. Global well-being, with shared resources and sufficiency, not militarism and profit, also is a vision contrary to patriarchy, capitalism, and white supremacy. Feminist ritual thealogy names its political agenda as justice and well-being for women. It eliminates hierarchy, names women's truths and experiences, envisions options, allows for personal and social healing, and discovers resources to deal with vulnerability and loss, so that change is not so scary.

The final question posed by Hartsock and Bunch is, "How will the strategy weaken the links between these institutions?" First, images of god/dess as cyclic and organic weaken the links between these pillars of Western society. Seeing life as whole and organic means that personal and public, spirituality and politics, history and nature, and black and white are not separate entities that need to compete or be in layers. Seeing god/dess in terms of mutuality, rather than superiority, weakens the links, as does seeing god/dess in need of our care. Capitalism, patriarchy, and white supremacy are all overturned by the concept of mutuality—to give care as well as receive care, to be healers and givers rather than abusers and only receivers. Justice also destroys the links between these powers by eliminating violence, seeking small economic and social structures rather than monostructures and multinationals, giving reproductive freedom to women, having women leaders, and valuing all people equally. The shape of justice in this new creation is substantive justice, not the procedural justice currently used to protect men and property. Feminist ritual thealogy contributes to the breaking down of the links between capitalism, patriarchy, and white supremacy by creating safe space for women to meet, hear each other, and discover the links. It encourages communities of diversity and justice-seeking friends. It invites bringing chaos out of order and welcomes laughing, playing, and creating. Feminist ritual thealogy uncovers the history of the three institutions and the history of women's resistance. It blossoms with options and alternative ways of being in the world.

Testing the theoretical insights developed with the tools offered in chapter 18, "Analysis," reveals that the quest for a nonsexist god/dess, the visions of justice, and feminist ritual thealogy can contribute to justice and well-being in the world. These understandings and visions for action can contribute to the elimination of patriarchy and the creation of a humane society. They can lead toward a feminist culture where women are central autonomous moral and religious agents, with sufficient material goods for well-being. They give women involvement in naming and shaping the common good and in creating new symbol systems, ideologies, and structures. They can give visions and understandings of a nonsexist deity.

How Can and Do Religious Rituals Challenge and Nurture Feminists in Their Work for Justice and Well-Being in the World?

In the words of women in the project:

> The rituals keep me on the path. They confirm my sense of self and my self-worth. Through spirituality and ritual, I am able to stay connected. There is validation. They center me. They keep me sane.

> Making justice is my lifework. . . . My spirituality helps me have a sense of how the world should be and empowers me to work toward that. Sometimes rituals give a glimpse of how the world could and should be.

> Ritual is connecting with the deepest part of ourselves and cuts us to the core. Rituals give groundedness in our core—which I perceive to be connected to God. And once we've caught that vision, we are changed. Ritual also creates community. It breaks down the barriers and lets people experience the holy. It is transpersonal—like an everflowing stream. We cannot connect with it without being changed. It is a birthing.

Feminist ritual does create the possible. It lets women know that beauty, safety, embodiment, naming ourselves and our experiences, our losses and our visions, our vulnerabilities and our diversities is divine work in a grounded politic of justice and well-being. It lets us know that the holy is in our communities, our healing, our resistance and undermining, our inner wisdom.

How can and do religious rituals challenge and nurture feminists in our work for justice and well-being in the world? Rituals do this by taking women's experience seriously and creating new insights into the holy. They do it by evoking new thealogical categories and understandings that fit for feminist women and that invite ongoing critique and formulation. They do this by setting new agendas for substantive justice to create a more peaceful, mutual, sustainable, and sufficient future, one that allows all affected to participate in naming and shaping of the common good. Feminist ritual thealogy calls for transforming political spiritualities that can be acted out in feminist communities. It interweaves the personal, the political, justice, well-being, nurture, challenge, wholeness, and holiness into a new creation.

How can and do religious rituals challenge and nurture feminists in their work for justice and well-being in the world? Safely, with love and tenderness and healing for ourselves, each other, and the whole of creation.

Appendix

Data Collection

The following nine questions were the basis of the interviews conducted with the thirty-six women of this study.

1. Statistical information about the respondent:
   a. name
   b. age range: 20–30, 30–45, 45–60, over 60
   c. single   committed relationship
   d. citizenship
   e. What kind of background, understanding of, or involvement do you have with the women's movement?
2. How would you describe your spirituality at this point in your life?
3. What kind of rituals do you participate in? (individual and group)
4. Are rituals important to you? Why or why not?
5. Have there been changes over the years in the rituals you do/ value?
6. Does it matter to you that you are a woman, as you do rituals?
7. What kinds of political work (formal and informal) do you do toward justice in the world?
8. Do you make connections between your work for justice and your religious rituals?
9. How do your religious rituals affect your sense of personal well-being?

Because the theoretical base of qualitative method encourages the accumulation of sufficient data for saturation, the questions can be varied to follow up on an area raised by the interviewee or to elicit more data from a less-talkative interviewee. This means that along with the basic questions, other questions specifically tailored to the person being interviewed may have been asked in the interview.

STUDY GUIDE

Introduction

This Study Guide has been prepared to be used by women who are coming together, seeking alternative material for study and ritual. Its goal is to provide study material for groups who are struggling with what their theological/thealogical understandings are and for feminists who are seeking a nonsexist god/dess. A major assumption in this project is that all women should be able to be involved in the naming and shaping of the common good. Thus, participation in the work to understand feminist ritual thealogy is ongoing. As women come together to enter into discussion of feminist ritual thealogy, it will develop and change to fit those women who are engaged in the study. This Study Guide invites that kind of interaction with the work. Such engagement is also a form of politicization. As women name their experience and its impact in community, they can be empowered toward solidarity in the feminist agenda of social change toward justice and well-being for women.

The three purposes, then, for this Study Guide are (1) to encourage thoughtful use of this book and discussion of its contents, (2) to bring groups together for study and experiences of feminist ritual thealogy, and (3) to increase politicization of women toward change in the world.

The Study Guide is set up simply and is based on the assumption that groups of feminists who are gathering to work through this project have some expertise in the area of small-group interaction and process.[1] Groups of five to eight people would work most easily. Option 1 is for groups who want to do their own work.

---

1. For women unfamiliar with group theory, some useful resources for understanding how to work in small groups effectively are Women's Self-Help Network, *Working Together for Change: Women's Self-Help Handbook,* vol. 1 (Ptarmigan Press, 1372 Island Highway, Campbell River, BC V9W 2E1); *A Board/Staff Handbook for Women's Organizations,* "Leadership" and "Program Planning" units (available from Saskatchewan

For Option 2 a program design is set for various parts of the book, consisting of discussion questions, exercises, and rituals to help participants use the material and relate it to their own lives. The sessions vary—some focus more on engagement in the rituals, others on intellectual discussion of meaning, others on exercises to engage women in their own experience. Many of the sessions have a list of questions, some (or all) of which could be used, depending on the size, interest, and time-frame of the group. The sessions are designed to last an hour or an hour and a half but could take longer, depending on how many women are in the group, how talkative members are, and how deeply they choose to share. Each group could adapt the material to suit its own inclinations around their differing priorities. Option 2 is based on the assumption that people would have read the relevant section of the book before attending the group session to work on the subject.

Option 1

Spend some time going through the section of the Introduction entitled "One Feminist Theological/Thealogical Method" and discussing points from it. The book is based on the method, and it is a method that can easily be used to gain new theological/thealogical insight. I have used it in short feminist gatherings and workshops, in semester-long academic courses, and in research projects. One way for a group to use this book would be to study the method together, interview each other using the interview questions outlined in the Appendix, and then work through the method, step by step, using the interview data as the beginning point for your own feminist ritual thealogy.

Option 2—Program Sessions

Session 1—"Introduction: Motives and Methods"

Goal: to provide an opportunity for the group members to get to know each other and to make commitments to the study project.

Although this session focuses on the "Context" and "Limits" sections of the Introduction, it will be helpful to read the whole of the Introduction to understand the context and method of the work.

Activities:
1. Go around the circle, with each woman giving her name, three descriptions of herself, and what the descriptors mean to her. (E.g., I

Women's Resources, 2398 Scarth St., Regina); David Johnson and Frank Johnson, *Joining Together: Group Theory and Group Skills* (Englewood Cliffs, N.J.: Prentice-Hall, 1975).

described myself in the Introduction as a person of faith, a feminist, and a Canadian.)

2. A second round could ask, Why does faith or spirituality matter to you? or Why are you interested in feminist ritual thealogy?

3. Spend some time discussing what you want from the group and what kinds of commitments you are willing to make to be part of the group.

4. Do another round focusing on the questions, What informs your priorities for action at this point in your life? and What limits are you aware of in your understandings?

Closing ritual: A simple closing ritual would be a final round in which each person, one at a time, turns to the one next to her, saying, "I am [Name], and I give you my hand," until the circle is complete with everyone holding hands. Conclude with a blessing such as, "Our hands reach out and touch in hope. May our burdens be lightened and our joys made abundant by our sharing, and may our spirits yearn for more until we meet again."

Session 2—Chapter 1, "Defining the Problem as Patriarchy"

Goal: to connect personal experiences of patriarchy as a problem to the experience of other women and to the political environment.

Discussion questions:

1. How have you been affected by patriarchy personally—in your work, your relationships, your community?

2. How does your experience relate to the experiences of five women in chapter 1: *(a)* the woman on social assistance, *(b)* the women without pensions, *(c)* the farm women, *(d)* the physiotherapy aide, and *(e)* the woman with husband and children?

3. What are the relationships of patriarchy, classism, racism, and heterosexism in your community?

4. Talk about the ways patriarchy is used to keep women "in their place" (several are mentioned). What laws are used to keep capitalist patriarchy in place, at the expense of women? If you could change one law, what would it be? How might you go about that change?

Closing ritual: Use the ritual "Rite of Mind-Cleansing from the Pollution of Sexism" on pages 133–34 of *Women-Church*, by Rosemary Radford Ruether. Or do a simple ritual where each woman names the evils and powers of patriarchy that she wants to be rid of, then extinguishes a candle, as the group says together, "Powers of patriarchy, be gone!" When everyone has extinguished a candle, each person turns around in a circle to claim the turning around of the powers of evil into powers of good. Each woman can then relight a candle, saying one of her hopes for change toward justice and well-being for women. Close with a blessing such as, "Go with courage to work toward justice and peace."

Session 3—Chapter 2, "Feminism"

Goal: to explore different understandings and definitions of feminism.

Discussion questions:
1. Describe your coming to feminist consciousness and what feminism has meant and now means to you.
2. What does the phrase "the personal is political" mean to you?
3. Do you like the idea of a nonaligned feminism, or does adhering to a particular stream of feminist understanding have more appeal for you?
4. What does feminist spirituality mean to you? What is your experience in this area?
5. How would you define or describe feminism?

Closing ritual:
1. With some quiet background music, take time, individually, to write a Haiku poem from your definition or description of feminism. Haiku is a form of Japanese poetry with seventeen syllables—five in the first line, seven in the second, and five in the third. It picks up moods and impressions more than making concrete statements.
2. Take a few minutes to go around the circle, each saying her name and briefly how she is feeling at this point. Be silent for a moment, and then share the Haiku poems. Close by repeating one of the Haiku as a blessing or by listening to or singing a feminist song.

Session 4—Chapter 3, "Justice"

Goal: to explore one's own values in relation to justice and to create opportunity for commitment to justice.

Activities:
1. Each person is given a sheet of paper. On it, draw one large circle with a smaller circle inside it. The center of the inside circle will represent your core beliefs and values. The outer circle will represent "the pale." A pale is a pointed stake used in making an enclosure, with several such posts making up the fence of an enclosure, often

the enclosure that fortified a village against the enemy. So the line— the pale—of the outer circle will allow you to place things within the pale or beyond the pale. Things inside the pale are ones that you value, or could live with. Things beyond the pale are things you do not approve of, or that are outside your value system.

2. One member should read the following list of items, with all members individually placing them inside or beyond the pale: capital punishment, in-vitro fertilization for wealthy couples, adult-only retirement communities, sadomasochistic sex between consenting adults, abortion in the first trimester, bringing Romanian children for adoption in North America, refusing anesthetic at childbirth, banning books that question whether or not the Holocaust happened, lesbian-only communities, abortion in the third trimester, strenuous outdoor activities that involve challenge and risk, euthanasia, whites-only communities, in-vitro fertilization for welfare couples, sending Canadian Native children to the United States to be adopted there, banning books on home abortions, having men at a feminist event.

3. Work alone for a few minutes to think about the beliefs, values, and convictions that contributed to your decisions about where to place each of the situations. Place some words about the values and convictions and beliefs that went into your placement of the situations inside the smaller circle in the center of the larger circle.

4. Move into pairs and share where you placed each of the situations. Have any placements changed recently? What has influenced that change? Out of this reflection, is there anything that you want to change in the values, convictions, beliefs circle?

5. Identify a situation in which you chose to tolerate injustice for the sake of preserving community. Identify another situation in which you chose to challenge injustice, knowing that in doing so, you risked splitting the community.

What values were you seeking to honor in each? Which values were compromised? With whom were you seeking to stand? To whom did you hold yourself accountable? How do these connect with the values in the center of your pale? [2]

Closing ritual: Use "Women Crossing Worlds: In Solidarity and Friendship," from *Water Wheel* 2, no. 4 (Winter 1989–90). Or have enough candles for each person to light three in this ceremony. On the first round, each woman can light a candle, naming people from the past who have worked toward justice for women. When everyone

2. This program design, called "Beyond the Pale," was designed by Dorothea Hudec and Ann Naylor for use at "Embracing Diversity: Overcoming Sameness" (Saskatchewan Christian Feminist Network event at PCTC, November 8–12, 1990).

has lit one candle, the group can say together, "We celebrate these heros/heras from the past."

On the second round, each woman can light a candle, naming a person or group of people who are working for justice for women today. When the second round is completed, everyone can say, "We celebrate these heros/heras of the present."

The third round involves lighting a candle and expressing a hope for someone in the future to work for justice in a particular area or as a sign of the beginning of new projects for justice for women. When all of the candles are lit, the group can say, "We celebrate these heros/heras of the future."

Session 5—Chapter 4, "Rituals," and Chapter 24, "Criteria for Feminist Rituals"

Goal: to become familiar with theories about rituals and to share experiences that reflect the theory.

Discussion questions:
1. Describe a meaningful worship/ritual experience in your life. Which qualities of ritual does it connect with in the two chapters read?
2. What feelings and moods are evoked as you listen to others describe rituals that are meaningful to them?
3. From your perspective, what are the similarities and differences between feminist rituals and other forms of religious rituals?
4. How do rituals connect with your daily life and work?
5. How do the rituals you do embody justice?
6. Which of the criteria for rituals are important to you? How do these get lived out in your group?

Closing ritual: In many cultures masks are worn for the performance of rituals. Often the mask allows the individual to became a persona and to move from the sphere of ordinary life to the realm of mystery. The qualities of rituals—exaggeration, framing, condensation of meaning—allow the mask to bring out a quality or characteristic that might ordinarily go unnoticed.

Take time to create ritual masks from paper, cloth, ribbons, feathers, sequins, paints, and other decorative materials. In the ritual, embody the quality that you want your mask to represent by having each woman in turn put on her mask and name herself or her quality through drama and action (e.g., "I am Peacock—proud and beautiful" as she struts around the circle). Conclude with everyone joining in a parade with singing and dancing or with a tape such as Cris

Williamson's "Song of the Soul" (on *The Changer and the Changed*) or Susan Savell's "Wild Horses" (on *Recovering Joy*).

Session 6— Part 2, "New Names for Theology/Thealogy"

Goal: to enable each participant to enter into the feminist thealogical categories in a holistic way.

Activities:

1. Before the group session, read all of part 2. Pick two of the categories that are meaningful to you. Journal about them and about how you have known the holy in that way. Put one of the categories into an art form to share with your group—a picture, a story, a song, a poem, or a dance. Create a ritual with the other one.

2. In the group, have check-in time, with everyone saying a bit about where they are at and what the exercise was like for them.

3. Share the art creations with the group.

4. Talk about the rituals and choose one that seems good to do together as the ritual for the evening. Then do it.

Session 7—Chapter 18, "Analysis"

Goal: to become aware of community issues that affect women's lives and to practice skills of social analysis.

Activities:

1. On a large sheet of mural paper draw a circle. Inside it place things that the participants do during the day. (Have them call out while someone draws or writes the various things into the circle—e.g., eats breakfast, drives to work, does children's laundry, shops for groceries, teaches a class.) Choose three or four of the activities from inside the circle, and outside the circle write or draw who benefits from those activities—use red for self, green for family or community, purple for corporate power. Push at this; go beyond the initial responses. (E.g., from the activity of driving the kids to school there are benefits to the family through assisting children to get their education, to the community through providing care for children, and to the service station owner by buying gas for your car.) Talk about the connections between the three colors and between your lives and the lives of others in the community and world shown through the mural.[3]

---

3. Based on "Everyday Economics" exercise in Joan Kuyek, *Managing the Household* (United Church of Canada, Division of Mission in Canada, 1989).

2. Pick one issue that has arisen in the discussion (either one worked on or one from the initial list) that you would like to see changed. Name five specific and concrete strategies that would help to bring about change.

3. Look at the questions posed by Bunch and Hartsock to see how your strategies measure against their tools of analysis.

Closing ritual: Have symbols of the four directions, one in each corner of the room: east (air—feathers, mobile; new beginnings), south (fire—candles, sun mandalas; warmth, sensuousness), west (water—bowls of water; source of all life), and north (earth—stones, earth, salt; groundedness and strength).

Acknowledge the four directions by turning to each one and welcoming its powers.

If women feel safe and comfortable with the symbolic action of binding, then bind each woman's hands with fine red thread. Call out loud together three times, "What is it that binds you?" and give time for the women to respond with those things that come to mind.

Then call out aloud, "Where must you go to be free?" repeating it as women go and stand in the corner of the room that represents freedom for her. When everyone has chosen a direction and moved to the corners, raise power by howling, gathering energy, or chanting (e.g., "Where must you go to be free?" repeated over and over). When the energy is high, break the bonds and be free.

When everyone is free, turn to each direction and say, "Women of the east are free"; "Women of the south (west, north) are free." All turn to the center at the end and say, "Our bonds are broken. We are free."[4]

Session 8—Chapter 19, "Functions of Rituals"

Goal: to identify some of the functions of rituals in our society and individual lives.

Discussion questions:
1. What functions, or roles, do rituals play in your life? How do these connect with, or differ from, those presented in chapter 19?

2. Share some rituals that you do that are similar to those outlined by Sarah—that is, personal rituals, seasonal rituals, community rituals, family/kin rituals. Are there any you would like to change or add to the ones you currently do?

---

4. This ritual is adapted from The Ritual Book of the Feminist Spiritual Community.

3. What kind of ritual would honor the ordinary in your life? What kind would be transformative?

4. What kinds of rituals have you been part of that were intended to undermine patriarchy? What kinds would you like to be involved in? Talk about what kind of political resistance you do. What actions are needed in your local community and in your country that require resistance? Talk about ways of breaking patterns in relationships and in public spheres. Choose one pattern that you want to break or one policy that you want to undermine.

5. Take time in the group to write one letter each to someone (your member of Parliament, your mayor, your school board, your church board, a local business, a multinational corporation), registering your concern about the particular policy or program that you want to see changed.

Closing ritual: Use a seasonal ritual from your tradition if there is one appropriate for the time of the year.

Or use a ritual of acting together. Sit back-to-back with someone, with as much of your backs touching as possible. Visualize breathing into your partner's back and receiving breath from your partner, giving and receiving in turn. After some time of doing this, change partners and face the new partner. Get in touch with your breath. As one person breathes out, the other person consciously breathes in. Reverse. Be conscious of the energy given and received.[5] Change partners again, and this time touch fingertips. First, one person can engage in a series of actions with the other person mirroring them, and then reverse roles. Again, be in touch with the energy. Conclude with a time of silence in a circle, holding hands, or with a blessing such as, "We have the power and energy to act together! May we do it wisely!"

Session 9—Chapter 20, "Symbols"

Goal: to examine overt and covert messages of symbols.

Activities:

1. Everyone should bring a simple symbol of feminist culture or spirituality, wrapped up to be given as a gift in the ritual.

2. Talk about the meaning of symbols and about symbols that are or have been important in your life.

3. Choose two rituals, using anything from a church bulletin, to a wedding service, to a national memorial such as Remembrance Day,

---

5. From Lyon, *Dance toward Wholeness*, p. 20.

to a family ritual celebration. Take time to look at the detail of the rituals, their symbols, and what they say in and behind the words (by action, innuendo, omission, or symbols) about sex, race, class, hierarchy, sexual orientation, and disability.

4. Take a few minutes to reflect on that exercise, sharing how you felt about it and what you learned from it.

5. Spend some time talking about symbols for transitions in women's lives. Then talk about the symbol of the crone, look at some rituals for croning, and think about what you would like to see in croning rituals. Two samples are given here. Others are in Rosemary Radford Ruether, *Women-Church*; Edna Ward, ed., *Celebrating Ourselves: A Crone Ritual Book*; and Barbara Walker, *Women's Rituals*.

A. A Ritual to Honor Carol on Her Fiftieth Birthday
December 14, 1990

The beginning: why we are here
Carol no. 1: Carol's Circle (Tune: Sarah's Circle)
>   Come now, join us, cast the circle (3x) . . . sisters all around.
>   All together, form a circle (3x) . . . sisters all around.
>   We are casting Carol's circle (3x) . . . sisters all around.

Crone-ological context:
The who, what, where, when, why of becoming a crone—Barb
Ringing in the years—Susan

The lighting of the three candles:
white, red, and black—Carol

Carol no. 2: Here We Are A-Croning
>   (Tune: Here We Come A-Caroling)

>   Here we are a-Caroling
>   Among the days so dark;
>   Here we are a-croning
>   To bless a new crone's start.

>   Chorus: Strength and wisdom to you,
>   And to you some humor, too
>   As you journey towards
>   Your amazing sagehood,
>   As you dance into raging sagehood.

>   Here we go a-Caroling,
>   Three wicks glow with their light;
>   Here we are a-croning,
>   The bells peal out with might.

>   Composed by Vicki and Susan,
>   with thanks to Mary Daly

Story-telling and appreciations:
an opportunity for everyone to share stories and appreciations of
   Carol

The croning: Ev and Lil and other crone friends

Giving of good wishes and symbols:
an opportunity for those in presentia and those in absentia to share
   their good wishes and/or symbols with Carol
an opportunity for Carol to respond

Carol no. 3: Women Let's Celebrate
               (Tune: Come Let Us Sing)

> Women, let's celebrate Carol's cronehood,
> She's come of age,
> This wonderful sage,
> Into the cackling band of crones;
> Carol leaps, bravely outrageous.
>
> Chorus: Cackling crones,
>   Cackling crones,
>   Shatter the universe,
>   Cackling crones.
>
> Women, let's celebrate cronology,
> Courage and strength,
> Wisdom and pride,
> Lead us and teach us to honour this life,
> Dreaming and dancing and singing.

Blessing:
> Carol, you are a strong woman,
> Surrounded by strong women.
>
> We are strong women
> Surrounded by strong women.

BLESSED BE!

B. From FSC Ritual Book—Croning for Betty and Micki

56 candles, bells, energy circle

Decade circle: Tonight we celebrate the first year of our community—the first cycle in our growing spiral. What we want to do
   now is create concentric circles within the larger one to celebrate
   the decades—the larger cycles—of each of our own lives. Each
   circle will represent a decade of our lives: the first, birth to 10
   years, then 10–20, 20–30, 30–40, 40–50, and 50–60. With each
   decade circle, think about what we have been through in that
   time. We will be story-telling or saying a phrase or word about

what was significant to us in that decade. For some of us it may well be that to say, "I survived," is enough.

[stand in concentric circles by decades]

We heard "I survived," often, and marriage, loss of self. Wonderfully, as the older women formed circles, it was a vision of gaining strength, wisdom, and new growth. When we were left with the 50+ women, we asked for those wishing to be celebrated as crones to remain standing.

We gather to celebrate Micki and Betty becoming fifty-six and entering the wise age.

M: Her proper title from now on is Young Crone. Who is the crone, you ask? A crone is a woman who has reached wisdom in her heart, who is called on in disputes to arbitrate, who is called on in despair to soothe the wounds. A young crone is everyone's older sister.

G: Who else is a crone, you ask? A young crone is the goddess in her third aspect. She is Mazera. She is Hecate. She is the goddess of unbound power.

M: Folklore has it that crones bring good luck when you see them on the street.

Closing ritual: Have all of the wrapped symbols on the table as well as enough brown paper bags for everyone and colored pencils/crayons. Have everyone write with their pencil or crayon on their paper bag symbols of patriarchy of which they want to be rid. Then blow up the paper bags and pop them, symbolizing the breaking of patriarchal power systems. (When this is done with laughter and gusto, it is quite powerful.) Then each woman unwraps the symbol she has brought, talks briefly about why she chose it, and offers it to the group. Then each person should take one of the gifts, explaining why she has chosen that one. End with a simple blessing such as, "We are the breakers and creators of symbol systems. May our lives be symbols of justice and well-being!"

Session 10—Chapter 21, "Feminist Spiritualities"

Goal: to analyze our values around feminist spirituality and to be in dialogue about them.

Activities:
1. Have three women with differences (e.g., different theological/ thealogical views; or a maiden, mother, and crone; or women of dif-

ferent races, physical abilities, or sexual orientations) talk about what it means to be themselves, at this stage of their life.

2. If the group is larger than five, break into trios to share insights and your own stories of times when you have been different from the majority. (Share in the total group if there are less than six.)

3. How have you changed by encountering difference? How have such encounters influenced your spirituality?

4. From your point of view, what are the limits to pluralism?

Closing ritual: Have a globe as a central image for people's attention. Pictures of women from around the world would also add to the atmosphere. The ritual focuses on the women and the earth. It begins with a guided meditation that could be led by a group member.

Take time to get comfortable and relax. Feel your body, with its aches and pains and stresses, and let it relax. Breathe in deeply and exhale slowly. Breathe in love from the universe. Feel connected to love in the universe. Be at one with the universe. . . . Slowly let yourself become the earth. Feel the textures of your body the earth. . . . See the colors, the tones, and the hues. . . . Listen to the sounds deep inside. Feel the open spaces of your body the earth. . . . Feel the hills, the mountains, the curves, the places where the wind blows over your surface easily, the hidden places, the oceans and the forest depths, the desert regions, the flowing streams, the soil that grows good things. You are one with the universe.

Sacred Ground

Sacred Ground—Where the holy stands
               Barefoot power
               fragile earth beneath the naked feet

Sacred Ground where the holy stands—
    bend down—touch this sacred ground—
gentle, fragile, careful tentative touch of earth and holy

Sacred Ground—oh so care full—
    To know You as one who is like and not other
    To know ourselves not as other but like
    To hear you who is like and other than call us by name,
    Joyful Mother, Cupfilled.

Sacred Ground—not so much to bend down to but to sit
                        upon. Earth.
    Earth of laughter and tears,
    Earth gathered up, scooped up, splashed in as mud between

the toes.
yet tear-watered mud in the joy and thickness.

Sacred Ground—the seeds of love within,
the womb-bearing place
the nourisher and lifeholder.

Hold carefully, gentle receive oh Sacred Ground a
holy-like love.

Judith Schenck

As Sacred Ground, you are one with all the women of the universe . . . past, present, and future. You love your deep connectedness with the women of every land—their colors, textures, smells, and
sounds. You love to hear the names of the countries in which they
dwell. In your heart you recite them daily as you long deep in your
heart for peace and justice in every land. [Here the names of all of
the countries of the world can be read out from Seager and Olson,
Women of the World, or from any current atlas. It takes about six minutes in a slow continuous voice.] You delight in the lands, in the sounds
of their names, in knowing there are strong vibrant women in every
land, and you hear the women singing. They sing a song with several
verses about peace, and by the end of the song you will have returned
to the body that is you and come back to this room together. [Play
Carolyn McDade's song "Women of the Earth, Arise in Every Land,"
from the tape *We Come with Our Voices,* or play some other song about
women's global solidarity.]

Take a few minutes to share anything from the meditation and
then close with a blessing such as, "Sacred Ground, hold carefully,
gently receive us, and bless us as we go."

Session 11—Chapter 22, "Leadership and Institutional Implications"

Goal: to explore from the book the meaning of the concepts about
leadership and structure, in relation to the activities of the group.

Activities:
1. Talk about the criteria for groups and leadership described in
this section of the book. What values do you hold around leadership
in groups? Brainstorm some criteria and values for positive leadership for rituals and liturgies.
2. Individually, draw your study group, using circles for each member, including yourself, in each of the following situations. Make the
circles large or small, close together or far apart, to show how you see

the interaction and power in the group. Where and how would you draw members of the group—during a discussion? when choosing how to get into small groups? during breaks or social times? during rituals? Share your drawings with the group.

3. Talk about what the criteria and values from the book mean for your group. Also add criteria and values from your brainstorming and from any insights from the group drawings. In what ways is the group leaderful, nonhierarchical, consistent between structure and leadership? Who participates easily, and who does not? What does this mean? What do you do with differences created by class, age, race, disability, or sexual orientation in the group? What do you do with demanding members? What difference does it make if you are a rural, urban, or mixed rural-urban group? What is your perception of yourself in the group? What do you value about how your group is working together? Are there any changes that you would like to make? Talk about differences and similarities in perception and what they mean to the people involved.

Closing ritual: If possible, use Diann Neu's "In Praise of Hands," *Water Wheel* 2, no. 1 (Winter 1989). Or use a simple commitment ceremony to the group. Start with a time of silence and grounding. Then go around the circle, with each woman saying how she is feeling about what was shared in the session. Each woman can light a candle to express her feelings. (E.g., I light this candle to burn away the hurt I feel because of . . . ; I light this candle as a sign of hope that we can continue to work together in the future as well as we have in the past, etc.) Close with a blessing by walking around the circle touching each person on the forehead, with a handclasp, or a hug, saying, "We are strong women, surrounded by strong women."

Session 12—Chapter 23, "Criteria for Feminist Theory, Thealogy, and Action"

Goal: to gain awareness of women's power to shape history through concrete actions.

Activities:

1. Everyone should bring one item that you have heard, seen, or read in the news that week. In choosing the story, focus on the meaning of the news story for you, for the women of your country, and for the women of the world.

2. In pairs or trios, choose five criteria from chapter 23 that you want to use as criteria for selecting and measuring your actions toward justice and well-being for women in the world.

3. Share the news stories you have brought in your trio, and then measure each of them against the five criteria you have chosen.

4. How would you "rewrite history"—that is, have the incident happen so that women were naming and shaping the common good, and so that it might meet your five criteria for bringing justice and well-being for women? Rewrite the story. (Have some extra newspapers present so that if all of the stories chosen by women are positive stories, you can choose some other ones to work with.)

Closing ritual: Conclude with a ritual of listening to Arlene Mantle's song "We're Writing Our Songs," from *On the Line,* and then sharing with the total group the news stories you have written in your small groups. Replay the song.

Session 13—Chapter 25, "Creation of Women's Culture through Arts"

Goal: to provide opportunity for women to gain insight into the role of arts in feminist ritual thealogy.

Activities:

1. Everyone should bring with them some art form to share in the ritual. It could be a story, a poem, a letter, a song, a dance, a visual art object or portrayal, or a photograph created by you or someone else.

2. Start the evening by listening to some feminist music such as "Bread and Roses" (on Judy Collins tape *So Early in the Spring*); "Trouble and Beauty," by Carolyn McDade (*This Tough Spun Web* tape); or "We Are a Gentle Angry People" (Holly Near and Ronnie Gilbert *Lifeline* tape).

3. What does the idea of women's culture suggest to you? How do your ideas connect with Lerner's, Daly's and Christ's as outlined in chapter 25?

4. What role do the arts play in your life? Which art form do you connect with most strongly? How does it connect with your feminist consciousness? What does it do for your spirituality?

Closing ritual: Each woman can share her art that she has brought. When she has finished speaking about it or doing it, have a moment of silence, and then say together, "[Name,] we celebrate your art. We celebrate you." Sing some feminist songs together to close.

Session 14—Chapter 26, "Actions and Strategies"

Goal: to explore a variety of options for actions and strategies toward justice and well-being for women.

Activities:

1. If you are going to use the "Dorcas" ritual, women need to bring with them garments or pieces of sewing, weaving, quilting, baby clothes, or sewn toys.

2. How is your life experience similar to, and different from, the experiences of the women in this chapter—the woman strategizing, the three mothers, the woman in ministry, Linda and Pat, Betty, the woman with her own business, the educator?

3. How do you link the personal and political?

4. Describe one action for personal well-being or justice that you did in the past week, and one action you did for interpersonal or global well-being or justice. Pick one that you want to do in the coming week.

Closing ritual: Use "With Dorcas Let Us Sew a Garment of Love to Cover Our World," by Martha Ann Kirk, in *Celebrations of Biblical Women's Stories* (Kansas City: Sheed and Ward, 1987). Or have a table set with symbols of the four directions: east—air; south—fire; west—water; north—earth. Begin with the chant "The earth, the air, the fire, the water."[6] Invite each woman to say how she connects with the four symbols. Which one(s) make you feel most at home? Which one connects you with women in a different part of the world? When everyone has spoken, turn to each direction and celebrate the symbols of earth, air, fire, and water, and the women who live in each of those directions in the world. Repeat the chant as a conclusion.

Session 15—"Conclusion: The Quest for a Nonsexist God/dess"

Goal: to challenge and nurture women's exploration of the holy.

Activities:

1. Begin the session with a silent circle, with time for centering. Close your eyes and repeat several times slowly the words of Ntozake Shange:

---

6. From tape by Libana, *A Circle Is Cast* (Libana, Inc., Box 530, Cambridge, MA 02140).

i found god in myself
and i loved her
i loved her fiercely.

Breathe the words in and out at least ten to fifteen times and sit with them silently.[7]

2. Did you get any new insights into the nature of the divine from this section of the book? Which of the aspects of the holy described were you able to relate to? Were there any you did not like or that disturbed you?

3. What is your favorite name or image of the holy at this point in your life? What were some of the images of the holy in your childhood? How would you describe the holy to a young child or a teenager?

4. Create a poem, prayer, chant, or mantra, using the different names and images appreciated by the women of the group.

Closing ritual: Use one of the ideas from Kathleen Fischer, *Women at the Well: Feminist Perspectives on Spiritual Direction* (New York: Paulist Press, 1988), "Women Experiencing and Naming God," pp. 69–73.

Or read the following poem:

God of Contrast[8]

God
        unnamed mystery
Friend
      rain
         lightning
           warmth
Tears and song
Malleable rock
The oppression of an imprisoned God
Powerless at the end of the bread line
Waiting,
Immanent power in the dancing circle
Hoping
Us
I am

---

7. From Maria Harris, *Dance of the Spirit* (New York: Bantam Books, 1989), p. 25.
8. A group reflection shared in a ritual at "Women and Men Explore Sexism and God Talk," Prairie Christian Training Centre, April 1984.

We will be who we will be
Blessed be!"

Women can then offer the poems, prayers, chants, or mantras that they wrote above. Conclude with a threefold blessing:

Ancient One, bless us with your presence!
Present One, bless us with your presence!
Holder of Dreams and Visions, bless us with your presence!
May we bathe in your light and love; may we feel you inside
and outside our bodies.
May you bless us to be life-giving, life-loving women.

Session 16—"Conclusion: The Shape of Justice"

Goal: to develop techniques for working toward justice for women in society.

Activities:
1. Drawing on the visions outlined in this section of the book and on your own visions of a just world, choose areas to work on. If there are enough group members, have two members work on each of the six areas in this section of the book (social, political, economic, cultural, physical, personal); if there are fewer members, choose the areas you prefer. Develop a brief or policy proposal around the area of concern. Think about what changes you want, what strategies you would propose to bring about the changes, and to whom you would need to address your concern. (E.g., you might want to work for change in family laws to equalize tax benefits for varying family forms. Think about what policies and laws would need to be changed and which federal and provincial departments have power in these areas.)
2. When you have completed your brief, spend time in the total group, role-playing presentation of the briefs to the body to whom you are sending them. (E.g., present the brief on changing laws regarding family forms to the Saskatchewan minister of the family.)
3. Debrief from the exercise, sharing any learnings and insights, as well as plans for action toward justice developed in the session.

Closing ritual: Have clay or play dough for this ritual. Each person should have a lump of clay or play dough. Relax and breathe deeply to get centered. Begin to feel the clay, play with it, get to know it. Shape it into a ball or sphere. Close your eyes and slowly and quietly work the clay and let it work you. Gradually form it into the shape of justice—not a preconceived form or a recognizable shape but an emerging shape that forms through your working with the clay. Take at least five to ten minutes for the molding. Sit with it. Allow it to speak to you about itself and about yourself. When everyone is ready, one by one place your creations on the ritual table with the words, "I offer this—the shape of justice." Conclude with a shared blessing such as, "May we always be shapers of justice and of the common good."[9]

Session 17—"Conclusion: Feminist Ritual Thealogy"

Goal: to integrate understandings of feminist ritual thealogy gained through the book.

Activities:
1. Beforehand, everyone should read the section in the Conclusion dealing with feminist ritual thealogy and also should look back at the entire book and course for learnings about what feminist ritual thealogy is and what it means in your lives.
2. How do feminism, spirituality, and politics come together for you? What role does ritual play in that integration?
3. Are there principles you would add to those outlined?
4. What new insights do you have about feminist ritual thealogy from the course? Take plenty of time for discussion and sharing insights gained, challenge and nurture received, and questions remaining.

Closing ritual: Have everyone lie on the floor in a fetal position, preferably in silence and darkness. Have one woman read the following section from Linda Ervin's poem "Groups of Words and Thoughts."

> In the
>   womb
>   we begin
> enclosed
>   and safe
> nurtured
>   by our
>   mother's
>   body
> soul
>   connected
>   to soul

---

9. The idea for this ritual comes from Harris, *Dance of the Spirit*, p. 82.

We are fed
and
encouraged
to
 grow
to take
the
 steps
to life
beyond
the womb

Then the women stand and form a birth canal with legs apart. Each
woman is pulled through the birth canal as a symbol of being born.
As each woman is "born," she can cry, "I am born a free, strong
woman!" and the other women can respond, "Blessed be!" When all
the women have survived the journey through the birth canal, stand
in a circle and listen to words from the poem "Easter," by Lorraine
Michael:

Nothing dies—not leaf, not grass, not tree, not animal.
We all give life to the other—over and over and over.
 I am part of an ongoing pouring out of life. . . .

My spirit reaches out in an
 unending burst of love.
 Resurrection
 LIFE UNENDING

Conclude by chanting together several times, "We are born free, strong
women!"

Session 18—"Conclusion: Testing the Theories"

Goal: to evaluate the experience of the study-ritual group and to bring
closure to it.

Activities:
 1. Take some time to evaluate the program. What worked for your
group? What did not work? What would have made it better in terms
of content? in terms of process?
 2. Having worked through one sample of the method, how might
you use the same method in gaining new thealogical insights?
 3. How would you respond to the question, How can and do reli-

gious rituals challenge and nurture feminists in their work for justice and well-being in the world?

4. Where will you go from here? What are the next steps in your journey?

Closing ritual: Repeat one of the rituals used in the course that worked well in your group. Or begin with a round in which each woman says her name and then gives a gift to each other member. (E.g., I am [Name], and I give you, [Name], the gift of play.) If the group is large, this part could be shortened by giving a gift only to the person sitting next to you.

When everyone has spoken, take a strand of ribbon and pass it around the circle, with each woman holding on to a portion of the ribbon and handing the ball on to the next person, so that eventually the ribbon forms a circle with each woman holding the strand. As the woman receives the first strand, she talks about what the group has meant to her. Pass a second ball of ribbon, with each woman naming one way she has changed during the course, or one thing she has learned. The third ribbon can represent hopes and commitments for the future. Conclude with a blessing such as, "Let us go from this place challenged and nurtured to work for justice and well-being for women in the world."

INDEX